# Mediterranean Euphoria

## Exploring the Delights of the Mediterranean Diet for a Fulfilling Lifestyle

### 500 Easy and Healthy Recipes for Inspired Everyday Eating

Lila West

# Table of contents

## Snack and Appetizer Recipes .............. 57

## Meat Recipes ................................................. 68

# Fish and Seafood Recipes ...................... 93

# Introduction

Welcome to an exhilarating exploration of one of the world's most cherished dietary approaches - the Mediterranean Diet! Highly praised globally and adored for its perfect balance of delicious allure and health benefits, this diet is not just a diet - it's truly a way of life.

The forthcoming pages of this cookbook aim to elucidate the Mediterranean diet and its myriad benefits, packed with answers to all your lingering questions, and arming you with all the knowledge needed to start a vibrant new chapter in your culinary journey.

The Mediterranean diet is anchored in the eating habits of people from Mediterranean countries like Greece, Italy, and Spain. It's a lifestyle that places a strong emphasis on simple, wholesome ingredients used in everyday meals - everything from bread, pasta, fruits, and vegetables to rice and potatoes. Let's not forget the pivotal role played by seafood, lean meats, healthy oils, and dairy products forming core components of this diet.

More than just a variety of palate-pleasing ingredients, adopting the Mediterranean diet means you'll enjoy a cornucopia of meals rich in calcium, protein, and vital nutrients. This diet has the potential to enhance your health, and if weight loss is on your agenda, you'll be pleased to hear it may even support shedding those extra pounds.

Isn't it indeed remarkable to note that a diet filled with some of the tastiest dishes from around the globe can also underpin a healthier lifestyle? The Mediterranean diet breaks the monotonous perception of "diet food," giving you an exciting world of culinary adventure while promoting vitality and wellness.

Embrace the Mediterranean diet today! With an infusion of warm, fresh, and savory Mediterranean tastes in every recipe, this cookbook may just be your golden ticket to overhauling your everyday dishes. Embark on your new life today, and savor the authentic taste of the Mediterranean!

# Top tips for starting your Mediterranean diet

Starting any new diet can be challenging, but the key to success is in preparation and maintaining balance. These are our top five tips to ensuring you get the most from your Mediterranean diet.

1. Balance your plate – A balanced plate is crucial in any diet to ensure that you are getting adequate macronutrients. Aim to have a portion of protein, healthy fat and carbohydrates at each meal.

2. Build your base – the basis for the Mediterranean diet relies upon a wide variety of vegetables, legumes and wholegrains. This should form the basis of your meal and cover 70% of your plate. From here you can add your healthy fats and protein choice.

3. Skip the sweets – The Mediterranean diet greatly eliminates refined sugars and processed foods. With a focus on natural whole foods, swap the desserts for fruits with a little Greek yogurt.

4. Keep the fats healthy – In contrast to popular opinion, fat doesn't make you fat. In fact healthy fats can provide a wide variety of health benefits and even contribute to weight loss. A key staple of the Mediterranean diet is the consumption of extra virgin olive oil, touted to prevent heart disease and provide anti-aging properties.

5. Reduce meat consumption – The Mediterranean diet focuses heavily on plant-based proteins and seafood. Although moderate portions of animal protein are included, red meat should be kept to a minimum and poultry eaten in moderation.

Starting a new diet need not be stressful and is a great opportunity to get creative in the kitchen. Using these top tips should be a good starting point to build your new diet.

# Better health with a Mediterranean diet

Unlike many diets which are created and adapted to achieve specific results, the Mediterranean diet simply adopts the healthful eating habits and ingredients of countries bordering the Mediterranean Sea. Naturally rich in vitamins and minerals and balanced with healthy carbs, fats and proteins, the Mediterranean diet has demonstrated a variety of benefits to health.

The region bordering the Mediterranean Sea is vast, so there is a large variety of cultural food influences that contribute to this diet. This means that unlike some diets, food choices are not restricted and there are plenty of delicious ingredients and combinations to choose from.

As a general rule, the Mediterranean diet focuses on a broad range of fruits, vegetables, healthy wholegrains and legumes. A moderate serving of fresh fish and seafood, small quantities of poultry, eggs and dairy products and occasional red meat. A glass or two of red wine is also approved!

The key benefits of this diet are that you are increasing your consumption of wholefoods in their natural form and eliminating, or greatly reducing, processed, refined and packaged foods.

By consuming more whole foods you will ensure a balanced and healthful diet rich in essential vitamins and minerals and nutrients crucial in fighting disease and maintaining a healthy immune system. The Mediterranean diet also provides an abundance of healthy fats which can contribute to good heart health, brain health and the health of the nervous system. What's more, a balanced Mediterranean diet has been shown to assist weight loss, prevent type 2 diabetes and contribute to a longer lifespan.

The recipes within this book will provide you with a wide variety of delicious Mediterranean inspired meals to help you kickstart your healthy new diet. We have also included a 4-week meal plan to help simplify things and provide you with a guideline to implement your new diet.

# Mediterranean approved foods list

The Mediterranean diet is an abundant source of plant-based foods, lean proteins and heart healthy fats. This list will provide you with an overview of foods that are approved on the Mediterranean diet.

### Meats

Although red meat may be consumed on the diet, this should be limited and eaten rarely. Meats to be eaten on occasion include:

Beef, lamb, pork, and goat.

### Poultry

Poultry may be consumed in moderation, organic is preferable where possible. These can include:

Chicken, duck and goose.

### Fish and Shellfish

Fish and shellfish are a popular element of the Mediterranean diet. Nutrient dense and a good source of omega 3, fish and shellfish can be enjoyed regularly. Some healthful examples include:

Salmon, cod, bass, tuna, mackerel, sardines, herring, trout, crab, shrimp, scallops, mussels, oysters and anchovies.

### Eggs

Eggs can provide a great source of nutrients as well as omega 3's, with pastured organic eggs providing the most health benefits. These may be eaten in moderation.

### Vegetables and leafy greens

Vegetables can be eaten abundantly on the Mediterranean diet and are a valuable source of antioxidants. Some popular Mediterranean vegetables are:

Tomatoes, eggplant, zucchini, spinach, artichokes, onions, cabbage, cucumber, mushrooms, bell peppers, fennel, leeks, kale, cabbage, broccoli, green beans, cauliflowers, carrots and potatoes.

### Fruits

A natural source of vitamins and minerals, fruit is frequently consumed as part of a balanced Mediterranean diet. Some popular choices are:

Lemons, limes, figs, dates, apples, strawberries, melon, grapes, oranges, pears, apricots, plums, pomegranates and peaches.

### Nuts and seeds

Nuts and seeds are a valuable source of nutrients and healthy fats and can be enjoyed frequently. These include:

Almonds, walnuts, pecans, macadamias, pistachios, filberts, pumpkin seeds, sunflower seeds, sesame seeds and pine nuts.

### Legumes

Legumes can be enjoyed frequently as part of a balanced Mediterranean diet and provide a generous source of vitamins, minerals and fiber. Popular choice are:

Chickpeas (garbanzo beans), lentils, cannellini beans, peas, haricot vert and okra.

### Wholegrains

Wholegrains feature heavily in the Mediterranean diet, providing multiple health benefits such as reducing the risk of heart disease. Healthful choices include:

Buckwheat, farro, spelt, oats, rice, bulgar, quinoa and sorghum.

### Fats and oils

Healthy fats are enjoyed liberally as part of the Mediterranean diet. Select organic options where possible to maximise the health benefits. These include:

Extra virgin olive oil, olives, tahini, avocado, nut butters.

### Herbs and Spices

Herbs and spices can be used abundantly within Mediterranean cooking to provide additional nutrients as well as flavor. Some popular options are:

Basil, parsley, mint, thyme, sage rosemary, oregano, marjoram ginger, cinnamon, cumin, paprika, saffron, ras el hanout and za'atar.

# Mediterranean diet non-approved foods list

The Mediterranean diet focuses on providing nutrients from a wide range of whole food sources. Whilst the priority is to eat vegetables, lean proteins, wholegrains, legumes and healthy fats, it is also important to eliminate heavily processed and refined food sources. Foods to avoid on the Mediterranean diet include:

### Processed foods

All heavily processed and refined foods are to be avoided such as:

Take-out, ready meals, sugary snacks, energy drinks, fizzy drinks, candy, artificial sweeteners, white bread.

### Trans fats and refined oils

High quality fats are an integral component of the Mediterranean diet whereas unhealthy trans fats are to be avoided completely. Avoid the following:

Vegetable oil, soya bean oil, margarine and spreads.

### Processed Meats

Whilst red meat should be limited, heavily processed meats should be avoided completely such as:

Hot dogs, sausages, bacon and hams that contain added fillers etc.

# Mediterranean diet four week meal plan

This meal plan has been compiled to provide a sample of some of our great Mediterranean inspired recipes. Use this as a template to get you started on your new diet, adapting as required to suit your needs.

Please ensure to factor in the recipe servings and adjust as necessary for the correct amount of people following the plan. Please note also to account for recipes that are being served as a dinner as well as lunch the following day.

## Week one meal plan

| DAY | BREAKFAST | LUNCH | DINNER | SNACK | DESSERT |
|---|---|---|---|---|---|
| **Monday** | Figs and Yogurt | Chickpea and Kale Soup | Pan Fried Cod with Olives and Tomatoes | | |
| **Tuesday** | Walnut Breakfast Oats | Chickpea and Kale Soup | Easy Chicken Bowls | Eggplant Chips | |
| **Wednesday** | Figs and Yogurt | Easy Chicken Bowls | Stuffed Eggplants | | |
| **Thursday** | Walnut Breakfast Oats | Summer | Beef with tomato Spaghetti | | |
| **Friday** | Figs and Yogurt | Summer | Salmon with Olives, Capers and Zucchini | | |
| **Saturday** | Mediterranean Fried Eggs | Broad Bean Toast | Mediterranean Shrimp and Veggies | | Simple Grilled Peaches |
| **Sunday** | Scrambled Eggs | Chicken Salad with Toasted Pita Bread | Pork and Chickpea Stew | | |

# Week two meal plan

| DAY | BREAKFAST | LUNCH | DINNER | SNACK | DESSERT |
| --- | --- | --- | --- | --- | --- |
| **Monday** | Breakfast Quinoa | Delicious Bean Soup | Pork and Chickpea Stew | | |
| **Tuesday** | Almond Breakfast Bars | Delicious Bean Soup | Tuna Steaks with Olives and Roasted Peppers and Tomatoes | | |
| **Wednesday** | Breakfast Quinoa | Salmon Gyros | Pan Fried Chicken with Delicious Summer Squash | Chickpeas Appetizer | |
| **Thursday** | Almond Breakfast Bars | Pan Fried Chicken with Delicious Summer Squash | Simple Pasta with Broccoli | | |
| **Friday** | Almond Breakfast Bars | Salmon Gyros | Baked Chicken Breasts with Brown Rice and Tomatoes | | |
| **Saturday** | Baked Egg and Tomato | Tasty Halloumi and Arugula Salad | Lamb Stew with Mint and Apricot | | Honey Baked Nectarines |
| **Sunday** | Eggplant and Tomato Breakfast Hash | Lamb Stew with Mint and Apricot | Orange Chicken Mix | | |

# Week three meal plan

| DAY | BREAKFAST | LUNCH | DINNER | SNACK | DESSERT |
|---|---|---|---|---|---|
| **Monday** | Arugula and Roasted Pepper Fritatta | Rich Chicken Soup | Morrocan Chickpeas | Eggplant Chips | |
| **Tuesday** | Quinoa Breakfast Muffins | Rich Chicken Soup | Salmon and Tomato Spread with Spicy Roasted Asparagus | | |
| **Wednesday** | Arugula and Roasted Pepper Fritatta | Salmon and Tomato Spread with Spicy Roasted Asparagus | Grilled Leg of Lamb with Caulliflower Couscous | | |
| **Thursday** | Quinoa Breakfast Muffins | Quick Chickpea and Bean Salad | Spaghetti with Grilled Veggies | | |
| **Friday** | Arugula and Roasted Pepper Fritatta | Quick Chickpea and Bean Salad | Sea Bass with Roasted Tomatoes and Italian Style Potatoes | | |
| **Saturday** | Breakfast Pancakes | Simple Shrimp Mix | Eggplant Stew | | |
| **Sunday** | Breakfast Pancakes | Eggplant Stew | Chicken with Pepperoncini with Roasted Potatoes | | Blueberry and Rosemary Dessert |

# Week four meal plan

| DAY | BREAKFAST | LUNCH | DINNER | SNACK | DESSERT |
|---|---|---|---|---|---|
| **Monday** | Breakfast Couscous | Vegetable Stew | Cabbage Rolls | Peppers Spread | |
| **Tuesday** | Berry Omelet | Vegetable Stew | Baked Chicken Thighs with Tasty Fennel Salad | | |
| **Wednesday** | Breakfast Couscous | Baked Chicken Thighs with Tasty Fennel Salad | Shrimp bake | | |
| **Thursday** | Berry Omelet | Fresh Orange and Mozzarella Salad | Pan Fried Garlic Chicken with Zucchini | | |
| **Friday** | Breakfast Couscous | Fresh Orange and Mozzarella Salad | Spicy Salmon with Lentils | | |
| **Saturday** | Greek Breakfast Burrito | Chickpea and Avocado Salad | Slow Cooked Chicken | | |
| **Sunday** | Spanish Baked Eggs | Slow Cooked Chicken | Lamb Meatballs with Morrocan Green Beans | | Mixed Berry and Yogurt Mousse |

# Breakfast Recipes

## Tomato Eggs Mix

*Prep Time*: 5 minutes | *Cook Time*: 5 minutes | *Servings*: 2

**Ingredients:**

- 1 tomato, chopped
- 1 tablespoon vegetable oil
- 1 cup baby spinach
- ½ cup feta cheese, cubed
- Salt and black pepper to taste
- 3 eggs

**Directions:**

Heat a pan with the oil over medium heat, add the eggs, tomato and the other ingredients except the cheese, toss and cook for 4 minutes. Add the cheese, stir the mix, cook for 1 minute more, divide between plates and serve.

**Nutrition:** calories 150, fat 2, fiber 0, carbs 2, protein 10

## Veggie and Eggs Salad

*Prep Time*: 10 minutes | *Cook Time*: 0 minutes | *Servings*: 4

**Ingredients:**

- ½ cup sun-dried tomatoes, chopped
- 8 eggs, hard-boiled, peeled and chopped
- ¼ cup olives, pitted and chopped
- 1 small cucumber, chopped
- 1 small red onion, finely chopped
- ½ cup Greek yogurt
- ¼ teaspoon cumin
- A splash of lemon juice
- Salt and black pepper to taste
- 1 and ½ teaspoon oregano

**Directions:**

In a bowl, combine the eggs with the olives, cucumber and the other ingredients except the yogurt and toss. Add the yogurt, toss the salad again and keep in the fridge until you serve it.

**Nutrition:** calories 230, fat 1, fiber 2, carbs 1.4, protein 7

## Quinoa, Eggs and Tomatoes Bowl

*Prep Time*: 10 minutes | *Cook Time*: 20 minutes | *Servings*: 6

**Ingredients:**

- 1 teaspoon onion powder
- ¼ cup Greek yogurt
- 12 eggs
- 1 teaspoon garlic powder
- Salt and black pepper to taste
- 1 teaspoon extra virgin olive oil
- 1 pint cherry tomatoes cut in halves
- 2 cups quinoa, already cooked
- 5 ounces baby spinach leaves
- 1 cup feta cheese, crumbled

**Directions:**

In a bowl, mix the eggs with the yogurts, onion powder and the other ingredients except the oil, spinach and tomatoes and toss. Heat a pan with the oil over medium high heat, add the spinach, stir and cook for 5 minutes. Add tomatoes, and the eggs mix, toss, cook everything for 15 minutes more stirring often, transfer to bowls and serve hot.

**Nutrition:** calories 357, fat 20, fiber 2, carbs 20, protein 23

## Walnut and Chia Oatmeal

*Prep Time*: 5 minutes | *Cook Time*: 0 minutes | *Servings*: 1

**Ingredients:**

- 2 tablespoons walnuts, chopped
- ½ cup oats
- ¾ cup almond milk
- 1 date, chopped
- 1 tablespoon chia seeds
- 1 tablespoon vanilla powder
- ½ teaspoon cinnamon

**Directions:**

In a bowl, combine the almond milk with the oats and the other ingredients. Stir well, keep in the fridge overnight and serve the next day cold.

**Nutrition:** calories 345, fat 18, fiber 3, carbs 38, protein 16

## Creamy Figs Bowls

*Prep Time:* 10 minutes | *Cook Time:* 5 minutes | *Servings:* 4

**Ingredients:**

- 8 ounces figs cut in halves
- 2 cups Greek yogurt
- 1 tablespoon
- honey
- A pinch of cinnamon
- ¼ cup pistachios, chopped

**Directions:**

Heat a pan over medium heat, add the figs and honey and cook them for 5 minutes. Divide yogurt into bowls, add caramelized figs and the other ingredients, toss gently and serve.

**Nutrition:** calories 200, fat 5, fiber 2, carbs 24, protein 5

## Spinach Frittata

*Prep Time:* 10 minutes | *Cook Time:* 20 minutes | *Servings:* 6

**Ingredients:**

- ¼ cup kalamata olives, pitted and chopped
- 6 eggs
- ½ cup milk
- ½ cup tomatoes, chopped
- ¼ cup black olives, pitted and chopped
- ¼ cup feta cheese, crumbled
- 1 cup spinach
- Salt and black pepper to taste
- 1 teaspoon oregano, dried
- A drizzle of olive oil

**Directions:**

Grease a baking dish with a drizzle of oil. In a bowl, combine the eggs with the milk and the other ingredients and whisk well. Pour this into the pan, bake in the oven at 400 degrees F for 20 minutes and serve hot.

**Nutrition:** calories 176, fat 3, fiber 7, carbs 21, protein 16

## Veggie and Eggs Bake

*Prep Time:* 10 minutes | *Cook Time:* 20 minutes | *Servings:* 6

**Ingredients:**

- 2 green bell peppers, chopped
- 2 garlic cloves, minced
- 3 tablespoons olive oil
- 1 yellow onion, chopped
- 1 teaspoon sweet paprika
- 1 teaspoon
- coriander, ground
- Salt and black pepper to taste
- A pinch of red pepper flakes
- ½ cup tomato sauce
- 6 tomatoes, chopped
- 6 eggs
- ¼ cup parsley, chopped
- ¼ cup mint, chopped

**Directions:**

Heat a pan with the oil over medium heat, add bell peppers, onion, garlic and the other ingredients except the eggs, tomatoes and tomato sauce and saute for 5 minutes. Add tomatoes and tomato sauce, stir and cook everything for another 5 minutes. Make 6 holes into this mix, crack an egg into each, cover pan, reduce heat and cook the mix for 10 minutes more. Divide the mix between plates and serve.

**Nutrition:** calories 300, fat 18, fiber 4, carbs 23, protein 1

# Mixed Veggie Casserole

*Prep Time: 10 minutes | Cook Time: 1 hour | Servings: 4*

## Ingredients:

- 2 garlic cloves, minced
- 3 tablespoons butter, melted
- 1 cup mushrooms, sliced
- 2 shallots, chopped
- 6 cups white bread, cubed
- 1 teaspoon marjoram, dried
- ½ cup artichoke hearts, chopped
- ¼ cup kalamata olives, pitted and cut
- in quarters
- 4 ounces mozzarella cheese balls, cut in halves
- 1/5 cup sun-dried tomatoes, marinated and chopped
- ¼ cup parmesan, grated
- 6 eggs
- 1 and ½ cups half and half
- Salt to taste
- ¼ cup basil, chopped

## Directions:

Heat up a small pan with 2 tablespoons butter over medium heat, add shallot, garlic, stir and cook for 2 minutes. Add mushrooms, marjoram and the other ingredients except the eggs, half and half and basil, stir, cook for 4 minutes and transfer to a bowl. Divide this mix into 4 baking cups greased with 1 tablespoon butter In a bowl, mix eggs with half and a half and whisk well. Divide this over the veggie mix and place in the oven at 325 degrees F and bake for 50 minutes. Scatter with fresh basil to serve.

**Nutrition:** calories 300, fat 6, fiber 8, carbs 20, protein 15

# Greek Pancakes

*Prep Time: 10 minutes | Cook Time: 5 minutes | Servings: 2*

## Ingredients:

- 6 ounces Greek yogurt
- ½ cup flour
- 1 egg
- 1 teaspoon baking soda

## Directions:

In a bowl, combine the egg with the yogurt and the other ingredients and whisk well. Heat a pan over medium high heat, spoon 1/2 of the batter into the pan, spread, cook for 2-3 minutes on each side and transfer to a plate. Repeat with the rest of the pancake batter and serve.

**Nutrition:** calories 111, fat 1.4, fiber 2, carbs 15, protein 10

# Veggie Squares

*Prep Time: 10 minutes | Cook Time: 50 minutes | Servings: 4*

## Ingredients:

- 2 yellow onions, cut into medium wedges
- 2 red bell peppers, cut into thin strips
- 1 teaspoon coriander
- 1 teaspoon cumin
- Salt and black pepper to taste
- Some thyme leaves
- 6 tablespoons olive
- oil
- A handful cilantro, chopped
- A handful parsley, chopped
- 1 puff pastry sheet
- 1 egg, whisked
- 6 eggs
- 12 teaspoons sour cream

## Directions:

In a bowl, mix onions with bell pepper, thyme, salt, pepper, oil, cumin and coriander, stir the mix, transfer to a baking dish, cook at 400 degrees F for 30 minutes, combine with half of the parsley and cilantro, toss and leave aside to cool down a bit. Roll out puff pastry, cut into 6 squares, place them on a lined baking sheet, prick them with a fork and keep in the fridge for 30 minutes. Brush the squares, whisked egg, spread 3 teaspoons sour cream on each, divide veggie mix, lift square edges a bit, place in the oven at 425 degrees F and bake for 10 minutes. Crack an egg in each, bake for 10 minutes, more, sprinkle the remaining herbs on each and serve.

**Nutrition:** calories 340, fat 20, fiber 3, carbs 20, protein 11

## Peppers Frittata

*Prep Time: 10 minutes | Cook Time: 45 minutes | Servings: 12*

**Ingredients:**

- 3 garlic cloves, minced
- 1 tablespoon olive oil
- 1 cup white onion, chopped
- 8 eggs, whisked
- 12 ounces canned roasted bell peppers, chopped
- 2 handfuls arugula, chopped
- Salt and black pepper to taste
- ¼ cup basil pesto
- 1 cup mozzarella cheese, shredded
- Cooking spray

**Directions:**

Heat a pan with the olive oil over medium high heat, add onion and garlic, stir and cook for 5 minutes. In a bowl, whisk eggs with arugula, red peppers, the rest of the ingredients and the onion saute and stir well. Pour into a lightly greased baking dish, place in the oven at 350 degrees F, bake for 45 minutes, slice and serve hot.

**Nutrition:** calories 200, fat 12, fiber 1, carbs 0, protein 10

## Bread Fritters and Syrup

*Prep Time: 10 minutes | Cook Time: 20 minutes | Servings: 6*

**Ingredients:**

- 2 eggs
- ½ cup milk
- 6 bread slices
- 1 teaspoon vanilla extract
*For the banana syrup:*
- 3 tablespoons whipping cream
- ¼ cup butter
- 2 tablespoons sugar
- 1 teaspoon vanilla
- ½ teaspoon cinnamon, ground
- A pinch of salt
- 2 tablespoons sugar
- 2 tablespoons butter

  extract
- ¼ teaspoon cinnamon, ground
- 2 bananas, chopped
- 4 tablespoons rum

**Directions:**

In a bowl, mix milk with eggs, salt, vanilla, ½ teaspoon cinnamon and 2 tablespoons sugar, stir well and dip each bread slice in this mix. Heat a pan with 2 tablespoons butter over medium high heat, add the bread, fry for 2 minutes on each side and transfer to a plate. Heat a pan with ¼ cup butter over medium high heat, add 2 tablespoons of sugar and the other ingredients for the syrup, toss, cook for 2 minutes and take off the heat. Spoon sauce over toasted slices and serve.

**Nutrition:** calories 180, fat 7, fiber 4, carbs 32, protein 5

## Veggie Omelet

*Prep Time: 10 minutes | Cook Time: 10 minutes | Servings: 4*

**Ingredients:**

- 6 eggs
- 2 cups fennel, chopped
- 1 tablespoon olive oil
- ¼ cup green olives, pitted and chopped
- 1 plum tomato, chopped
- 2 tablespoons parsley, chopped
- ¼ cup artichoke hearts, chopped
- Salt and black pepper to the taste
- ½ cup goat cheese, crumbled

**Directions:**

Heat up a pan with the oil over medium heat, add the artichokes, fennel and the other ingredients except the eggs, salt and pepper, stir and cook for 5 minutes. In a bowl, mix eggs with salt and pepper, whisk well, add to the pan, stir gently and cook for 5 minutes. Divide the omelet between plates and serve.

**Nutrition:** calories 210, fat 12, fiber 1, carbs 6, protein 5

## Cheesy Frittata

*Prep Time: 10 minutes | Cook Time: 45 minutes | Servings: 6*

**Ingredients:**

- 1 cup red bell pepper, chopped
- 2 tablespoons butter
- 1 yellow onion, chopped
- 1 and ½ cups spinach
- ½ cup milk
- Salt and black
- pepper to taste
- 8 eggs
- 1 teaspoon olive oil
- 2 ounces feta cheese, crumbled
- 1 cup tomato, chopped
- 1 tablespoon basil, chopped

**Directions:**

Heat a pan with butter over medium high heat, add onion, spinach and bell pepper, stir, cook for 10 minutes and take of the heat. In a bowl, mix eggs with salt, pepper, cheese and the spinach and onion mix and stir well. Heat another pan with olive oil over medium heat, add the eggs, spread evenly, sprinkle the tomatoes and basil on top and bake at 350 degrees F for 35 minutes. Cut the frittata and serve.

**Nutrition:** calories 250, fat 13, fiber 0, carbs 12, protein 17

## Potato Salad

*Prep Time:* 5 minutes | *Cook Time:* 22 minutes | *Servings:* 4

**Ingredients:**

- 17 ounces gold potatoes, cubed
- 1 tablespoon olive oil
- 2 smoked salmon fillets, skinless, boneless and flaked
- 1 small broccoli, florets separated
- 8 eggs, whisked
- 1 teaspoon mint, chopped

**Directions:**

Put the potatoes in a pot, add water to cover and cook over medium heat for 10 minutes. Add broccoli, cook everything for 5 minutes more, drain and place in a bowl. Heat a pan with the oil over medium heat, add the eggs, potatoes and the other ingredients, toss, cook for 7 minutes, divide into bowls and serve.

**Nutrition:** calories 220, fat 12, fiber 4, carbs 7, protein 5

## Zucchini and Peppers Sandwich

*Prep Time:* 10 minutes | *Cook Time:* 15 minutes | *Servings:* 6

**Ingredients:**

- 1 tablespoons dill, chopped
- 5 eggs
- 1 tablespoon cream cheese
- 1 zucchini, grated
- ½ cup jarred roasted peppers
- 1 tablespoon kalamata olives, pitted and chopped
- 1 whole wheat baguette
- Cooking spray
- Salt and pepper to taste

**Directions:**

In a bowl, mix eggs with salt, pepper and dill and stir well. Heat up a pan over medium high heat, add cooking spray and zucchinis, stir and cook for 3 minutes. Add egg mix, and the remaining ingredients except the baguette, stir and cook for 10 minutes more. Cut baguette in half, spread egg mix on one-half and top with the other and serve.

**Nutrition:** calories 160, fat 12, fiber 2, carbs 15, protein 17

## Cheese and Eggs Pitas

*Prep Time:* 10 minutes | *Cook Time:* 10 minutes | *Servings:* 4

**Ingredients:**

- 6 eggs
- 2 shallots, chopped
- 1 teaspoon vegetable oil
- 1/3 cup smoked ham, chopped
- 1/3 cup sweet green
- pepper, chopped
- ¼ cup brie cheese
- Salt and black pepper to taste
- 4 lettuce leaves
- 2 whole wheat pita breads

**Directions:**

Heat a pan with the oil over medium heat, add green pepper and shallots, stir and cook for 5 minutes. Add the eggs and the other ingredients except the pitas, mustard and lettuce and cook for another 5 minutes. Cut pitas in half, open pockets, spread 1 teaspoon mustard in each pocket, add 1 lettuce leaf, spread eggs mix and serve.

**Nutrition:** calories 350, fat 7, fiber 2.3, carbs 24, protein 20

## Avocado Toast

*Prep Time:* 10 minutes | *Cook Time:* 0 minutes | *Servings:* 3

**Ingredients:**

- 1 avocado, pitted and mashed
- 3 whole grain bread slices, toasted
- Juice of ½ lemon
- Salt and black
- pepper to taste
- 2 tablespoons feta cheese
- ¼ teaspoon paprika
- 4 cherry tomatoes, cut in halves

**Directions:**

In a bowl, mix avocado with salt, pepper and the other ingredients except the bread and tomatoes and toss. Spread this on toasted bread slices, top with cherry tomatoes and serve.

**Nutrition:** calories 249, fat 18, fiber 3, carbs 18, protein 9

## Couscous and Apricots Bowls

*Prep Time: 15 minutes* | *Cook Time: 5 minutes* | *Servings: 4*

### Ingredients:

- 3 cups low fat milk
- 1 cinnamon stick
- ½ cup apricots, dried and chopped
- 1 cup couscous, uncooked
- ¼ cup currants,
- dried
- A pinch of salt
- 6 teaspoons brown sugar
- 4 teaspoons butter, melted

### Directions:

Heat a pan with the milk and the cinnamon stick over medium heat for about 5 minutes and take off the heat. Add the couscous and the other ingredients, stir, cover and leave aside for 15 minutes. Discard cinnamon stick, divide into bowls and serve.

**Nutrition:** calories 250, fat 6.5, fiber 4, carbs 24, protein 10

## Chickpeas and Eggs Bowls

*Prep Time: 10 minutes* | *Cook Time: 10 minutes* | *Servings: 4*

### Ingredients:

- 3 cups baby spinach
- 1 tablespoon ginger, grated
- ½ cup yellow onion, chopped
- Salt and black pepper to taste
- 1 tablespoon sweet paprika
- 15 ounces canned chickpeas, drained
- ¼ cup olive oil
- 4 eggs

### Directions:

Heat a pan with the oil over medium-high heat. Add spinach, ginger, chickpeas and the other ingredients except the eggs, toss and cook for 5 minutes. Make 4 holes in the mix, crack an egg in each, cover pan, cook for 5 minutes more, divide into bowls and serve.

**Nutrition:** calories 230, fat 6, fiber 3, carbs 14, protein 6

## Tomato and Olives Omelet

*Prep Time: 10 minutes* | *Cook Time: 15 minutes* | *Servings: 4*

### Ingredients:

- 6 eggs
- 1 tablespoon olive oil
- 1 cup green olives, pitted and chopped
- 1 plum tomato, chopped
- 2 tablespoons cilantro, chopped
- Salt and black pepper to taste
- ½ cup goats cheese, crumbled

### Directions:

Heat a pan with the oil over medium heat, add the tomato and olives, stir and cook for 5 minutes. In a bowl, mix eggs with salt and pepper, whisk well and add to the pan. Sprinkle cheese all over and bake in the oven at 325 degrees F for 10 minutes. Slice the omelet, divide between plates and serve with fresh cilantro on top.

**Nutrition:** calories 210, fat 2, fiber 1, carbs 3, protein 5

## Beans Pockets

*Prep Time: 10 minutes* | *Cook Time: 15 minutes* | *Servings: 4*

### Ingredients:

- 1 ½ tablespoons olive oil
- 1 tomato, chopped
- 1 garlic clove, minced
- 1 yellow onion, chopped
- ¼ cup parsley, chopped
- 1 teaspoon cumin,
- ground
- 15 ounces canned fava beans
- ¼ cup lemon juice
- A pinch of red pepper flakes
- Salt and black pepper to taste
- 4 warm whole wheat pita bread pockets

### Directions:

Heat a pan with the oil over medium heat, add onion, stir and cook for 5 minutes. Add garlic, tomato, beans and the other ingredients except the pita pockets, stir and cook over medium heat for 10 minutes. Fill pita pockets with fava bean mix, divide between plates and serve.

**Nutrition:** calories 150, fat 3, fiber 1, carbs 5, protein 5

# Almond Quinoa Bowls

*Prep Time: 10 minutes | Cook Time: 0 minutes | Servings: 4*

## Ingredients:

- 2 cups low fat milk
- 1 teaspoon cinnamon powder
- ¼ cup almonds, chopped
- 1 cup quinoa, cooked
- 1 teaspoon vanilla extract
- 2 tablespoons honey
- 2 dates, dried, pitted and chopped
- 5 apricots, dried and chopped

## Directions:

In a bowl, combine the milk with the quinoa and the other ingredients, stir, set aside for 10 minutes and then serve for breakfast.

**Nutrition:** calories 180, fat 11, fiber 4, carbs 7, protein 5

# Muffin Toast

*Prep Time: 10 minutes | Cook Time: 5 minutes | Servings: 2*

## Ingredients:

- 2 tomatoes, sliced
- 2 eggs, hard-boiled, peeled and sliced
- ¼ cup goats cheese, crumbled
- 1 English muffin,
- halved and toasted
- 1 tablespoon olive oil
- A pinch of chipotle chili powder

## Directions:

Drizzle the oil over each muffin half, and divide tomato, cheese and the other ingredients on each Broil the muffin toast under medium heat for 5 minutes. Divide between 2 plates and serve.

**Nutrition:** calories 145, fat 2, fiber 2, carbs 5, protein 2

# Radicchio and Fennel Salad

*Prep Time: 20 minutes | Cook Time: 0 minutes | Servings: 4*

## Ingredients:

- 1 tablespoon red wine vinegar
- 2 garlic cloves, minced
- 1 teaspoon mustard
- ¼ cup olive oil
- 1 tablespoon lemon juice
- Sea salt and black pepper to taste
- ½ cup kalamata olives, pitted and chopped
- 1 tablespoon parsley, chopped
- 10 cups mixed radicchio and lettuce leaves, torn
- 2 endives, roughly chopped
- 3 medium navel oranges, peeled and cut into medium segments
- 2 bulbs fennel, roughly chopped

## Directions:

In a bowl, mix the olives with the radicchio and the other ingredients, toss and serve for breakfast.

**Nutrition:** calories 100, fat 1, fiber 2, carbs 3, protein 2

# Raspberry Smoothie Bowls

*Prep Time: 5 minutes | Cook Time: 0 minutes | Servings: 2*

## Ingredients:

- 2 bananas, peeled and roughly chopped
- 2 cups raspberries
- ½ cup Greek yogurt
- ½ cup low fat milk
- Coconut flakes, toasted for serving

## Directions:

In a blender, combine the raspberries with the yogurt and the other ingredients except the coconut flakes, pulse well and divide into 2 bowls. Top with coconut flakes and serve right away.

**Nutrition:** calories 100, fat 1, fiber 8, carbs 5, protein 4

# Farro Bowls

*Prep Time: 10 minutes* | *Cook Time: 4 minutes* | *Servings: 2*

## Ingredients:

- 1 tablespoon olive oil
- A pinch of salt and black pepper
- 1 bunch spinach, chopped
- 1 avocado, pitted,
- peeled and chopped
- 1 garlic clove, minced
- 2 cups farro, already cooked
- 1 tomato, chopped

## Directions:

Heat a pan with the oil over medium heat, add garlic, stir and cook for 1 minute. Add the farro and the remaining ingredients, toss, cook everything over medium heat for another 3 minutes, divide into bowls and serve.

**Nutrition:** calories 120, fat 1, fiber 3, carbs 3, protein 6

# Almond Granola Bars

*Prep Time: 40 minutes* | *Cook Time: 4 minutes* | *Servings: 12*

## Ingredients:

- 12 dates, pitted and chopped
- 1 teaspoon vanilla extract
- ¼ cup honey
- ½ cup rolled oats
- ¾ cup cranberries,
- dried
- ¼ cup almond butter
- 1 cup almonds, toasted and chopped
- ¼ cup pumpkin seeds

## Directions:

Put the almond butter in a small saucepan over medium heat, heat up, add the vanilla and the other ingredients, toss for 1 minute, take off the heat, cool down, arrange everything on a lined baking sheet and press well. Keep in the freezer for 30 minutes, divide into 12 pieces and serve for breakfast when you are on the run.

**Nutrition:** calories 140, fat 1, fiber 3, carbs 2, protein 3

# Spinach and Eggs Sandwich

*Prep Time: 5 minutes* | *Cook Time: 6 minutes* | *Servings: 4*

## Ingredients:

- 8 multigrain sandwich slices
- 4 teaspoons olive oil
- 1 tablespoon rosemary, chopped
- 4 eggs
- A pinch of salt and
- black pepper
- 2 cups baby spinach leaves
- 4 tablespoons feta cheese, crumbled
- 1 tomato, cut into 8 slices

## Directions:

Brush the bread slices with half of the oil, arrange on a lined baking sheet and toast in the oven at 375 degrees F for 5 minutes. Heat a pan with the remaining oil over medium heat, add the eggs and the rosemary, stir and cook for 4 minutes. Arrange 4 toasted slices on a plate, divide the eggs, cheese, and spinach on each of these slices. Arrange 2 tomato slices on each of the 4 slices, top with the other 4 slices of bread and serve the sandwiches for breakfast.

**Nutrition:** calories 185, fat 11, fiber 4, carbs 12, protein 8

# Potato Frittata

*Prep Time: 10 minutes* | *Cook Time: 1 hour and 5 minutes* | *Servings: 4*

## Ingredients:

- 28 ounces small potatoes, cut into medium wedges
- 1 yellow onion, chopped
- 3 ounces pancetta, chopped
- 2 garlic cloves, minced
- 1 ½ tablespoons olive oil
- 2 eggs, whisked
- 2 ounces goat cheese, crumbled
- A pinch of salt and black pepper
- A bunch of parsley, chopped

## Directions:

Put potatoes in a large saucepan, add water to cover, add salt, cook over medium heat for 15 minutes, drain and transfer to a bowl. Heat ½ tablespoon olive oil in a saucepan over low heat, add onion, garlic and pancetta, stir, cook for 15 minutes and add over potatoes. Add cheese and eggs, salt, pepper and parsley and stir everything well. Heat a pan with remaining oil over medium heat, add potato mix, cook for 15 minutes on each side, slice, divide between plates and serve for breakfast.

**Nutrition:** calories 250, fat 4, fiber 4, carbs 7, protein 10

# Berry and Egg Mix

*Prep Time: 5 minutes | Cook Time: 5 minutes | Servings: 1*

**Ingredients:**

- 1 egg, whisked
- ½ teaspoon olive oil
- 1 teaspoon cinnamon powder
- 1 tablespoon almond milk
- 3 ounces cottage cheese
- 4 ounces mixed raspberries and blueberries

**Directions:**

In a bowl, mix the egg with milk, cinnamon and the other ingredients except the oil and toss. Heat up a pan with the oil over medium heat, add the berry mix, spread into the pan, cook for 5 minutes, transfer to a plate and serve.

**Nutrition:** calories 140, fat 1, fiber 4, carbs 6, protein 10

# Eggs and Salad

*Prep Time: 10 minutes | Cook Time: 5 minutes | Servings: 2*

**Ingredients:**

- A handful cherry tomatoes, halved
- 1 cucumber, sliced
- 1 avocado, pitted, peeled and chopped
- 2 tablespoons parsley, chopped
- 1 red bell pepper, chopped
- 1 tablespoon basil, chopped
- 1 tablespoon olive oil a drizzle more
- ¼ cup pine nuts, toasted
- Sea salt to taste
- 2 eggs

**Directions:**

In a large bowl mix tomatoes, cucumber And the other ingredients except the eggs and a drizzle of oil and toss. Heat a pan with a drizzle of oil over medium heat, crack eggs and fry them. Divide mixed salad into 2 bowls, top each with an egg and serve for breakfast.

**Nutrition:** calories 140, fat 3, fiber 4, carbs 6, protein 5

# Fruit Salad

*Prep Time: 5 minutes | Cook Time: 0 minutes | Servings: 2*

**Ingredients:**

- 1 white grapefruit, peeled and cut into small segments
- 1 pink grapefruit, peeled and cut into
- small segments
- 1 teaspoon pistachios, chopped
- 1 tablespoon agave nectar

**Directions:**

In a bowl, mix the grapefruit with the nectar and the other ingredients, toss and serve.

**Nutrition:** calories 100, fat 1, fiber 2, carbs 2. protein 1

# Salmon Frittata

*Prep Time: 5 minutes | Cook Time: 10 minutes | Servings: 4*

**Ingredients:**

- 17 ounces red potatoes, boiled and cubed
- 1 tablespoon olive oil
- 2 salmon fillets,
- skinless and boneless
- 8 eggs, whisked
- 1 teaspoon parsley, chopped

**Directions:**

Heat a pan with the oil over medium heat, the eggs mixed with the potatoes and the other ingredients, spread into the pan, cook for 10 minutes, divide between plates and serve.

**Nutrition:** calories 140, fat 7, fiber 3, carbs 12, protein 3

## Tomato and Mushroom Salad

*Prep Time:* 10 minutes | *Cook Time:* 7 minutes | *Servings:* 6

### Ingredients:

- ½ pounds mushrooms, sliced
- 1 tablespoon extra virgin olive oil
- 3 garlic cloves, minced
- 1 teaspoon basil, dried
- Salt and black pepper to taste
- 1 tomato, diced
- 3 tablespoons lemon juice
- ½ cup water
- 1 tablespoons coriander, chopped

### Directions:

Heat a pan with the oil over medium heat, add mushrooms, stir and cook for 3 minutes. Add the rest of the ingredients, cook everything for 4 minutes more, divide into bowls and serve for breakfast.

**Nutrition:** calories 140, fat 4, fiber 4, carbs 7, protein 4

## Lentils Bowls

*Prep Time:* 10 minutes | *Cook Time:* 10 minutes | *Servings:* 4

### Ingredients:

- ½ cup almonds, toasted chopped
- 1 apple, cored, peeled and chopped
- 3 tablespoons maple syrup
- 4 cups low fat milk
- ½ cup red lentils
- ½ teaspoon cinnamon powder
- ½ cup cream of wheat
- ½ cup cranberries, dried
- 1 teaspoon vanilla extract

### Directions:

In a bowl, mix apple with 1 tablespoon maple syrup and almonds, stir and leave aside. Put milk in a saucepan, heat over medium heat, add the lentils and the remaining ingredients, stir, bring to a simmer and cook for 10 minutes. Divide into bowls, top each with apple mixture and serve.

**Nutrition:** calories 150, fat 2, fiber 1, carbs 3, protein 5

## Ham Frittata

*Prep Time:* 10 minutes | *Cook Time:* 15 minutes | *Servings:* 3

### Ingredients:

- 1 yellow onion, chopped
- 2 tablespoons butter
- 1 cup potatoes, boiled and chopped
- ¼ cup parsley, chopped
- ¾ cup ham, finely chopped
- 4 eggs
- ¾ cup lentils, cooked
- 2 tablespoons half and half
- Salt and black pepper to taste
- ½ cup cherry tomatoes, halved
- ¾ cup cheddar cheese, shredded

### Directions:

Heat a pan with the butter over medium heat, add onions, stir and cook for 2 minutes. Add the ham, eggs and the other ingredients except the tomatoes and cheese, spread the mix into the pan and cook for 8 minutes. Arrange halved tomatoes and shredded cheese on top, place under preheated broiler and broil for 5 minutes. Divide between plates and serve for breakfast.

**Nutrition:** calories 156, fat 3, fiber 2, carbs 5, protein 7

## Lentils Granola and Yogurt

*Prep Time:* 10 minutes | *Cook Time:* 1 hour | *Servings:* 4

### Ingredients:

- ½ cup red lentils, soaked for 12 hours and drained
- ¼ cup pumpkin seeds, toasted
- 3 tablespoons hemp seeds
- 2 teaspoons olive oil
- ¼ cup rolled oats
- ¼ cup coconut,
- shredded and toasted
- 1 tablespoon honey+ 1 teaspoon
- 1/3 cup cranberries, dried
- 1 tablespoon orange zest, grated
- 1 cup Greek yogurt
- 1 cup blackberries

### Directions:

Spread lentils on a lined baking sheet, place in the oven at 370 degrees F and roast them for 30 minutes, flipping them occasionally. Mix pumpkin seeds with hemp seeds, oats, coconut, roasted lentils, and the other ingredients except the yogurt, berries and 1 teaspoon honey, toss, spread into a pan and bake at 370 degrees F for 20 minutes. Put half of the yogurt in a bowl, add half of the lentil granola and half of the berries. Add remaining yogurt and lentil mix, drizzle 1 teaspoon honey on top and serve.

**Nutrition:** calories 132, fat 2, fiber 3, carbs 5, protein 4

# Tuna Muffin Sandwich

*Prep Time:* 10 minutes | *Cook Time:* 3 minutes | *Servings:* 2

### Ingredients:

- 1 English muffin, halved
- 6 ounces canned tuna, drained and flaked
- 2 tablespoons
- tomato sauce
- A pinch of sea salt and black pepper
- 2 mozzarella slices
- 1 teaspoon oregano, dried

### Directions:

Spread tomato sauce on each muffin half, divide the tuna and the other ingredients on each, place in the oven at 325 degrees F, bake for 3 minutes and serve hot.

**Nutrition:** calories 110, fat 1, fiber 2, carbs 3, protein 4

# Fish and Eggs Bake

*Prep Time:* 5 minutes | *Cook Time:* 15 minutes | *Servings:* 4

### Ingredients:

- 10 ounces canned tuna, drained and flaked
- 5 eggs, whisked
- ½ cup feta cheese,
- shredded
- Salt and black pepper to taste
- 3 teaspoons olive oil

### Directions:

In a bowl, mix tuna with eggs, and the other ingredients and whisk well. Pour into a lightly greased dish which, place in the oven at 370 degrees F and bake for 15 minutes. Divide the mix between plates and serve.

**Nutrition:** calories 143, fat 2, fiber 4, carbs 5, protein 7

# Tuna Sandwich

*Prep Time:* 5 minutes | *Cook Time:* 0 minutes | *Servings:* 2

### Ingredients:

- 6 ounces canned tuna, drained and flaked
- 1 tablespoon mayonnaise
- 4 slices whole wheat bread
- A pinch of sea salt
- and black pepper
- A handful baby spinach
- 1 tablespoon feta cheese, crumbled
- A splash of white wine vinegar

### Directions:

In a bowl, mix tuna with mayo, vinegar, salt, pepper and whisk well. Divide tuna and the other ingredients on half of the bread, top with the other 2 bread slices and serve.

**Nutrition:** calories 112, fat 2, fiber 1, carbs 2, protein 3

# Simple Scramble

*Prep Time:* 10 minutes | *Cook Time:* 6 minutes | *Servings:* 2

### Ingredients:

- 4 sun dried tomatoes, chopped
- 2 eggs whisked
- 1 teaspoon olive oil
- A small handful of mixed salad leaves
- ½ tablespoon feta cheese, crumbled

### Directions:

Heat a pan with the olive oil over medium heat, add eggs and the other ingredients except the salad leaves, toss and scramble them for 6 minutes. Divide the scramble between 2 plates and serve with salad leaves on the side.

**Nutrition:** calories 140, fat 2, fiber 1, carbs 5, protein 3

# Spinach and Fruits Salad

*Prep Time:* 10 minutes | *Cook Time:* 0 minutes | *Servings:* 4

## Ingredients:

- 5 lettuce leaves, roughly chopped
- 1 peach, stone removed and chopped
- 1 cup baby spinach, chopped

*For the dressing:*

- 1 tablespoon lime juice
- 1 tablespoon tahini
- 1 tablespoon date syrup
- ½ mango, peeled and chopped
- 10 strawberries, halved
- 1 tablespoon hemp seeds
- 1 cucumber, sliced
- 1 tablespoon coconut water
- ½ teaspoon spirulina powder

## Directions:

In a salad bowl, mix lettuce with spinach, mango, and the other ingredients, toss and serve right away for breakfast.

**Nutrition:** calories 130, fat 2, fiber 3, carbs 5, protein 3

# Spinach Muffins

*Prep Time:* 10 minutes | *Cook Time:* 35 minutes | *Servings:* 6

## Ingredients:

- 1 cup quinoa
- 2 cups water
- 1 cup spinach, torn
- 1 small yellow onion, chopped
- 2 eggs
- ¼ cup cheddar cheese, grated
- ½ teaspoon garlic powder
- Sea salt and black pepper to taste
- ½ teaspoon oregano, dried
- A drizzle of olive oil

## Directions:

Put water in a pan, heat over medium heat, add quinoa, stir, simmer for 10 minutes, take off heat and leave aside. Heat a pan with some oil over medium heat, add the onion and spinach, stir and cook for 2-3 minutes. In a bowl, mix quinoa with spinach, onion, eggs and the other ingredients and stir well. Divide mix into a greased muffin pan, place in the oven at 350 degrees F and bake for 20 minutes.

**Nutrition:** calories 87, fat 3, fiber 1, carbs 5, protein 4

# Roasted Potato and Pepper Bake

*Prep Time:* 10 minutes | *Cook Time:* 45 minutes | *Servings:* 6

## Ingredients:

- 2 pounds potatoes, peeled and sliced
- ½ white onion, sliced
- 1 teaspoon garlic powder
- 1 red bell pepper, chopped
- 2 tablespoons olive oil
- Sea salt and black pepper to taste

## Directions:

Spread the potatoes on a lined baking sheet, add the other ingredients, toss, place in the oven at 425 degrees F and bake for 45 minutes, stirring often. Divide between plates and serve warm for breakfast.

**Nutrition:** calories 160, fat 3, fiber 3, carbs 7, protein 3

# Tapioca and Coconut Pudding

*Prep Time: 30 minutes | Cook Time: 15 minutes | Servings: 3*

**Ingredients:**

- ¼ cup pearl tapioca
- ¼ cup sugar
- 2 cups water
- ½ cup coconut flakes
- 1 and ½ teaspoon lemon juice

**Directions:**

Put tapioca in a pan, add water, stir, cover and leave aside for 30 minutes. Add the rest of the ingredients, toss, cook over medium heat for 15 minutes, divide into breakfast bowls and serve.

**Nutrition:** calories 120, fat 1, fiber 3, carbs 5, protein 2

# Beans Tortillas

*Prep Time: 10 minutes | Cook Time: 25 minutes | Servings: 4*

**Ingredients:**

- 1 yellow onion, chopped
- 2 garlic cloves, minced
- 1 tablespoon olive oil
- 1 small green bell pepper, sliced
- 3 cups canned pinto beans, drained
- 2 hot chili peppers, chopped
- 4 tablespoon cilantro, chopped
- 1 teaspoon cumin, ground
- A pinch of salt
- 8 whole wheat Greek tortillas
- Salsa for serving
- 1 cup cheddar cheese, shredded
- Lettuce leaves shredded for serving
- Black olives, pitted and chopped for serving

**Directions:**

Heat a pan with oil over medium heat, add onion and cook for 3 minutes stirring occasionally. Add garlic, stir and cook for 1 minute. Add green pepper, beans, chili peppers, salt, cilantro and cumin and cook for 10 minutes more. Mash everything using a potato masher, stir and cook for 5 minutes more. Divide this on each tortilla, divide the remaining ingredients as well, roll and serve for breakfast.

**Nutrition:** calories 132, fat 2, fiber 4, carbs 5, protein 3

# Cauliflower Hash

*Prep Time: 10 minutes | Cook Time: 1 hour | Servings: 4*

**Ingredients:**

- 2 cups cauliflower florets
- 8 medium potatoes
- 2 cups white mushrooms, roughly chopped
- 6 tomatoes, cubed
- 1 yellow onion, chopped
- 1 small garlic clove, minced
- ¼ teaspoon onion powder
- 3 tablespoons basil, chopped
- 3 tablespoons parsley, chopped

**Directions:**

Place potatoes in oven at 350 degrees F, bake for 45 minutes, leave aside to cool down, peel, chop them roughly and arrange on a lined baking sheet. Add the rest of the ingredients, toss, bake at 350 degrees F for 15 minutes more. Divide the mix between plates and serve for breakfast.

**Nutrition:** calories 143, fat 1, fiber 1, carbs 3, protein 4

# Stuffed Tomato

*Prep Time: 10 minutes | Cook Time: 30 minutes | Servings: 2*

**Ingredients:**

- 2 eggs
- 2 tomatoes, tops cut off and insides scooped out
- 1 teaspoon parsley, chopped
- Salt and black pepper to taste

**Directions:**

Season tomato cups with salt and pepper and arrange them on a lined baking sheet. Crack an egg into each tomato cup, sprinkle the parsley on top, bake in the oven at 350 degrees F for 30 minutes, divide between plates and serve.

**Nutrition:** calories 162, fat 1, fiber 2, carbs 4, protein 4

# Tomato Sandwich

*Prep Time: 5 minutes | Cook Time: 5 minutes | Servings: 1*

**Ingredients:**

- 1 English muffin, halved and toasted
- 1 tablespoon mayonnaise
- 3 bacon slices, halved
- Salt and black pepper to taste
- 2 tomato slices

**Directions:**

Heat a pan over medium heat, add bacon, cook for 5 minutes, transfer to paper towels, drain excess grease and leave aside. Spread the mayo on each muffin halves, arrange tomato and bacon on one half, season with salt and pepper, top with the other muffin half and serve.

**Nutrition:** calories 110, fat 1, fiber 2, carbs 2, protein 1

# Potato and Cucumbers Salad

*Prep Time: 15 minutes | Cook Time: 20 minutes | Servings: 6*

**Ingredients:**

- 2 pounds new potatoes, halved
- 2 tomatoes, cut in medium segments
- 2 bell peppers, chopped
- 1 cucumber, chopped
- 1 small red onion, sliced
- ½ cup kalamata olives, pitted and sliced
- 4 ounces feta cheese, crumbled
- ¼ cup lemon juice
- ½ cup olive oil
- 1 tablespoon oregano, chopped
- 1 tablespoon mustard
- Salt and black pepper to taste
- 1 teaspoon sugar
- 2 garlic cloves, minced

**Directions:**

Put potatoes in a pan, add water to cover, add salt, bring to a boil over medium high heat, cook for 20 minutes, drain, leave aside to cool down, cut into cubes and put in a salad bowl. Add tomatoes, and the other ingredients, toss to coat and keep in the fridge until you serve it.

**Nutrition:** calories 132, fat 1, fiber 2, carbs 5, protein 5

# Bulgur and Salmon Bowls

*Prep Time: 40 minutes | Cook Time: 10 minutes | Servings: 4*

**Ingredients:**

- 1 pound salmon fillet, skinless and boneless
- 1 tablespoon olive oil +1 teaspoon
- 1 cup bulgur
- 1 cup parsley, chopped
- 2 medium
- cucumbers, sliced
- ¼ cup mint, chopped
- 3 tablespoons lemon juice
- 1 small red onion, sliced
- Salt and black pepper to taste
- 2 cup hot water

**Directions:**

Heat a pan with 1 teaspoon oil over medium heat, add salmon, season with salt and pepper, cook for 5 minutes on each side, take off heat, transfer to a plate and cool down for about 15 minutes. In a bowl, mix bulgur with hot water, stir, cover, leave aside for 25 minutes, drain and transfer to another bowl. Add the salmon and the other ingredients, toss, divide into bowls and serve.

**Nutrition:** calories 142, fat 2, fiber 1, carbs 4, protein 7

# Quinoa and Asparagus Salad

*Prep Time: 10 minutes | Cook Time: 10 minutes | Servings: 4*

**Ingredients:**

- ½ cup peas
- 2 and ½ cups asparagus, roughly chopped
- 3 bacon slices, cooked and chopped
- 1 tablespoon butter
- 3 tablespoons white vinegar
- 1 and ¾ cups quinoa
- 2 teaspoons mustard
- Salt and black
- pepper to taste
- 5 ounces baby spinach
- ½ cup parsley, chopped
- 1 tablespoon thyme, chopped
- 1 tablespoon tarragon, chopped
- 3 tablespoons almonds, chopped

**Directions:**

Put water in a saucepan, bring to a boil over medium high heat, add peas and asparagus, boil for 2 minutes, drain, rinse under cold water, put in a bowl and set aside. Heat up a pan with the butter, mustard and viegar over medium high heat, add quinoa, salt and pepper and cook for 1 minute. Transfer quinoa to a bowl, add asparagus and peas mix, thyme, bacon and the other ingredients, toss and serve.

**Nutrition:** calories 187, fat 4, fiber 2, carbs 4, protein 6

## Strawberry Salad

*Prep Time: 5 minutes* | *Cook Time: 0 minutes* | *Servings: 6*

**Ingredients:**

- 3 tablespoons mayonnaise
- 2 tablespoons low fat milk
- 1 tablespoon poppy seeds
- 10 ounces romaine lettuce leaves, torn
- 2 bunches spinach, chopped
- 1 tablespoon white wine vinegar
- 1 cup strawberries sliced
- 2 tablespoons almonds, toasted and chopped

**Directions:**

In a salad bowl, mix the lettuce with strawberries and the other ingredients, toss to coat and serve right away.

**Nutrition:** calories 148, fat 6, fiber 6, carbs 6, protein 4

## Asparagus and Beans Bowls

*Prep Time: 10 minutes* | *Cook Time: 22 minutes* | *Servings: 6*

**Ingredients:**

- 1 tablespoon parmesan, grated
- A pinch of sea salt and black pepper
- 1 tablespoon lemon juice
- 2 cups fava beans
- 1 shallot, chopped
- 2 bunches asparagus, trimmed
- 1 cup peas
- ½ cup olive oil + 3 tablespoons
- 4 bacon slices, cooked and crumbled

**Directions:**

In a bowl, mix parmesan with lemon juice, 3 tablespoons olive oil, salt and pepper and whisk well. Put water and a pinch of salt in a saucepan, add fava beans, cook for 4 minutes over medium heat, drain, transfer to a bowl and leave aside. Heat the same pan over medium heat, add asparagus and peas, stir, cook for 3 minutes, drain and add to fava beans. Heat a small pan with ½ cup olive oil over medium high heat, add shallot, stir, cook for 10 minutes and add to asparagus mix. Add the parmesan dressing, toss and serve for breakfast.

**Nutrition:** calories 164, fat 3, fiber 1, carbs 3, protein 2

## Lime Corn Bowls

*Prep Time: 10 minutes* | *Cook Time: 20 minutes* | *Servings: 6*

**Ingredients:**

- 8 ears of corn, husks removed
- 3 tablespoons mayonnaise
- 2/3 cup feta cheese, crumbled
- ¼ cup lime juice
- 1 lime cut into 4 wedges
- 1/3 cup chives, chopped
- Salt and black pepper to the taste

**Directions:**

Preheat your grill to 450 degrees F. Brush corn with mayo, season with salt and pepper, place on preheated grill over medium heat and cook for 12 minutes, turning it occasionally. Cut kernels from cobs, transfer to a bowl, add the rest of the ingredients, toss and serve for breakfast.

**Nutrition:** calories 132, fat 2, fiber 3, carbs 5, protein 4

## Potato and Sausage Hash

*Prep Time: 10 minutes* | *Cook Time: 15 minutes* | *Servings: 6*

**Ingredients:**

- ½ pound breakfast sausage, ground
- 2 cups red potatoes, cubed
- 1 yellow onion, chopped
- 1 cup broccoli florets, chopped
- 1 cup cherry tomatoes, cubed
- 2 tablespoons olive oil
- ½ tablespoon dill, chopped
- 1 teaspoon oregano, dried
- 1 teaspoon thyme, dried
- A pinch of salt and black pepper

**Directions:**

Heat a skillet with the oil over medium heat. Add the potatoes and cook for 5 minutes. Add the sausage and cook for 5 minutes more. Add the rest of the ingredients, cook the mix for 5 more minutes, divide into bowls and serve for breakfast.

**Nutrition:** calories 143, fat 2, fiber 1, carbs 2, protein 3

# Eggplant Salad

*Prep Time: 20 minutes* | *Cook Time: 25 minutes* | *Servings: 4*

## Ingredients:

- 1 eggplant, chopped
- ½ cup extra-virgin olive oil
- ½ pound cherry tomatoes, halved
- A pinch of sea salt and black pepper
- 4 eggs, poached
- 1 teaspoon hot sauce
- ¼ cup basil, chopped
- ¼ cup mint, chopped

## Directions:

In a bowl, mix eggplant with salt, stir, leave aside for 20 minutes, drain excess liquid and transfer to another bowl. Heat a pan with half the olive oil over medium high heat, add the eggplant, cook for 3 minutes on each side and return to the bowl. Heat the same pan with remaining oil over medium heat, add tomatoes, stir and cook for 8 minutes. Return eggplant to the pan, add the rest of the ingredients except the eggs, toss and cook for 1 minute. Divide between plates, top with poached eggs and serve for breakfast.

**Nutrition:** calories 132, fat 1, fiber 2, carbs 2, protein 2

# Veggie Ciabatta

*Prep Time: 10 minutes* | *Cook Time: 25 minutes* | *Servings: 2*

## Ingredients:

- 2 tablespoons olive oil
- 1 eggplant, sliced
- 4 slices cheddar cheese
- Salt and black pepper to taste
- 4 tablespoons basil pesto
- 1 avocado, pitted, peeled and chopped
- 2 ciabatta rolls, halved

## Directions:

Mix eggplant with oil, season with salt and pepper to taste, toss, arrange on a baking sheet and bake at 360 degrees F for 20 minutes, flipping the eggplant slices halfway. Arrange the ciabatta rolls on another baking sheet, place them in the oven next to the eggplant slices and brown them for a 5 minutes. Take rolls out of the oven, spread the pesto, divide the eggplant slices, avocado and cheese slices on 2 ciabatta halves. Top with the other 2 ciabatta halves, divide between 2 plates and serve.

**Nutrition:** calories 150, fat 6, fiber 2, carbs 7, protein 4

# Eggplant Spread

*Prep Time: 10 minutes* | *Cook Time: 15 minutes* | *Servings: 8*

## Ingredients:

- ¼ cup extra-virgin olive oil + a drizzle
- 1 eggplant, sliced
- Salt and black pepper to taste
- 2 and ½ tablespoons lemon juice
- ¼ cup Greek yogurt
- 1 cup arugula
- 1 cup mixed green, yellow, red and orange cherry tomatoes, halved
- 1 garlic clove, minced
- 1 ounce parmesan, grated
- 2 tablespoon mint, torn

## Directions:

Brush eggplant slices with olive oil, place on preheated grill pan over medium heat, cook them for 6 minutes on each side and transfer them to a plate. Transfer eggplant to a blender, add salt, pepper, 1 tablespoon lemon juice, yogurt and garlic and blend well. In a bowl, mix tomatoes with mint, arugula, remaining lemon juice and a drizzle of oil, salt and pepper to taste and toss to coat. Divide the eggplant spread into bowls, top with the tomato salad and serve on toasted bread for breakfast.

**Nutrition:** calories 185, fat 1, fiber 2, carbs 3, protein 3

## Lamb and Chickpeas Stew

*Prep Time:* 10 minutes | *Cook Time:* 1 hour and 20 minutes | *Servings:* 6

### Ingredients:

- 1 and ½ pounds lamb shoulder, cubed
- 3 tablespoons olive oil
- 1 cup yellow onion, chopped
- 1 cup carrots, cubed
- 1 cup celery, chopped
- 3 garlic cloves, minced
- 4 rosemary springs, chopped
- 2 cups chicken stock
- 1 cup tomato puree
- 15 ounces canned chickpeas, drained and rinsed
- 10 ounces baby spinach
- 2 tablespoons black olives, pitted and sliced
- A pinch of salt and black pepper

### Directions:

Heat up a pot with the oil over medium-high heat, add the meat, salt and pepper and brown for 5 minutes. Add carrots, celery, onion and garlic, stir and sauté for 5 minutes more. Add the rosemary, stock, chickpeas and the other ingredients except the spinach and olives, stir and cook for 1 hour. Add the rest of the ingredients, cook the stew over medium heat for 10 minutes more, divide into bowls and serve.

**Nutrition:** calories 340, fat 16, fiber 3, carbs 21, protein 19

## Chorizo and Lentils Stew

*Prep Time:* 10 minutes | *Cook Time:* 35 minutes | *Servings:* 4

### Ingredients:

- 4 cups water
- 1 cup carrots, sliced
- 1 yellow onion, chopped
- 1 tablespoon extra-virgin olive oil
- ¾ cup celery, chopped
- 1 and ½ teaspoon garlic, minced
- 1 and ½ pounds gold potatoes, roughly chopped
- 7 ounces chorizo, cut in half lengthwise and thinly sliced
- 1 and ½ cup lentils
- ½ teaspoon smoked paprika
- ½ teaspoon oregano
- Salt and black pepper to taste
- 14 ounces canned tomatoes, chopped
- ½ cup cilantro, chopped

### Directions:

Heat a saucepan with oil over medium high heat, add onion, garlic, celery and carrots, stir and cook for 4 minutes. Add the chorizo, stir and cook for 1 minute more. Add the rest of the ingredients except the cilantro, stir, bring to a boil, reduce heat to medium-low and simmer for 25 minutes. Divide the stew into bowls and serve with the cilantro sprinkled on top. Enjoy!

**Nutrition:** calories 400, fat 16, fiber 13, carbs 58, protein 24

# Lamb and Potato Stew

*Prep Time:* 10 minutes | *Cook Time:* 2 hours | *Servings:* 4

## Ingredients:

- 2 and ½ pounds lamb shoulder, boneless and cut in small pieces
- Salt and black pepper to taste
- 1 yellow onion, chopped
- 3 tablespoons extra virgin olive oil
- 3 tomatoes, grated
- 1 and ½ cups chicken stock
- ½ cup dry white wine
- 1 bay leaf
- 2 and ½ pounds gold potatoes, cut into medium cubes
- ¾ cup green olives

## Directions:

Heat a saucepan with the oil over medium high heat, add the lamb, brown for 10 minutes, transfer to a platter and keep warm for now. Heat the pan again, add onion, stir and cook for 4 minutes. Add tomatoes, stir, reduce heat to low and cook for 15 minutes. Return lamb meat to pan, add wine and the rest of the ingredients except the potatoes and olives, stir, increase heat to medium high, bring to a boil, reduce heat again, cover pan and simmer for 30 minutes. Add potatoes and olives, stir, cook for 1 more hour, divide into bowls and serve.

**Nutrition:** calories 450, fat 12, fiber 4, carbs 33, protein 39

# Meatball and Pasta Soup

*Prep Time:* 10 minutes | *Cook Time:* 40 minutes | *Servings:* 4

## Ingredients:

- 12 ounces pork meat, ground
- 12 ounces veal, ground
- Salt and black pepper to taste
- 1 garlic clove, minced
- 2 garlic cloves, sliced
- 2 teaspoons thyme, chopped
- 1 egg, whisked
- 3 ounces Manchego, grated
- 2 tablespoons extra virgin olive oil
- 1/3 cup panko
- 4 cups chicken stock
- A pinch of saffron
- 15 ounces canned tomatoes, crushed
- 1 tablespoons parsley, chopped
- 8 ounces pasta

## Directions:

In a bowl, mix veal with pork, 1 garlic clove, 1 teaspoon thyme, ¼ teaspoon paprika, salt, pepper to taste, egg, manchego, panko, stir very well and shape medium meatballs out of this mix. Heat a pan with 1 ½ tablespoons oil over medium high heat, add half of the meatballs, cook for 2 minutes on each side, transfer to paper towels, drain grease and put on a plate. Repeat this with the rest of the meatballs. Heat a saucepan with the rest of the oil, add sliced garlic, stir and cook for 1 minute. Add the remaining ingredients and the meatballs, stir, reduce heat to medium low, cook for 25 minutes and season with salt and pepper. Cook pasta according to instructions, drain, put in a bowl and mix with ½ cup soup. Divide pasta into soup bowls, add soup and meatballs on top, sprinkle parsley all over and serve.

**Nutrition:** calories 380, fat 17, fiber 2, carbs 28, protein 26

# Peas Soup

*Prep Time:* 10 minutes | *Cook Time:* 10 minutes | *Servings:* 4

## Ingredients:

- 1 teaspoon shallot, chopped
- 1 tablespoon butter
- 1-quart chicken stock
- 2 eggs
- 3 tablespoons lemon juice
- 2 cups peas
- 2 tablespoons parmesan, grated
- Salt and black pepper to taste

## Directions:

Heat a saucepan with the butter over medium high heat, add shallot, stir and cook for 2 minutes. Add stock, lemon juice, some salt and pepper and the whisked eggs. Add more salt and pepper to taste, peas and parmesan cheese, stir, cook for 3 minutes, divide into bowls and serve.

**Nutrition:** calories 180, fat 39, fiber 4, carbs 10, protein 14

# Minty Lamb Stew

*Prep Time:* 10 minutes | *Cook Time:* 1 hour and 45 minutes | *Servings:* 4

## Ingredients:

- 3 cups orange juice
- ½ cup mint tea
- Salt and black pepper to taste
- 2 pounds lamb shoulder chops
- 1 tablespoon mustard, dry
- 3 tablespoons canola oil
- 1 tablespoon ras el hanout
- 1 carrot, chopped
- 1 yellow onion, chopped
- 1 celery rib, chopped
- 1 tablespoon ginger, grated
- 28 ounces canned tomatoes, crushed
- 1 tablespoon garlic, minced
- 2-star anise
- 1 cup apricots, dried and cut in halves
- 1 cinnamon stick
- ½ cup mint, chopped
- 15 ounces canned chickpeas, drained
- 6 tablespoons yogurt

## Directions:

Put orange juice in a saucepan, bring to a boil over medium heat, take off heat, add tea leaves, cover and leave aside for 3 minutes, strain this and leave aside. Heat a saucepan with 2 tablespoons oil over medium high heat, add lamb chops seasoned with salt, pepper, mustard and rasel hanout, toss, brown for 3 minutes on each side and transfer to a plate. Add remaining oil to the saucepan, heat over medium heat, add ginger, onion, carrot, garlic and celery, stir and cook for 5 minutes. Add orange juice, star anise, tomatoes, cinnamon stick, lamb, apricots, stir and cook for 1 hour and 30 minutes. Transfer lamb chops to a cutting board, discard bones and chop. Bring sauce from the pan to a boil, add chickpeas and mint, stir and cook for 10 minutes. Discard cinnamon and star anise, divide into bowls and serve with yogurt on top.

**Nutrition:** calories 560, fat 24, fiber 11, carbs 35, protein 33

# Spinach and Orzo Soup

*Prep Time: 10 minutes | Cook Time: 10 minutes | Servings: 4*

**Ingredients:**

- ½ cup orzo
- 6 cups chicken soup
- 1 and ½ cups parmesan, grated
- Salt and black pepper to taste
- 1 and ½ teaspoon
- oregano, dried
- ¼ cup yellow onion, finely chopped
- 3 cups baby spinach
- 2 tablespoons lemon juice
- ½ cup peas, frozen

**Directions:**

Heat a saucepan with the stock over high heat, add oregano, orzo, onion, salt and pepper, stir, bring to a boil, cover and cook for 10 minutes. Take soup off the heat, add salt and pepper to taste and the rest of the ingredients , stir well and divide into soup bowls. Serve right away.

**Nutrition:** calories 201, fat 5, fiber 3, carbs 28, protein 17

# Minty Lentil and Spinach Soup

*Prep Time: 10 minutes | Cook Time: 30 minutes | Servings: 6*

**Ingredients:**

- 2 tablespoons olive oil
- 1 yellow onion, chopped
- A pinch of salt and black pepper
- 2 garlic cloves, minced
- 1 teaspoon coriander, ground
- 1 teaspoon cumin, ground
- 1 teaspoon sumac
- 1 teaspoon red
- pepper, crushed
- 2 teaspoons mint, dried
- 1 tablespoon flour
- 6 cups veggie stock
- 3 cups water
- 12 ounces spinach, torn
- 1 and ½ cups brown lentils, rinsed
- 2 cups parsley, chopped
- Juice of 1 lime

**Directions:**

Heat up a pot with the oil over medium heat, add the onions, stir and sauté for 5 minutes. Add garlic, salt, pepper, coriander, cumin, sumac, red pepper, mint and flour, stir and cook for another minute. Add the stock, water and the other ingredients except the parsley and lime juice, stir, bring to a simmer and cook for 20 minutes. Add the parsley and lime juice, cook the soup for 5 minutes more, ladle into bowls and serve.

**Nutrition:** calories 170, fat 7, fiber 6, carbs 22, protein 8

# Chicken and Apricots Stew

*Prep Time: 10 minutes | Cook Time: 2 hours and 10 minutes | Servings: 4*

**Ingredients:**

- 3 garlic cloves, minced
- 1 tablespoon parsley, chopped
- 20 saffron threads
- 3 tablespoons cilantro, chopped
- Salt and black pepper to taste
- 1 teaspoon ginger, ground
- 2 tablespoons olive
- oil
- 3 red onions, thinly sliced
- 4 chicken drumsticks
- 5 ounces apricots, dried
- 2 tablespoons butter
- ¼ cup honey
- 2/3 cup walnuts, chopped
- ½ cinnamon stick

**Directions:**

Heat a pan over medium high heat, add saffron threads, toast them for 2 minutes, transfer to a bowl, cool down and crush. Add the chicken pieces, 1 tablespoon cilantro, parsley, garlic, ginger, salt, pepper, oil and 2 tablespoons water, toss really well and keep in the fridge for 30 minutes. Arrange onion on the bottom of a saucepan. Add chicken and marinade, add 1 tablespoon butter, place on stove over medium high heat and cook for 15 minutes. Add ¼ cup water, stir, cover pan, reduce heat to medium-low and simmer for 45 minutes. Heat a pan over medium heat, add 2 tablespoons honey, cinnamon stick, apricots and ¾ cup water, stir, bring to a boil, reduce to low and simmer for 15 minutes. Take off heat, discard cinnamon and leave to cool down. Heat a pan with remaining butter over medium heat, add remaining honey and walnuts, stir, cook for 5 minutes and transfer to a plate. Add chicken to apricot sauce also season with salt, pepper and the rest of the cilantro, stir, cook for 10 minutes and  serve on top of walnuts.

**Nutrition:** calories 560, fat 10, fiber 4, carbs 34, protein 44

# Fish and Veggie Stew

*Prep Time:* 10 minutes | *Cook Time:* 1 hour and 30 minutes | *Servings:* 4

## Ingredients:

- 6 lemon wedges, pulp separated and chopped and some of the peel reserved
- 2 tablespoons parsley, chopped
- 2 tomatoes, cut in halves, peeled and grated
- 2 tablespoons cilantro, chopped
- 2 garlic cloves, minced
- ½ teaspoon paprika
- 2 tablespoons water
- ½ cup water
- ½ teaspoon cumin,
- ground
- Salt and black pepper to taste
- 4 bass fillets
- ¼ cup olive oil
- 3 carrots, sliced
- 1 red bell pepper, sliced lengthwise and thinly cut in strips
- 1 and ¼ pounds potatoes, peeled and sliced
- ½ cup olives
- 1 red onion, thinly sliced

## Directions:

In a bowl, mix tomatoes with lemon pulp, cilantro, parsley, cumin, garlic, paprika, salt, pepper, 2 tablespoons water, 2 teaspoons oil and the fish, toss to coat and keep in the fridge for 30 minutes. Heat a saucepan with the water and some salt over medium high heat, add potatoes and carrots, stir, cook for 10 minutes and drain. Heat a pan over medium heat, add bell pepper and ¼ cup water, cover, cook for 5 minutes and take off heat. Coat a saucepan with remaining oil, add potatoes and carrots, ¼ cup water, onion slices, fish and its marinade, bell pepper strips, olives, salt and pepper, toss gently, cook for 45 minutes, divide into bowls and serve.

**Nutrition:** calories 440, fat 18, fiber 8, carbs 43, protein 30

# Tomato Soup

*Prep Time:* 60 minutes | *Cook Time:* 2 minutes | *Servings:* 4

## Ingredients:

- ½ green bell pepper, chopped
- ½ red bell pepper, chopped
- 1 and ¾ pounds tomatoes, chopped
- ¼ cup bread, torn
- 9 tablespoons extra virgin olive oil
- 1 garlic clove,
- minced
- 2 teaspoons sherry vinegar
- Salt and black pepper to taste
- 1 tablespoon cilantro, chopped
- A pinch of cumin, ground

## Directions:

In a blender, mix green and red bell peppers with tomatoes, salt, pepper, 6 tablespoons oil, and the other ingredients except the bread and cilantro, and pulse well. Keep in the fridge for 1 hour. Heat up a pan with remaining oil over medium high heat, add bread pieces, and toast them for 1 minute. Divide cold soup into bowls, top with bread cubes and cilantro then serve.

**Nutrition:** calories 260, fat 23, fiber 2, carbs 11, protein 2

# Chickpeas Soup

*Prep Time:* 10 minutes | *Cook Time:* 35 minutes | *Servings:* 4

## Ingredients:

- 1 bunch kale, leaves torn
- Salt and black pepper to taste
- 3 tablespoons olive oil
- 1 celery stalk, chopped
- 1 yellow onion,
- chopped
- 1 carrot, chopped
- 30 ounces canned chickpeas, drained
- 14 ounces canned tomatoes, chopped
- 1 bay leaf
- 3 rosemary sprigs
- 4 cups veggie stock

## Directions:

In a bowl, mix kale with half of the oil, salt and pepper, toss to coat, spread on a lined baking sheet, cook at 425 degrees F for 12 minutes and leave aside to cool down. Heat a saucepan with remaining oil over medium high heat, add carrot, celery, onion, some salt and pepper, stir and cook for 5 minutes. Add the rest of the ingredients, toss and simmer for 20 minutes. Discard rosemary and bay leaf, puree using a blender and divide into soup bowls. Top with roasted kale and serve.

**Nutrition:** calories 360, fat 14, fiber 11, carbs 53, protein 14

# Fish Soup

*Prep Time:* 10 minutes | *Cook Time:* 35 minutes | *Servings:* 6

## Ingredients:

- 2 garlic cloves, minced
- 2 tablespoons olive oil
- 1 fennel bulb, sliced
- 1 yellow onion, chopped
- 1 pinch saffron, soaked in some orange juice for 10 minutes and drained
- 14 ounces canned tomatoes, peeled
- 1 strip orange zest
- 6 cups seafood stock
- 10 halibut fillet, cut into big pieces
- 20 shrimp, peeled and deveined
- 1 bunch parsley, chopped
- Salt and white pepper to taste

## Directions:

Heat a saucepan with oil over medium high heat, add onion, garlic and fennel, stir and cook for 10 minutes. Add saffron, tomatoes, orange zest and stock, stir, bring to a boil and simmer for 20 minutes. Add fish and shrimp, stir and cook for 6 minutes. Sprinkle parsley, salt and pepper, divide into bowls and serve.

**Nutrition:** calories 340, fat 20, fiber 3, carbs 23, protein 45

# Shrimp Soup

*Prep Time:* 30 minutes | *Cook Time:* 5 minutes | *Servings:* 6

## Ingredients:

- 1 English cucumber, chopped
- 3 cups tomato juice
- 3 jarred roasted red peppers, chopped
- ½ cup olive oil
- 2 tablespoons sherry vinegar
- 1 teaspoon sherry vinegar
- 1 garlic clove, mashed
- 2 baguette slices, cut into cubes and toasted
- Salt and black pepper to taste
- ½ teaspoon cumin, ground
- ¾ pounds shrimp, peeled and deveined
- 1 teaspoon thyme, chopped

## Directions:

In a blender, mix cucumber with tomato juice, red peppers and pulse well, bread, 6 tablespoons oil, 2 tablespoons vinegar, cumin, salt, pepper and garlic, pulse again, transfer to a bowl and keep in the fridge for 30 minutes. Heat a saucepan with 1 tablespoon oil over high heat, add shrimp, stir and cook for 2 minutes. Add thyme, and the rest of the ingredients, cook for 1 minute and transfer to a plate. Divide cold soup into bowls, top with shrimp and serve. Enjoy!

**Nutrition:** calories 230, fat 7, fiber 10, carbs 24, protein 13

# Chili Watermelon Soup

*Prep Time:* 4 hours | *Cook Time:* 5 minutes | *Servings:* 4

## Ingredients:

- 3 pounds watermelon, sliced
- ½ teaspoon chipotle chili powder
- 2 tablespoons olive oil
- Salt to taste
- 1 tomato, chopped
- 1 tablespoon shallot, chopped
- ¼ cup cilantro, chopped
- 1 small cucumber, chopped
- 1 small Serrano chili pepper, chopped
- 3 and ½ tablespoons lime juice
- ¼ cup crème Fraiche
- ½ tablespoon red wine vinegar

## Directions:

In a bowl, mix 1 tablespoon oil with chipotle powder, stir and brush the watermelon with this mix. Put the watermelon slices preheated grill pan over medium high heat, grill for 1 minute on each side, cool down, chop and put in a blender. Add cucumber and the rest of the ingredients except the vinegar and the lime juice and pulse well. Transfer to bowls, top with lime juice and vinegar, keep in the fridge for 4 hours and then serve.

**Nutrition:** calories 115, fat 0, fiber 2, carbs 18, protein 2

# Halibut and Veggies Stew

*Prep Time:* 10 minutes | *Cook Time:* 50 minutes | *Servings:* 4

## Ingredients:

- 1 yellow onion, chopped
- 2 tablespoons oil
- 1 fennel bulb, stalks removed, sliced and roughly chopped
- 1 carrot, thinly sliced crosswise
- 1 red bell pepper, chopped
- 2 garlic cloves, minced
- 3 tablespoons tomato paste
- 16 ounces canned chickpeas, drained
- ½ cup dry white wine
- 1 teaspoon thyme, chopped
- A pinch of smoked paprika
- Salt and black pepper to taste
- 1 bay leaf
- 2 pinches saffron
- 4 baguette slices, toasted
- 3 and ½ cups water
- 13 mussels, debearded
- 11 ounces halibut fillets, skinless and cut into chunks

## Directions:

Heat a saucepan with the oil over medium high heat, add fennel, onion, bell pepper, garlic, tomato paste and carrot, stir and cook for 5 minutes. Add wine, stir and cook for 2 minutes. Add the rest of the ingredients except the halibut and mussels, stir, bring to a boil, cover and boil for 25 minutes. Add, halibut and mussels, cover and simmer for 6 minutes more. Discard unopened mussels, ladle into bowls and serve with toasted bread on the side.

**Nutrition:** calories 450, fat 12, fiber 13, carbs 47, protein 34

# Cucumber Soup

*Prep Time:* 10 minutes | *Cook Time:* 6 minutes | *Servings:* 4

## Ingredients:

- 3 bread slices
- ¼ cup almonds
- 4 teaspoons almonds
- 3 cucumbers, peeled and chopped
- 3 garlic cloves, minced
- ½ cup warm water
- 6 scallions, thinly sliced
- ¼ cup white wine vinegar
- 3 tablespoons olive oil
- Salt to taste
- 1 teaspoon lemon juice
- ½ cup green grapes, cut in halves

## Directions:

Heat a pan over medium high heat, add almonds, stir, toast for 5 minutes, transfer to a plate and leave aside. Soak bread in warm water for 2 minutes, transfer to a blender, add almost all the cucumber, salt, the oil, garlic, 5 scallions, lemon juice, vinegar and half of the almonds and pulse well. Ladle soup into bowls, top with reserved ingredients and 2 tablespoons grapes and serve.

**Nutrition:** calories 200, fat 12, fiber 3, carbs 20, protein 6

# Chickpeas, Tomato and Kale Stew

*Prep Time:* 10 minutes | *Cook Time:* 30 minutes | *Servings: 4*

Ingredients:

- 1 yellow onion, chopped
- 1 tablespoon extra-virgin olive oil
- 2 cups sweet potatoes, peeled and chopped
- 1 ½ teaspoon cumin, ground
- 4-inch cinnamon stick
- 14 ounces canned tomatoes, chopped
- 14 ounces canned chickpeas, drained
- 1 ½ teaspoon honey
- 6 tablespoons orange juice
- 1 cup water
- Salt and black pepper to taste
- ½ cup green olives, pitted
- 2 cups kale leaves, chopped

Directions:

Heat a saucepan with the oil over medium high heat, add onion, cumin and cinnamon stir and cook for 5 minutes. Add potatoes and the rest of the ingredients except the kale, stir, cover, reduce heat to medium-low and cook for 15 minutes. Add kale, stir, cover again and cook for 10 minutes more. Divide into bowls and serve.

Nutrition: calories 280, fat 6, fiber 9, carbs 53, protein 10

# Chicken and Rice Soup

*Prep Time:* 10 minutes | *Cook Time:* 30 minutes | *Servings: 4*

Ingredients:

- ½ cup water
- Salt and black pepper to taste
- 6 cups chicken stock
- ¼ cup lemon juice
- 1 chicken breast,
- boneless, skinless and cut into thin strips
- ½ cup white rice
- 6 tablespoons mint, chopped

Directions:

Put the water in a saucepan, add salt, ½ cup stock, stir, bring to a boil over medium heat, add rice, stir, reduce temperature to low, cover, simmer for 20 minutes, take off heat and cool down. Put remaining stock in another saucepan, bring to a boil over medium heat, add chicken, rice and the rest of the ingredients, stir, simmer for 10 minutes more, divide into bowls and serve.

Nutrition: calories 180, fat 2, fiber 1, carbs 21, protein 20

# Veggie Stew

*Prep Time:* 10 minutes | *Cook Time:* 50 minutes | *Servings: 4*

Ingredients:

- 3 eggplants, chopped
- Salt and black pepper to taste
- 6 zucchinis, chopped
- 2 yellow onions, chopped
- 3 red bell peppers, chopped
- 56 ounces canned tomatoes, chopped
- A handful black olives, pitted and chopped
- A pinch of allspice,
- ground
- A pinch of cinnamon, ground
- 1 teaspoon oregano, dried
- A drizzle of honey
- 1 tablespoon garbanzo bean flour mixed with 1 tablespoon water
- A drizzle of olive oil
- A pinch of red chili flakes
- 3 tablespoons Greek yogurt

Directions:

Heat a saucepan with the oil over medium high heat, add bell peppers, onions, some salt and pepper, stir and sauté for 4 minutes. Add eggplant and the rest of the ingredients except the flour, olives, chili flakes and the yogurt, stir, bring to a boil, cover, reduce heat to medium-low and cook for 45 minutes. Add the remaining ingredients except the yogurt, stir, cook for 1 minute, divide into bowls and serve with some Greek yogurt on top.

Nutrition: calories 80, fat 2, fiber 4, carbs 12, protein 3

# Side Dish Recipes

## Escarole Saute

*Prep Time: 10 minutes | Cook Time: 20 minutes | Servings: 4*

### Ingredients:

- 4 escarole heads, leaves separated and roughly chopped
- 14 ounces canned tomatoes, chopped
- Salt and black pepper to taste
- 2 garlic cloves, minced
- ¼ pound sobrassada salami, chopped
- ½ teaspoon red pepper, crushed
- 3 tablespoons olive oil
- ¼ cup panko breadcrumbs
- 1 tablespoon oregano, chopped
- 2 tablespoons parmesan, grated

### Directions:

Heat a pan with 2 tablespoons oil over medium heat, add garlic, red pepper and sobrassada, stir and cook for 2 minutes. Add escarole, salt, pepper, tomatoes and oregano, stir, bring to a boil, reduce heat to low, cook for 15 minutes and transfer to a bowl, Heat another pan with remaining oil over medium heat, add panko and the parmesan, stir, cook for 1 minute, sprinkle over the escarole saute and serve as a side dish.

**Nutrition:** calories 60, fat 3.5, fiber 4, carbs 5, protein 3

## Creamy Eggplant Mix

*Prep Time: 10 minutes | Cook Time: 10 minutes | Servings: 4*

### Ingredients:

- 1 eggplant, diced
- 5 tablespoons olive oil
- 3 shallots, chopped
- 3 garlic cloves, minced
- Salt and black pepper to taste
- A handful dill, chopped
- ½ cup Greek yogurt

### Directions:

Heat a pan with oil over medium high heat, add shallots and garlic, stir and cook for 3 minutes. Add eggplant and the rest of the inrgedients, stir and cook for 10 minutes. Divide between plates and serve as a side dish.

**Nutrition:** calories 254, fat 21, fiber 4, carbs 14, protein 5

## Artichoke and Tomato Saute

*Prep Time: 10 minutes | Cook Time: 12 minutes | Servings: 4*

### Ingredients:

- 1 small yellow onion, chopped
- 2 garlic cloves, minced
- Salt and black pepper to taste
- ½ cup white wine
- 2 tomatoes, chopped
- 9 ounces artichoke
- hearts, frozen
- 1 tablespoon extra-virgin olive oil
- 1 strip lemon zest
- A handful basil, chopped
- 3 tablespoons water
- A few black olives, pitted and chopped

### Directions:

Heat a pan with oil over medium high heat, add onion, garlic and some salt, stir and cook for 5 minutes. Add wine, stir and cook for 3 minutes. Add tomatoes, artichokes, and the rest of the ingredients, stir and cook for 6 minutes. Divide the saute between plates and serve.

**Nutrition:** calories 145, fat 7.6, fiber 8, carbs 18, protein 5

## Broccoli Mix

*Prep Time: 10 minutes | Cook Time: 10 minutes | Servings: 4*

### Ingredients:

- 2 bunches broccoli rabe
- 2 garlic cloves, minced
- 1 tablespoon olive oil
- ¼ cup jarred cherry
- peppers, chopped
- 2 tablespoons liquid from the peppers
- Salt and black pepper to taste
- Some parmesan, grated for serving

### Directions:

Put broccoli in a saucepan, add water to cover, bring to a boil over medium heat, cook for 7 minutes, drain and put in a bowl. Heat a pan with the oil over medium high heat, add garlic and peppers, stir and cook for 2 minutes. Add liquid from the jar, the broccoli and the other ingredients, toss, cook for another 2 minutes, divide between plates and serve as a side dish.

**Nutrition:** calories 177, fat 8, fiber 3, carbs 16, protein 13

# Cinnamon Couscous and Cauliflower

*Prep Time:* 10 minutes | *Cook Time:* 10 minutes | *Servings:* 4

## Ingredients:

- 1 and ½ cups couscous, already cooked
- 3 tablespoons olive oil
- 3 cups cauliflower florets
- 1 shallot, chopped
- Salt and pepper to taste
- A pinch of cinnamon, ground
- ¼ cup dates, chopped
- A splash of red wine vinegar
- A handful parsley, chopped

## Directions:

Place cooked couscous in a bowl, add 1 tablespoon oil, toss to coat and leave aside. Heat a pan with remaining oil over medium high heat, add shallot, stir and cook for 2 minutes. Add cauliflower florets dates, salt, pepper and cinnamon, stir and cook for 5-6 minutes. Add couscous, and the other ingredients, toss, cook for 1 minute, divide between plates and serve.

**Nutrition:** calories 345, fat 11, fiber 5, carbs 55, protein 9

# Balsamic Lentils Mix

*Prep Time:* 10 minutes | *Cook Time:* 1 hour | *Servings:* 4

## Ingredients:

- ½ cup celery, chopped
- ½ cup carrot, chopped
- ½ cup onion, chopped
- ½ cup red bell pepper, chopped
- ½ teaspoon coriander, chopped
- 1 tablespoon olive oil
- ½ cup dry white wine
- ½ teaspoon marjoram, dried
- 1 cup lentils, rinsed
- 2 teaspoons kalamata olives, pitted and chopped
- 8 ounces ruby chard, leaves torn
- 2 tablespoons sun-dried tomatoes, chopped
- Salt and black pepper to taste
- 2 and ½ cups water
- 1 teaspoon balsamic vinegar

## Directions:

Heat a saucepan with the oil over medium high heat, add celery, carrot, onion, coriander, bell pepper, marjoram, salt and pepper, stir and cook for 4 minutes. Add wine, stir and cook for 3 minutes. Add lentils, tomatoes, olives and water, stir, bring to a boil, reduce heat and simmer for 40 minutes. Add chard, salt, pepper and the vinegar, stir and cook for 6-7 minutes more. Transfer to plates and serve as a side dish.

**Nutrition:** calories 180, fat 3.5, fiber 9, carbs 24, protein 10

# Cauliflower and Almonds Mix

*Prep Time:* 10 minutes | *Cook Time:* 30 minutes | *Servings:* 4

### Ingredients:

- ½ cauliflower head, florets separated
- 12 small carrots
- 1 tablespoon olive oil
- 1 tablespoon harissa paste
- Salt and black pepper to taste
- A handful mint, chopped
- 2 tablespoons almonds, toasted and chopped

### Directions:

In a bowl, mix cauliflower florets with carrots, harissa, salt, pepper and oil, toss to coat, spread on a lined baking sheet and cook at 400 degrees F for 30 minutes. Divide between plates, sprinkle mint and almonds on top and serve.

**Nutrition:** calories 70, fat 4, fiber 2, carbs, 6, protein 2

# Oregano Potatoes

*Prep Time:* 10 minutes | *Cook Time:* 50 minutes | *Servings:* 4

### Ingredients:

- 6 red potatoes, cut into medium wedges
- Salt and black pepper to taste
- 2 tablespoons extra
- virgin olive oil
- 1 teaspoon lemon zest, grated
- 1 teaspoon oregano, dried

### Directions:

In a bowl, mix potatoes with salt, pepper and oil, toss to coat and arrange on a lined baking sheet. Cover and place in the oven at 425 degrees F and bake for 20 minutes. Take potatoes out of oven, toss them a bit, place back in oven again and roast for 20 minutes. Take out of the oven, add the rest of the ingredients, cook for a further 10 minutes, divide them among plates and serve.

**Nutrition:** calories 190, fat 7, fiber 3, carbs 30, protein 3

# Roasted Creamy Carrots

*Prep Time:* 10 minutes | *Cook Time:* 45 minutes | *Servings:* 4

### Ingredients:

- 3 tablespoons olive oil
- 16 slender carrots, peeled
- Salt and black pepper to taste
- ½ teaspoon lemon
- zest, grated
- 1/3 cup yogurt
- 1 garlic clove, minced
- A pinch of cumin, ground
- 2 teaspoons honey

### Directions:

In a bowl, mix carrots with salt and pepper, spread on a lined baking sheet and cook at 425 degrees F for 20 minutes. In a bowl, mix yogurt with the rest of the ingredients except the honey and toss. Take carrots out of oven, drizzle honey, place in the oven again and roast for 25 minutes. Transfer carrots to a platter, drizzle yogurt mix all over and serve.

**Nutrition:** calories 200, fat 12, fiber 5, carbs 20, protein 3

# Sherry Squash Mix

*Prep Time:* 10 minutes | *Cook Time:* 10 minutes | *Servings:* 4

### Ingredients:

- 3 ounces chorizo, cut in half lengthwise and thinly sliced
- 2 and ½ tablespoon extra-virgin olive oil
- ½ teaspoon smoked paprika
- 10 ounces baby
- squash, sliced
- 1 tablespoon sherry vinegar
- 15 ounces canned chickpeas, drained
- Salt and black pepper to taste

### Directions:

Heat a pan with 1 ½ tablespoons oil over high heat, add chorizo, cook for 1 minute and transfer to a bowl. Heat the pan again, add squash, chickpeas, chorizo and the other ingredients stir, cook for 5 minutes, transfer to a platter and serve as a side dish.

**Nutrition:** calories 240, fat 12, fiber 6, carbs 21, protein 10

# Parmesan Bulgur

*Prep Time:* 10 minutes | *Cook Time:* 20 minutes | *Servings:* 4

Ingredients:

- 1 cup bulgur
- 2 cups chicken stock
- 1 tablespoon butter
- 1 tablespoon extra-virgin olive oil
- 6 ounces mushrooms, chopped
- 1 teaspoon garlic, minced
- Salt and black pepper to taste
- ½ cup parmesan, grated
- 2 tablespoons parsley, finely chopped
- ½ cup cashews, toasted and chopped

Directions:

Put stock in a saucepan, bring to a boil over medium high heat, add bulgur, reduce temperature to medium-low, cover and simmer for 12 minutes. Heat a pan with the oil and butter over medium heat, add mushrooms, garlic, salt and pepper, stir and cook for 10 minutes. Take bulgur off heat, uncover the pan, fluff a bit, add sautéed mushrooms, and the rest of the ingredients, stir, divide between plates and serve as a side dish.

Nutrition: calories 330, fat 15, fiber 4, carbs 35, protein 11

# Chives Rice

*Prep Time:* 10 minutes | *Cook Time:* 5 minutes | *Servings:* 4

Ingredients:

- 3 tablespoons butter
- 1 cup jasmine rice
- 2 tablespoons chives, chopped
- Salt and black
- pepper to taste
- ¼ cup pine nuts
- 2 teaspoons lemon juice

Directions:

Cook rice according to package instructions, fluff with a fork and leave aside. Heat a pan with the butter over medium high heat, add pine nuts, rice and the ther ingre stir and brown for 3 minutes. Add chives, lemon juice, rice, salt and pepper, stir, cook for 2 minutes. Divide among plates and serve.

Nutrition: calories 280, fat 14, fiber 1, carbs 34, protein 5

# Minty Beans

*Prep Time:* 10 minutes | *Cook Time:* 6 minutes | *Servings:* 4

Ingredients:

- 2 tablespoons olive oil
- 1 and ½ pounds green beans
- Salt and black pepper to taste
- 2 tablespoons tahini
- 1 teaspoon lemon zest, grated
- 1 tablespoon lemon juice
- 2 tablespoons water
- 2 tablespoons mint leaves, chopped
- A pinch of red pepper flakes, crushed

Directions:

Put green beans in a steamer basket, season with salt and pepper, place over a saucepan filled with 1 inch water, bring to a boil and cook for 5 minutes. Transfer the beans to a bowl, add the rest of the ingredients, toss to coat, divide between plates and serve.

Nutrition: calories 179, fat 11, fiber 5, carbs 14, protein 5

# Almond Peas Mix

*Prep Time:* 10 minutes | *Cook Time:* 5 minutes | *Servings:* 4

Ingredients:

- ½ cup almonds, blanched
- 2 teaspoons lemon juice
- ¼ cup extra virgin olive oil
- ½ cup water
- 1 and ½ teaspoons garlic, minced
- 1 pound sugar snap peas
- Salt and black pepper to taste

Directions:

In a blender, mix almonds with lemon juice, olive oil, water, garlic, salt and pepper, blend for 3 minutes, and transfer to a bowl. Heat a saucepan with water over medium high heat, add salt and peas, cook for 1 minute, drain them, transfer to a bowl filled with ice water, cool down, drain again, divide between plates, drizzle the almonds sauce all over and serve as a side dish.

Nutrition: calories 240, fat 23, fiber 4, carbs 12, protein 7

# Corn and Tapenade

*Prep Time: 10 minutes | Cook Time: 4 minutes | Servings: 4*

## Ingredients:

- 4 ears of corn
- 4 ounces green olives, pitted
- ½ teaspoon anchovy paste
- 1 teaspoon thyme,
- chopped
- Salt and black pepper to taste
- 2 tablespoons extra virgin olive oil

## Directions:

In a blender, mix the olives with the anchovy paste and the other ingredients except the corn and pulse well. Shuck corn, place in a large saucepan filled with boiling water, cover, take the saucepan off heat and leave aside for 5 minutes. Drain corn, arrange on plates, drizzle the tapenade over each piece and serve.

**Nutrition:** calories 160, fat 10, fiber 4, carbs 20, protein 3

# Quinoa and Sun-dried Tomatoes Mix

*Prep Time: 10 minutes | Cook Time: 35 minutes | Servings: 6*

## Ingredients:

- 4 cups chicken stock
- 2 cups red quinoa, rinsed and drained
- 1 yellow onion, chopped
- 2 tablespoons vegetable oil
- 1 tablespoon garlic, minced
- 1 teaspoon lemon
- zest, grated
- 2 tablespoons lemon juice
- ½ cup sun-dried tomatoes, chopped
- Salt and black pepper to taste
- 2 tablespoons olive oil
- ½ cup basil, chopped

## Directions:

Heat a pan over medium high heat, add quinoa, fry for 8 minutes stirring often and transfer to a plate. Put the stock in a saucepan, bring to a boil over medium heat, add quinoa, stir, cover and cook for 15 minutes. Heat a pan with the vegetable oil over medium heat, add onion and garlic, stir and cook for 8 minutes. In a bowl, mix lemon zest with lemon juice, salt, pepper, olive oil, quinoa, tomatoes, basil and onions mix, toss, divide between plates and serve.

**Nutrition:** calories 260, fat 11, fiber 4, carbs 41, protein 10

# Cheesy Couscous Mix

*Prep Time: 10 minutes | Cook Time: 0 minutes | Servings: 6*

## Ingredients:

- 2 cups couscous, cooked and cooled
- 1 cup broccoli florets, chopped
- 1 red bell pepper, chopped
- 1 tomato, cubed
- 15 ounces canned chickpeas, drained and rinsed
- ½ cup feta cheese, crumbled
- 2 teaspoons mustard
- 2 teaspoons lemon juice
- 1 tablespoon olive oil
- A pinch of salt and black pepper

## Directions:

In a large bowl, mix the couscous with broccoli, bell pepper, tomato, chickpeas and the other ingredients, toss, divide between plates and serve.

**Nutrition:** calories 200, fat 11, fiber 5, carbs 12, protein 6

# Carrots and Kale Saute

*Prep Time: 10 minutes | Cook Time: 45 minutes | Servings: 4*

## Ingredients:

- 1 tablespoon mint, chopped
- 1 tablespoon parsley, chopped
- 1 tablespoon green olives, pitted and chopped
- 4 and ½ tablespoons olive oil
- 2 teaspoons capers, drained and chopped
- ½ teaspoon lemon zest, grated
- 1 and ½ teaspoons
- sherry vinegar
- ¼ teaspoon cumin, ground
- ¼ teaspoon sugar
- Salt and black pepper to taste
- 1 and ¼ pounds carrots, chopped
- 5 shallots, cut into wedges
- 2 turnips, trimmed and roughly chopped
- 2 ounces kale leaves, thinly sliced

## Directions:

In a bowl, mix 1 ½ tablespoons olive oil with olives, parsley, mint, capers, lemon zest, vinegar, cumin, sugar and black pepper, and whisk well. Heat a pan with the rest of the oil over medium high heat, add turnips, shallots, carrots, salt and pepper, stir and cook for 30 minutes stirring often. Add kale, parsley and mint sauce, salt and pepper, stir, take off heat and serve as a side dish.

**Nutrition:** calories 104, fat 7, fiber 2.6, carbs 10, protein 2

## Lemon Fennel Wedges

*Prep Time: 10 minutes | Cook Time: 2 hours | Servings: 4*

**Ingredients:**

- 3 lemon slices, cut in quarters
- Salt and black pepper to taste
- 3 tablespoons extra
- virgin olive oil
- 1 tablespoon water
- 2 fennel bulb, cut in halves and sliced into medium wedges

**Directions:**

Place fennel wedges in a baking dish, add the rest of the ingredients, toss to coat, cover with tin foil, place in the oven at 375 degrees F and bake for 1 hour and 40 minutes. Uncover, place back in oven, bake for 20 minutes more, divide between plates and serve.

**Nutrition:** calories 190, fat 11, fiber 9, carbs 22, protein 4

## Leeks Saute

*Prep Time: 10 minutes | Cook Time: 1 hour | Servings: 4*

**Ingredients:**

- 2 pounds leeks, white and green parts separated and halved
- 1 tablespoon dry white wine
- 12 thyme sprigs
- 1 tablespoon water
- Salt and black pepper to taste
- ¼ cup olive oil

**Directions:**

Arrange leeks in a baking dish and add thyme sprigs on top. Add the rest of the ingredients, toss to coat, cover the dish with tin foil, place in the oven at 375 degrees F and bake for 45 minutes. Uncover the dish, bake leeks for 15 minutes more, discard thyme, divide between plates and serve as a side dish.

**Nutrition:** calories 180, fat 13, fiber 2, carbs 14, protein 1

## Garlic Asparagus Mix

*Prep Time: 30 minutes | Cook Time: 15 minutes | Servings: 4*

**Ingredients:**

- 5 tablespoons olive oil
- 1 garlic head
- 2 tablespoons shallot, chopped
- Salt
- Black pepper to taste
- 1 and ½ teaspoons
- white wine vinegar
- 1 and ½ pound asparagus
- 2 slices ciabatta bread
- ½ teaspoon red wine vinegar

**Directions:**

Season garlic with salt, pepper and 1 tablespoon olive oil, arrange on a baking tray and bake at 350 degrees F for 40 minutes. Squeeze garlic into a bowl, add salt, pepper and 2 tablespoons of oil and leave aside. In a bowl, mix shallot with the white vinegar, red vinegar, the rest of the oil, salt, pepper and the asparagus, stir well and leave aside for 30 minutes. Preheat your grill pan over medium high heat, add asparagus in and cook for 10 minutes. Meanwhile, spread roasted garlic mix over bread and grill it for a few minutes. Divide asparagus on plates, drizzle vinegar mix all over and serve as a side dish.

**Nutrition:** calories 132, fat 1, fiber 2, carbs 4, protein 4, carbs 3

# Cucumber Salad

*Prep Time: 1 hour | Cook Time: 0 minutes | Servings: 12*

## Ingredients:

- 2 cucumbers, chopped
- 2 tomatoes, chopped
- ½ cup green bell pepper, chopped
- 1 yellow onion, chopped
- 1 jalapeno pepper, chopped
- 1 garlic clove, minced
- 1 teaspoon parsley, chopped
- 2 tablespoons lime juice
- 2 teaspoons cilantro, chopped
- ½ teaspoon dill weed, dried
- Salt to taste

## Directions:

In a large salad bowl, mix the cucumbers with the tomatoes, peppers and the other ingredients and toss well. Place in the fridge about 1 hour before serving. Serve as a side dish.

**Nutrition:** calories 132, fat 3, fiber 1, carbs 2, protein 4

# Chili Cucumber Mix

*Prep Time: 10 minutes | Cook Time: 5 minutes | Servings: 2*

## Ingredients:

- 1 large cucumber, chopped
- 1 tablespoon butter
- Salt to taste
- 1 red chili pepper, dried
- ½ teaspoon cumin, ground
- 1 tablespoon lemon juice
- 3 tablespoons peanuts, chopped
- 1 teaspoon cilantro, chopped

## Directions:

In a bowl, mix cucumber with salt, leave aside for 10 minutes, drain well, pat dry and transfer to a bowl. Heat a pan with the butter over medium heat, add chili pepper and cumin, stir well and cook for 30 seconds. Add peanuts, cucumber and the rest of the ingredinets, toss and serve as a side dish.

**Nutrition:** calories 142, fat 6, fiber 5, carbs 12, protein 5

# Beet and Walnuts Mix

*Prep Time: 10 minutes | Cook Time: 1 hour | Servings: 4*

## Ingredients:

- 4 fresh beets
- Salt and black pepper to taste
- ½ cup olive oil + a drizzle
- ¼ cup lemon juice
- 8 slices goats cheese, crumbled
- 1/3 cup walnuts, chopped
- 8 lettuce leaves

## Directions:

Arrange beets on a lined, baking sheet, add a drizzle of oil, season with some salt and pepper, place in the oven at 400 degrees F and bake for 1 hour. Peel beets, cut them and transfer to a bowl. Add the rest of the ingredients, toss to coat, divide between plates and serve.

**Nutrition:** calories 121, fat 1, fiber 2, carbs 3, protein 3

# Balsamic Beets

*Prep Time: 10 minutes | Cook Time: 30 minutes | Servings: 6*

## Ingredients:

- 3 medium beets, sliced
- 1/3 cup balsamic vinegar
- 1 teaspoon rosemary, chopped
- 1 garlic clove, minced
- ½ teaspoon Italian seasoning
- A drizzle of olive oil

## Directions:

In a bowl, mix rosemary with vinegar, garlic, Italian seasoning and the beets, toss and leave aside for 10 minutes. Place beets and the marinade on aluminum foil pieces, add a drizzle of oil, seal edges, place on preheated grill pan over medium heat and cook for 25 minutes. Unwrap beets, peel, cube them, divide between plates and serve as a side dish.

**Nutrition:** calories 100, fat 2, fiber 2, carbs 2, protein 4

# Hot Assorted Squash

*Prep Time:* 10 minutes | *Cook Time:* 10 minutes | *Servings:* 6

Ingredients:

- 4 medium assorted squash, thinly sliced
- ¼ teaspoon red pepper flakes, crushed
- 2 tomatoes, chopped
- 2 tablespoons feta cheese, crumbled
- ¼ cup Greek yogurt
- 1 tablespoon olive oil
- 1 tablespoon cilantro, chopped

Directions:

Arrange the squash slices on a preheated grill. Brush them with the oil, and cook over medium heat for 6 minutes on each side. In a bowl, mix the grilled squash with the rest of the ingredients, toss and serve as a side dish.

Nutrition: calories 170, fat 7, fiber 1, carbs 8, protein 6

# Eggplant and Mayo Mix

*Prep Time:* 10 minutes | *Cook Time:* 5 minutes | *Servings:* 6

Ingredients:

- 1/3 cup homemade mayonnaise
- 2 tablespoons balsamic vinegar
- A pinch of salt and black pepper
- 1 tablespoon lime juice
- 2 big eggplants, sliced
- ¼ cup cilantro, chopped
- ¼ cup olive oil

Directions:

In a small bowl, mix mayonnaise with vinegar, cilantro, lime juice and black pepper, stir well and leave aside. Brush each eggplant slice with some olive oil, season with salt and pepper, place on preheated grill pan over medium high heat, cook for 5 minutes on each side, divide between plates, drizzle the mayo all over and serve.

Nutrition: calories 100, fat 1, fiber 2, carbs 2, protein 2

# Sage Barley Mix

*Prep Time:* 10 minutes | *Cook Time:* 1 hour | *Servings:* 4

Ingredients:

- 1 tablespoon butter
- 1 yellow onion, chopped
- 4 parsnips, roughly chopped
- 10 sage leaves, chopped
- 1 garlic clove, minced
- 14 ounces barley
- ½ tablespoon parmesan, grated
- 6 cups hot veggie stock
- Salt and black pepper

Directions:

Heat a pan with the butter over medium high heat, add onion, some salt and pepper, stir and cook for 5 minutes. Add parsnips and cook for 10 more minutes. Add barley and the other ingredients except the parmesan, stir well, bring to a simmer and cook for 40 minutes. Add parmesan, stir, divide between plates and serve.

Nutrition: calories 132, fat 1, fiber 1, carbs 2, protein 2

# Lentil and Beets Salad

*Prep Time:* 15 minutes | *Cook Time:* 30 minutes | *Servings:* 4

Ingredients:

- 7 ounces lentils
- 3 tablespoons capers, chopped
- Juice of 1 lemon
- Zest and juice from 1 lemon
- 1 red onion, chopped
- 3 tablespoons olive oil
- 14 ounces canned chickpeas, drained
- 8 ounces already cooked beetroot, chopped
- 1 small handful parsley, chopped
- Salt and pepper to taste

Directions:

Put lentils in a saucepan, add water to cover, bring to a simmer over medium heat, boil for 20 minutes, drain and leave aside. Put lemon juice from 1 lemon in a bowl, add onion, salt and pepper, whisk and leave aside. In a second bowl, combine lemon juice and zest from the second lemon in a bowl with oil, salt, pepper and the capers, and toss. In a large bowl, combine chickpeas with lentils, capers, onions mix, salt and pepper, toss and serve.

Nutrition: calories 132, fat 1, fiber 2, carbs 2, protein 3

# Potato and Yogurt Sauce

*Prep Time:* 10 minutes | *Cook Time:* 1 hour | *Servings:* 4

## Ingredients:

- 4 tablespoons olive oil
- 1 garlic clove, minced
- 4 medium sweet potatoes
- 1 shallot, chopped
- 14 ounces canned
- chickpeas, drained
- 3 ounces baby spinach
- Zest and juice from 1 lemon
- A small bunch dill, chopped

*For the tahini yogurt:*

- 1 ½ tablespoons Greek yogurt
- ½ tablespoon pine nuts
- 2 tablespoons tahini
- paste
- 4 ounces pomegranate seeds
- Salt and pepper to taste

## Directions:

Wrap potatoes in foil, arrange them on a lined baking sheet, place in the oven at 350 degrees F and cook them for 1 hour. Meanwhile, heat a pan with 1 tablespoon olive oil over medium high heat, add shallot, garlic, chickpeas, spinach and dill, stir, cook for 4 minutes and take off the heat. In a bowl, mix remaining oil with lemon zest, juice and chickpeas, stir and mash everything with a potato masher. In another bowl, mix yogurt with tahini, salt and pepper and stir well. Take potatoes out of oven, unwrap, split them lengthwise, divide between plates, stuff with chickpeas mix, drizzle tahini mix all over and serve with pine nuts and pomegranate seeds on top.

**Nutrition:** calories 120, fat 1, fiber 1, carbs 2, protein 2

# Cabbage and Chickpeas Sauté

*Prep Time:* 10 minutes | *Cook Time:* 20 minutes | *Servings:* 2

## Ingredients:

- 2 tablespoons olive oil
- 1 yellow potato, cubed
- 2 garlic cloves, minced
- 1 green cabbage,
- shredded
- 1 cup canned chickpeas, drained
- 1 teaspoon sweet paprika
- A pinch of salt and black pepper

## Directions:

Heat a pan with the oil over medium heat, add the potatoes, salt and pepper, stir and sauté for 10 minutes. Add the rest of the ingredients, stir, cook for 10 minutes more, divide between plates and serve.

**Nutrition:** calories 182, fat 6, fiber 6, carbs 11, protein 6

# Mushroom and Lemon Rice

*Prep Time:* 10 minutes | *Cook Time:* 30 minutes | *Servings:* 4

## Ingredients:

- 2 cups chicken stock
- 1 yellow onion, chopped
- 10 ounces mixed mushrooms, sliced
- 2 garlic cloves, minced
- 8 ounces wild and basmati rice
- Juice and zest of 1 lemon
- A small bunch of chives, chopped
- 6 tablespoons light goats cheese with herbs, crumbled
- Salt and black pepper to taste

## Directions:

Heat a pot with 2 tablespoons of stock over medium high heat, add onion, stir and cook for 5 minutes. Add stock, mushrooms and garlic and cook for further 2 minutes. Add rice, and the rest of the ingredients except the cheese, stir, bring to a simmer, cover and cook for 25 minutes. Divide between plates and serve with the cheese sprinkled on top.

**Nutrition:** calories 142, fat 1, fiber 2, carbs 2, protein 2

# Worcestershire Baked Potatoes

*Prep Time:* 10 minutes | *Cook Time:* 1 hour and 10 minutes | *Servings:* 4

**Ingredients:**

- 4 potatoes, scrubbed and pricked with a fork
- 1 carrot, chopped
- 1 tablespoon olive oil
- 1 celery stalk, chopped
- 2 tomatoes, chopped
- A splash of water
- 1 teaspoon sweet
- paprika
- 14 ounces canned haricot beans, drained
- 1 teaspoon Worcestershire sauce
- Salt and black pepper to taste
- 2 tablespoons chives, chopped

**Directions:**

Place potatoes on a lined baking sheet, place in the oven and bake at 350 degrees F for 1 hour. Heat a pan with the oil over medium heat, add celery, carrots and the other ingredients except the chives, toss, and cook for 20 minutes stirring often. Take potatoes out of oven, split them, spoon beans mix in each, sprinkle chives on top, arrange on plates and serve as a side dish.

**Nutrition:** calories 123, fat 1, fiber 2, carbs 2, protein 1

# Bulgur and Kale Salad

*Prep Time:* 10 minutes | *Cook Time:* 15 minutes | *Servings:* 6

**Ingredients:**

- 4 ounces bulgur wheat
- 4 ounces kale
- A bunch of mints, chopped
- A bunch of scallions, chopped
- ½ cucumber, chopped
- A pinch of cinnamon powder
- A pinch of allspice
- 6 tablespoons olive oil
- Zest and juice from ½ lemon
- 4 ounces feta cheese, crumbled

**Directions:**

Put bulgur in a bowl, cover with hot water and set aside for 10 minutes. Put kale in a food processor and gently pulse. Drain bulgur, transfer to another bowl and mix with kale, mint and the other ingredients. Toss, divide between plates and serve as a side dish.

**Nutrition:** calories 100, fat 1, fiber 2, carbs 2, protein 4

# Beans and Spinach Mix

*Prep Time:* 10 minutes | *Cook Time:* 25 minutes | *Servings:* 4

**Ingredients:**

- 4 teaspoons olive oil
- 1 garlic clove, minced
- ½ teaspoon smoked paprika
- ¾ cup veggie stock
- 1 yellow onion, sliced
- 1 red bell pepper,
- chopped
- 15 ounces canned butter beans, drained
- 4 cups baby spinach
- ½ cup goats cheese, shredded
- 2 teaspoon sherry vinegar

**Directions:**

Heat a pan with the oil over medium heat, add garlic, stir and cook for 30 seconds. Add onion, beans and the other ingredients except the cheese and vinegar, stir and cook for 10 minutes. Add cheese and vinegar, divide between plates and serve.

**Nutrition:** calories 140, fat 1, fiber 2, carbs 2, protein 2

# Brown Rice Pilaf

*Prep Time:* 10 minutes | *Cook Time:* 40 minutes | *Servings:* 4

**Ingredients:**

- 2 cups brown rice
- 1 shallot, chopped
- A pinch of salt and black pepper
- 1 red bell pepper, chopped
- 1 zucchini, grated
- 1 carrot, grated
- ¼ cup parsley,
- chopped
- ¼ cup olive oil
- ½ teaspoon oregano, dried
- ¼ teaspoon sweet paprika
- ½ teaspoon thyme, dried
- 4 cups water

**Directions:**

Heat a pan with half the olive oil over medium heat, add shallot, bell pepper and the other ingredients except the rice, water and parsley, stir and cook for 5 minutes. Add the rice, parsley and water, stir, bring to a simmer and cook for 35 minutes. Divide the rice between plates and serve as a side dish.

**Nutrition:** calories 182, fat 11, fiber 4, carbs 8, protein 5

# Millet and Spring Onions Mix

*Prep Time: 10 minutes | Cook Time: 20 minutes | Servings: 6*

**Ingredients:**

- 4 tablespoons olive oil
- 1 cup millet
- 2 small bunches green onions, chopped
- 2 tomatoes, chopped
- ½ cup cilantro, chopped
- 5 drops hot sauce
- 6 cups cold water
- ½ cup lemon juice
- Salt and black pepper to taste

**Directions:**

Heat up a pan with 2 tablespoons oil over medium high heat, add millet, stir and cook for 4 minutes. Add water, bring to a boil, cover and boil for 20 minutes. Transfer millet to a bowl, add the rest of the ingredients, toss, divide between plates and serve.

**Nutrition:** calories 163, fat 1, fiber 2, carbs 5, protein 3

# Quinoa and Greens Mix

*Prep Time: 10 minutes | Cook Time: 0 minutes | Servings: 4*

**Ingredients:**

- 1 cup quinoa, cooked
- 1 avocado, chopped
- 1 medium bunch collard greens, chopped
- 1 handful strawberries, sliced
- 4 tablespoons
- walnuts, chopped
- 2 tablespoons white wine vinegar
- 4 tablespoons tahini
- 4 tablespoons cold water
- 1 tablespoon maple syrup

**Directions:**

In a bowl, mix tahini with maple syrup, water and vinegar and pulse well. In a salad bowl, mix collard green leaves with avocado and the other ingredients except the dressing and toss. Add the dressing, toss and serve.

**Nutrition:** calories 175, fat 3, fiber 3, carbs 5, protein 3

# Greek Corn Salad

*Prep Time: 10 minutes | Cook Time: 0 minutes | Servings: 4*

**Ingredients:**

- 1 tablespoon pumpkin seeds, roasted
- 2 tablespoons cilantro, chopped
- 4 tablespoons parsley, chopped
- 2 cups corn
- 1 cup radishes, sliced
- 2 avocados, peeled, pitted and chopped
- 3 tablespoons olive oil
- 4 tablespoons Greek yogurt
- 2 tablespoons lemon juice
- Salt and black pepper to taste

**Directions:**

In a bowl, mix the corn with radishes, and the other ingredients, toss, divide between plates and serve as a side dish.

**Nutrition:** calories 170, fat 6, fiber 4, carbs 5, protein 3

# Beet and Dill Salad

*Prep Time: 15 minutes | Cook Time: 0 minutes | Servings: 6*

**Ingredients:**

- 2 pounds beets, baked, peeled and cubed
- 2 tablespoons olive oil
- 1 tablespoon lemon juice
- 2 tablespoons red wine vinegar
- 1 cup blue cheese,
- crumbled
- 3 small garlic cloves, minced
- 4 green onions, chopped
- 5 tablespoons dill, chopped
- Salt and black pepper to taste

**Directions:**

In a bowl, mix the beets with the oil and the other ingredients and toss well. Leave in the fridge for 15 minutes and then serve as a side dish.

**Nutrition:** calories 180, fat 2, fiber 3, carbs 2, protein 3

# Mozzarella Broccoli and Quinoa Mix

*Prep Time:* 10 minutes | *Cook Time:* 30 minutes | *Servings:* 5

## Ingredients:

- 2 and ½ cups quinoa
- 4 and ½ cups veggie stock
- ½ teaspoon salt
- 2 tablespoons pesto sauce
- 2 tablespoons arrowroot powder
- 12 ounces mozzarella cheese
- 2 cups spinach
- 12 ounces broccoli
- 1/3 cup parmesan
- 3 green onions, chopped

## Directions:

Put quinoa, green onions, stock, arrowroot powder, pesto sauce and salt in a baking dish. Put broccoli in a heatproof bowl, place in the microwave, cook on high for 5 minutes and leave a side. Add the broccoli over the quinoa, also add the rest of the ingredients and toss. Place in the oven at 400 degrees F and bake for 30 minutes. Divide between plates and serve.

**Nutrition:** calories 210, fat 2, fiber 2, carbs 3, protein 3

# Basil Pea Mix

*Prep Time:* 10 minutes | *Cook Time:* 0 minutes | *Servings:* 8

## Ingredients:

- 60 ounces peas
- 1 yellow bell pepper, chopped
- 2 ounces Cheddar cheese, grated
- ½ cup mayonnaise
- 3 tablespoon basil, dried
- 2 tablespoons red onion, chopped
- 2 teaspoons chili
- pepper, chopped
- 1 teaspoon apple cider vinegar
- 1 teaspoon sugar
- Salt and black pepper to taste
- 1 teaspoon garlic powder
- A drizzle of hot sauce

## Directions:

In a salad bowl, combine the peas with the cheese, pepper and the other ingredients, toss and serve. cold as a side dish.

**Nutrition:** calories 120, fat 2, fiber 1, carbs 2, protein 3

# Milky Potato Mash

*Prep Time:* 10 minutes | *Cook Time:* 40 minutes | *Servings:* 10

## Ingredients:

- 2 pounds gold potatoes, cut into small pieces
- 1 ½ cup fresh ricotta cheese
- Sea salt and black pepper to taste
- ½ cup low fat milk
- 3 tablespoons butter

## Directions:

Put potatoes in a large saucepan, add water to cover, add a pinch of salt, bring to a simmer over medium heat, cook for 20 minutes then drain and mash well. Add the rest of the ingredients, whisk well, divide into 10 ramekins, broil for 10 minutes and serve as a side dish.

**Nutrition:** calories 180, fat 3, fiber 1, carbs 2, protein 3

# Brown Rice Pilaf

*Prep Time:* 5 minutes | *Cook Time:* 50 minutes | *Servings:* 4

## Ingredients:

- 1 tablespoon olive oil
- 1 cup brown rice
- 1 yellow onion, chopped
- 1 tablespoon tomato paste
- 2 tomatoes, cubed
- A pinch of salt and black pepper
- 1 tablespoon basil, chopped
- 2 cups hot water

## Directions:

Heat a pan with the oil over medium high heat. Add the onion, tomatoes, salt, pepper and the tomato paste, stir and cook for 5 minutes. Add the rest of the ingredients, stir, bring to a simmer and cook over medium heat for 45 minutes. Divide the mix between plates and serve as a side dish.

**Nutrition:** calories 187, fat 7, fiber 4, carbs 7, protein 3

# Greek Barley Mix

*Prep Time:* 15 minutes | *Cook Time:* 30 minutes | *Servings:* 4

## Ingredients:

- ½ cup barley
- 1 and ½ cup water
- ½ cup Greek yogurt
- Salt and black pepper to taste
- 2 tablespoons olive oil
- 1 teaspoon mustard
- 1 tablespoon lemon juice
- 2 celery stalks, sliced
- ¼ cup mint, chopped
- 1 apple, cored and chopped

## Directions:

Put barley in a pan, add water and some salt, bring to a boil, cover, simmer for 25 minutes, drain, arrange on a baking sheet and leave aside. In a bowl, mix the barley with the yogurt and the remaining ingredients, toss to coat and serve.

**Nutrition:** calories 132, fat 2, fiber 3, carbs 3, protein 1

# Couscous and Pine Nuts Mix

*Prep Time:* 10 minutes | *Cook Time:* 10 minutes | *Servings:* 4

## Ingredients:

- 10 ounces couscous
- 1 ½ cup hot water
- ½ cup pine nuts
- 2 garlic cloves, minced
- 3 tablespoons olive oil
- 15 ounces canned chickpeas, rinsed
- ½ cup raisins
- 2 bunches Swiss chard
- Salt and black pepper to taste

## Directions:

Put couscous in a bowl, add water, stir, cover and leave aside for 10 minutes. Meanwhile, heat a pan over medium high heat, add pine nuts, toast them for 4 minutes, transfer to a plate and leave aside. Return pan to medium heat, add oil and heat, add garlic, stir and cook for 1 minute. Add raisins and the rest of the ingredients as well as the couscous and pine nuts, toss, cook for 1-2 minutes more, divide between plates and serve.

**Nutrition:** calories 153, fat 2, fiber 3, carbs 6, protein 4

# Lemon Cabbage Mix

*Prep Time:* 2 hours and 10 minutes | *Cook Time:* 0 minutes | *Servings:* 4

## Ingredients:

- 12 ounces red cabbage, shredded
- 1 carrot, shredded
- ¼ cup lemon juice
- ¼ cup olive oil
- A pinch of salt and black pepper
- 1 tablespoon sweet paprika

## Directions:

In a bowl, mix the cabbage with the carrot and the other ingredients, toss, keep in the fridge for 2 hours and serve as a side dish.

**Nutrition:** calories 153, fat 6, fiber 4, carbs 8, protein 5

# Chickpeas and Tomato Mix

*Prep Time:* 10 minutes | *Cook Time:* 25 minutes | *Servings:* 4

## Ingredients:

- 1 yellow onion, chopped
- 2 tablespoons olive oil
- 2 garlic cloves, minced
- 2 teaspoons spice mix
- 28 ounces canned chickpeas, drained
- 14 ounces canned tomatoes, chopped
- 2 cups veggie stock
- 2 zucchinis, chopped
- 6 ounces green beans, halved
- 2 cups couscous, cooked
- 2 tablespoons coriander, chopped
- ½ cup figs, dried and chopped
- Salt and pepper to taste

## Directions:

Heat a pan with the oil over medium high heat, add onion, stir and cook for 3-4 minutes. Add garlic, chickpeas and the other ingredients except the couscous, bring to a boil, cover and simmer for 20 minutes. Divide couscous on serving plates, add veggie mix and serve.

**Nutrition:** calories 200, fat 1, fiber 2, carbs 3, protein 4

# Tomato and Cheese Salad

*Prep Time: 10 minutes* | *Cook Time: 0 minutes* | *Servings: 4*

**Ingredients:**

- 4 pounds heirloom tomatoes, sliced
- 1 yellow bell pepper, chopped
- 1 green bell pepper, chopped
- 1 red onion, chopped
- Sea salt and black pepper to taste
- 4 ounces feta cheese, crumbled
- ½ teaspoon oregano, dried
- 2 tablespoons mint, chopped
- A drizzle of olive oil

**Directions:**

In a salad bowl, mix the tomatoes with the peppers and the other ingredients, toss, leave aside for 10 minutes and serve right away.

**Nutrition:** calories 142, fat 1, fiber 1, carbs 1, protein 2

# Balsamic Tomato Salad

*Prep Time: 6 minutes* | *Cook Time: 6 minutes* | *Servings: 4*

**Ingredients:**

- 20 ounces tomatoes, cut in wedges
- 2 tablespoons olive oil
- 1 and ½ tablespoons balsamic vinegar
- 1 teaspoon sugar
- 1 garlic clove, minced
- 8 ounces baby bocconcini, drain and torn
- 1 cup basil, chopped
- Salt and black pepper to taste

**Directions:**

In a bowl, mix the tomatoes with the bocconcini and the other ingredients, toss to coat and serve right away.

**Nutrition:** calories 121, fat 1, fiber 1, carbs 2, protein 2

# Cucumber and Tomato Salad

*Prep Time: 10 minutes* | *Cook Time: 5 minutes* | *Servings: 6*

**Ingredients:**

- 1 tablespoon olive oil
- 1 cucumber, chopped
- 2 pints colored cherry tomatoes, halved
- Salt and black pepper to taste
- 1 red onion, chopped
- 3 tablespoons red wine vinegar
- 1 garlic clove, minced
- 1 bunch basil, chopped
- 1 teaspoon honey

**Directions:**

In a bowl, mix the tomatoes with the cucumber and the other ingredients, toss to coat and serve.

**Nutrition:** calories 153, fat 2, fiber 1, carbs 2, protein 2

# Tomato and Avocado Mix

*Prep Time: 10 minutes* | *Cook Time: 0 minutes* | *Servings: 4*

**Ingredients:**

- 1 cucumber, chopped
- 1 pound tomatoes, chopped
- 2 avocados, pitted, peeled and chopped
- 1 small red onion, sliced
- 2 tablespoons olive oil
- 2 tablespoons lemon juice
- ¼ cup cilantro, chopped
- Sea salt and black pepper to taste

**Directions:**

In a salad bowl, combine the tomatoes with the avocados and the other ingredients, toss to coat and serve right away.

**Nutrition:** calories 173, fat 1, fiber 1, carbs 2, protein 2

# Peppers and Tomato Salad

*Prep Time: 10 minutes | Cook Time: 1 hour | Servings: 5*

### Ingredients:

- 1 red bell pepper
- 1 green bell pepper
- 7 tomatoes
- 1 eggplant, cut into thin strips
- 2 tablespoons tomato paste
- Salt and black
- pepper to taste
- A pinch of cayenne pepper
- 4 garlic cloves, crushed
- ¼ cup extra-virgin olive oil

### Directions:

Place bell peppers on stove burners, roast them until they turn black, transfer to a bowl, cover, leave them to cool down, peel, cut into thin strips, put in a bowl and leave aside. Put some water in a sauepan, bring to a boil over medium high heat, add tomatoes, steam them for 1 minute, transfer to a bowl filled with ice water, allow them to cool down. Heat a pan with oil over medium high heat, add eggplant strips, stir and cook for 8 minutes. Add peppers, tomatoes and all the other ingredients, toss, reduce heat and cook for 30 minutes. Divide between plates and serve as a side dish.

**Nutrition:** calories 200, fat 1, fiber 2, carbs 2, protein 4

# Pecorino Rice and Tomatoes

*Prep Time: 10 minutes | Cook Time: 25 minutes | Servings: 4*

### Ingredients:

- 5 cups chicken stock
- 1 garlic clove, minced
- 1 yellow onion, chopped
- 10 ounces sun dried tomatoes in olive oil, chopped
- 1 ½ cup Arborio rice
- Salt and black pepper to taste
- 1 ½ cup pecorino, grated
- 1 cup white wine
- 2 tablespoons butter
- ¼ cup basil leaves, chopped

### Directions:

Heat a saucepan over medium high heat, add dried tomatoes, onions, garlic, salt and pepper, stir and cook for 2 minutes. Add wine, 3 cups stock and rice, stir well and cook for another 10 minutes. Add remaining stock, stir again, cover saucepan, place in the oven at 425 degrees F and bake for 15 minutes. Take risotto out of oven, add cheese, basil and butter, stir until they melt, divide between plates and serve as a side dish.

**Nutrition:** calories 110, fat 1, fiber 1, carbs 2, protein 2

# Honey Cucumber Mix

*Prep Time: 30 minutes | Cook Time: 0 minutes | Servings: 8*

### Ingredients:

- 4 cucumbers, sliced
- ¼ cup red onion, chopped
- 1 garlic clove, minced
- 1 tablespoon dill, chopped
- 4 tablespoons lemon
- juice
- 1 and ½ tablespoons honey
- 1 and ½ tablespoons olive oil
- A pinch of salt and black pepper

### Directions:

In a bowl, mix the cucumbers with the onion, honey and the other ingredients, toss well, leave aside for 30 minutes and serve as a side dish.

**Nutrition:** calories 132, fat 11, fiber 5, carbs 8, protein 6

# Greek Salad

*Prep Time: 10 minutes | Cook Time: 0 minutes | Servings: 4*

### Ingredients:

- 1 large English cucumber, chopped
- 1 avocado, pitted, peeled and chopped
- 2 tomatoes, chopped
- 1 tablespoon lime juice
- 3 tablespoons olive oil
- 2 teaspoons balsamic vinegar
- 1 teaspoon Greek herb salad dressing mix

### Directions:

In a bowl, mix the cucumber with the tomatoes, avocado and the other ingredients, toss to coat and serve.

**Nutrition:** calories 100, fat 1, fiber 1, carbs 2, protein 2

## Sesame Cucumber Mix

*Prep Time: 6 minutes | Cook Time: 0 minutes | Servings: 6*

**Ingredients:**

- 2 big cucumbers, sliced
- ½ cup balsamic vinegar
- 2 tablespoons olive
- oil
- Sesame seeds, toasted for serving
- Salt and black pepper to taste

**Directions:**

In a bowl, mix the cucumbers with the vinegar and the other ingredients, toss to coat and serve.

**Nutrition:** calories 100, fat 1, fiber 1, carbs 1, protein 1

## Walnut Cucumber Salad

*Prep Time: 10 minutes | Cook Time: 0 minutes | Servings: 4*

**Ingredients:**

- 2 cucumbers, chopped
- 8 dates, pitted and sliced
- ¾ cup fennel, sliced
- 2 tablespoons chives, chopped
- ½ cup walnuts,
- chopped
- 2 tablespoons lemon juice
- 4 tablespoons olive oil
- Salt and black pepper to taste

**Directions:**

In a salad bowl, mix the cucumbers with the dates and the other ingredients, toss to coat and serve right away as a side dish.

**Nutrition:** calories 90, fat 1, fiber 1, carbs 2, protein 2

## Cilantro Tomato Salad

*Prep Time: 5 minutes | Cook Time: 0 minutes | Servings: 6*

**Ingredients:**

- 1 and ½ pounds tomatoes, cubed
- 1 cucumber, cubed
- 2 chili peppers, chopped
- 1 cup corn
- ¼ cup cilantro, chopped
- 2 tablespoons white
- vinegar
- 1 tablespoons lemon juice
- 2 tablespoons olive oil
- 1 small red onion, chopped
- Salt and black pepper to taste

**Directions:**

In a bowl, combine the tomatoes with the cucumber and the other ingredients, toss and serve cold as a side salad.

**Nutrition:** calories 193, fat 6, fiber 4, carbs 7, protein 4

## Beet and Herbs Salad

*Prep Time: 10 minutes | Cook Time: 2 minutes | Servings: 8*

**Ingredients:**

- 4 small beets, peeled and sliced
- 3 cucumbers, sliced
- 6 scallions, chopped
- 3 chili peppers, sliced
- Zest from 1 lemon, sliced
- 5 ounces dry ricotta, crumbled
- 2 cups mixed basil
- with mint, parsley and cilantro, chopped
- ¼ cup white wine vinegar
- 2 teaspoons poppy seeds
- ½ teaspoon sugar
- A drizzle of olive oil
- Salt and black pepper to taste

**Directions:**

In a salad bowl mix the beets with the cucumbers, scallions and the other ingredients, toss to coat, divide between plates and serve.

**Nutrition:** calories 112, fat 1, fiber 2, carbs 2, protein 2

# Snack and Appetizer Recipes

## Mini Burgers and Sauce

*Prep Time:* 5 minutes | *Cook Time:* 6 minutes | *Servings:* 16

### Ingredients:

*For the sauce:*
- ¾ cup Greek yogurt
- 1 teaspoon lemon zest, grated
- 1 garlic clove minced

*For the burgers:*
- 1 pound beef, ground
- ¼ cup bread crumbs
- 2 teaspoons lemon juice
- 1 tablespoon balsamic vinegar
- 1 teaspoon oregano, dried
- ¼ teaspoon dill, chopped
- A pinch of salt and black pepper
- 1 teaspoon thyme, chopped
- 3 garlic cloves, minced
- 16 mini pita breads, sliced in halves horizontally
- Cooking spray
- 1 cucumber, sliced

### Directions:

In a bowl, mix the yogurt with the lemon zest and the other ingredients for the sauce, whisk and leave aside for now. In a separate bowl mix the meat with the bread crumbs and the other ingredients except the pita breads, cucumber and cooking spray stir well and shape 16 small burgers out of this mix. Place the mini burgers on your preheated grill, grease them with cooking spray and cook for 3 minutes on each side. Divide the burgers on 16 of the pita bread halves, spread the sauce all over, divide the cucumber slices over the burgers and tip with the other pita halves, arrange on a platter and serve as an appetizer.

**Nutrition:** calories 210, fat 11, fiber 5, carbs 12, protein 7

## Tuna Rolls

*Prep Time:* 10 minutes | *Cook Time:* 0 minutes | *Servings:* 6

### Ingredients:

- 1 big cucumber, sliced lengthwise
- 1 tablespoon cilantro, chopped
- 1 tablespoon cranberries, dried
- 4 ounces canned sardines, drained and flaked
- 3 ounces canned tuna pate
- Salt and black pepper to taste
- 1 teaspoon lemon juice

### Directions:

In a bowl, mix sardines with tuna paste, salt and pepper to taste and lemon juice and mash everything well. Spoon this mix on each cucumber slice, add the rest of the ingredients on top, roll, arrange on a platter and serve.

**Nutrition:** calories 80, fat 1, fiber 2, carbs 2, protein 1

## Cheese Stuffed Tomatoes

*Prep Time:* 10 minutes | *Cook Time:* 2minutes | *Servings:* 24

### Ingredients:

- 24 cherry tomatoes, top cut off and insides scooped out
- 2 tablespoons olive oil
- A pinch of salt
- ¼ teaspoon red pepper flakes
- ½ cup feta cheese, cut into 24 pieces
- 1 tablespoon black olive paste
- 1 tablespoon water
- ¼ cup mint, torn

### Directions:

Season each tomato with pepper flakes and drizzle half of the oil. Insert a feta cheese cube in each tomato, place them under preheated broiler over medium heat and broil them for 2 minutes. In a bowl, mix the rest of the ingredients except the mint, whisk, spread on a platter, arrange the tomatoes on top and serve. with the mint sprinkled on top.

**Nutrition:** calories 110, fat 1, fiber 2, carbs 2, protein 2

## Tomato Toasts

*Prep Time: 10 minutes | Cook Time: 5 minutes | Servings: 6*

### Ingredients:

- 1 garlic clove, minced
- 4 tablespoons olive oil
- 5 tomatoes, chopped
- 1 tablespoon balsamic vinegar
- ¼ cup basil, chopped
- A pinch of red pepper flakes
- 14 slices whole wheat baguette
- Salt and black pepper to taste

### Directions:

In a bowl, mix tomatoes with 3 tablespoons oil and the other ingredients except the baguette and stir, Arrange bread slices on a lined baking sheet, place them in the oven at 350 degrees F, toast for 5 minutes, arrange on a platter, divide tomato mix on them, drizzle the remaining oil all over and serve as an appetizer.

**Nutrition:** calories 84, fat 1, fiber 1, carbs 1, protein 1

## Tomato and Watermelon Salsa

*Prep Time: 2 hours and 5 minutes | Cook Time: 0 minutes | Servings: 16*

### Ingredients:

- 3 yellow tomatoes, seedless and chopped
- 1 red tomato, seedless and chopped
- Salt and black pepper to taste
- 1 cup watermelon, seedless and chopped
- 1/3 cup red onion,
- chopped
- 1 mango, peeled, seedless and chopped
- 2 jalapeno peppers, chopped
- ¼ cup cilantro, chopped
- 3 tablespoons lime juice
- 2 teaspoons honey

### Directions:

In a bowl, combine the tomatoes with the watermelon and the other ingredients, toss, keep in the fridge for 2 hours and then serve.

**Nutrition:** calories 83, fat 2, fiber 1, carbs 2, protein 1

## Green Dip

*Prep Time: 15 minutes | Cook Time: 0 minutes | Servings: 4*

### Ingredients:

- 1 bunch spinach, roughly chopped
- 1 scallion, sliced
- 2 tablespoons mint,
- chopped
- ¾ cup sour cream
- Salt and black pepper to taste

### Directions:

Put some water in a saucepan, bring to a boil over medium heat, add spinach, cook for 20 seconds, rinse and drain well, chop and put in a bowl. Add the rest of the ingredients, blend with an immersion blender, stir well, leave aside for 15 minutes and then serve.

**Nutrition:** calories 110, fat 1, fiber 1, carbs 1, protein 5

## Basil Artichoke Spread

*Prep Time: 10 minutes | Cook Time: 30 minutes | Servings: 10*

### Ingredients:

- 8 ounces artichoke hearts
- ¾ cup basil, chopped
- ¾ cup green olive paste
- 1 cup parmesan cheese, grated
- 5 ounces garlic and herb cheese

### Directions:

In a food processor, mix artichokes with basil and the other ingredients, pulse well and spread into a baking dish. Place in the oven at 375 degrees F and bake for 30 minutes. Serve warm.

**Nutrition:** calories 152, fat 2, fiber 3, carbs 3, protein 1

# Lemon Cilantro and Avocado Dip

*Prep Time: 10 minutes | Cook Time: 0 minutes | Servings: 8*

## Ingredients:

- ½ cup sour cream
- 1 chili pepper, chopped
- Salt and pepper to taste
- 4 avocados, pitted, peeled and chopped
- 1 cup cilantro, chopped
- ¼ cup lemon juice
- Carrot sticks for serving

## Directions:

Put avocados in a blender and pulse a few times. Add the rest of the ingredients, pulse well, transfer to a bowl and serve as a snack.

**Nutrition:** calories 112, fat 1, fiber 2, carbs 2, protein 4

# Potato Chips and Dip

*Prep Time: 10 minutes | Cook Time: 10 minutes | Servings: 4*

## Ingredients:

- 2 ounces goats cheese, soft
- ¾ cup sour cream
- 1 shallot, minced
- 1 tablespoon chives, chopped
- 1 tablespoon lemon juice
- Salt and black pepper to taste
- ½ pound potatoes, sliced
- ½ pound purple potatoes, sliced
- 2 tablespoons extra virgin olive oil

## Directions:

In a bowl, mix the chives with the cream and the other ingredients except the potatoes and the oil and whisk. In another bowl, mix potato slices with salt and olive oil and toss to coat. Heat up a grill pan over medium high heat, add potato slices, grill for 5 minutes on each side, transfer them to a bowl and serve with the dip on the side.

**Nutrition:** calories 110, fat 2, fiber 2, carbs 2, protein 5

# Chickpeas and Arugula Salsa

*Prep Time: 10 minutes | Cook Time: 0 minutes | Servings: 6*

## Ingredients:

- 4 scallions, sliced
- 1 cup arugula, chopped
- 15 ounces canned chickpeas, chopped
- Salt and black pepper to taste
- 2 jarred red peppers, roasted and chopped
- 2 tablespoons olive oil
- 2 tablespoons lemon juice

## Directions:

In a bowl, mix the chickpeas with the arugula and the other ingredients, toss and serve.

**Nutrition:** calories 74, fat 2, fiber 2, carbs 6, protein 2

# Ginger Cilantro Dip

*Prep Time: 10 minutes | Cook Time: 0 minutes | Servings: 6*

## Ingredients:

- ½ cup ginger, sliced
- 2 bunches cilantro, chopped
- 3 tablespoons balsamic vinegar
- ½ cup olive oil
- 2 teaspoons sesame oil
- 2 tablespoons soy sauce

## Directions:

In a blender, combine the ginger with the cilantro and the other ingredients, pulse, divide into smaller bowls and serve.

**Nutrition:** calories 85, fat 3, fiber 3, carbs 8, protein 2

# Dill Dip

*Prep Time: 10 minutes | Cook Time: 0 minutes | Servings: 8*

**Ingredients:**

- 1 garlic clove, minced
- 2 cups Greek yogurt
- ¼ cup dill, chopped
- ¼ cup walnuts, chopped
- Salt and black pepper to taste

**Directions:**

In a bowl, mix the yogurt with the dill and the other ingredients, whisk well, stir again and serve.

**Nutrition:** calories 73, fat 2, fiber 1, carbs 2, protein 3

# Goats Cheese Dip

*Prep Time: 10 minutes | Cook Time: 0 minutes | Servings: 4*

**Ingredients:**

- ¼ cup mixed parsley and chives, chopped
- 8 ounces goat
- cheese, soft
- Black pepper to taste

**Directions:**

In a food processor mix the parsley with the cheese and black pepper, pulse well, divide into bowls and serve as a snack.

**Nutrition:** calories 152, fat 2, fiber 2, carbs 2, protein 1

# Cannelini Beans Dip

*Prep Time: 10 minutes | Cook Time: 0 minutes | Servings: 8*

**Ingredients:**

- 19 ounces canned cannellini beans, drained
- 3 scallions, chopped
- 1 garlic clove, minced
- 3 tablespoons olive
- oil
- Salt and black pepper to taste
- 1 tablespoon lemon juice
- 2 ounces prosciutto, chopped

**Directions:**

In a bowl, combine the beans with the scallions and the other ingredients, whisk well, divide into bowls and serve.

**Nutrition:** calories 62, fat 4, fiber 1, carbs 1, protein 3

# Cream Cheese Dip

*Prep Time: 10 minutes | Cook Time: 0 minutes | Servings: 6*

**Ingredients:**

- 12 ounces Greek cream cheese
- 1 big tomato, cut in quarters
- ¼ cup mayonnaise
- 2 garlic clove, minced
- 2 tablespoons yellow onion, chopped
- 1 celery stalk, chopped
- 1 teaspoon sugar
- 2 tablespoons lemon juice
- Salt and black pepper to taste
- 4 drops hot sauce

**Directions:**

In a blender, mix the cream cheese with the tomato and the other ingredients and pulse well. Transfer to a bowl and serve.

**Nutrition:** calories 74, fat 3, fiber 1, carbs 3, protein 4

# Pesto Dip

*Prep Time: 10 minutes | Cook Time: 0 minutes | Servings: 6*

**Ingredients:**

- 1 cup mayonnaise
- 7 ounces Greek basil pesto sauce
- Salt and black pepper to taste
- 1 cup sour cream

**Directions:**

In a bowl, combine the mayo with the pesto and the other ingredients, whisk and keep in the fridge until ready to serve.

**Nutrition:** calories 87, fat 2, fiber 0, carbs 1, protein 2

# Chips and Vinaigrette

*Prep Time: 1 hour and 10 minutes | Cook Time: 30 minutes | Servings: 4*

**Ingredients:**

- 2 beets, sliced

*For the vinaigrette:*

- 1/3 cup champagne vinegar
- A pinch of black pepper
- A pinch of sea salt

- 1 cup olive oil
- 1 teaspoon green tea powder

**Directions:**

Put the vinegar in a small saucepan and heat over medium heat. Add salt, pepper and green tea powder, whisk and keep in the fridge for 1 hour. Add beets slices and a pinch of salt, arrange them on a lined baking sheet and bake at 350 degrees F for 30 minutes. Leave them to cool down completely before serving with the vinaigrette on the side for your next party as a snack.

**Nutrition:** calories 100, fat 2, fiber 2, carbs 3, protein 2

# Zucchini Salsa

*Prep Time: 10 minutes | Cook Time: 0 minutes | Servings: 4*

**Ingredients:**

- ½ cup black olives, pitted and sliced
- 3 zucchinis, cut with a spiralizer
- 1 cup cherry tomatoes, halved
- Salt and black

*For the mint tea vinaigrette:*

- 1 tablespoon shallot, chopped
- ½ cup sunflower oil
- ½ cup olive oil
- ¼ cup apple cider

- pepper to taste
- 1 small red onion, chopped
- ½ cup canned chickpeas, drained
- ½ cup feta cheese, crumbled

- vinegar
- 2 teaspoons mint tea powder
- 1 teaspoon mustard

**Directions:**

In a bowl, mix the olives with the zucchinis and the other ingredients except the cheese and toss. Divide into smaller bowls, and serve with the cheese on top.

**Nutrition:** calories 200, fat 3, fiber 2, carbs 4, protein 2

# Olives and Hummus Dip

*Prep Time: 10 minutes | Cook Time: 0 minutes | Servings: 10*

**Ingredients:**

- 7 ounces hummus
- ½ cup kalamata olives, pitted and chopped
- 1 tablespoon Greek yogurt

- A pinch of salt and black pepper
- 1 avocado, pitted, peeled and chopped

**Directions**

In a blender, mix the hummus with the olives and the other ingredients, pulse well, divide into small cups and serve as an appetizer.

**Nutrition:** calories 130, fat 2, fiber 2, carbs 12, protein 5

# Chickpeas Spread

*Prep Time: 10 minutes | Cook Time: 0 minutes | Servings: 6*

## Ingredients:

- 16 ounces canned chickpeas, drained
- ¼ cup Greek yogurt
- 6 ounces roasted red peppers, minced
- Juice of 1 lemon
- 3 tablespoons tahini
- paste
- 1 tablespoon olive oil
- 3 garlic cloves, minced
- A pinch of salt and black pepper

## Directions:

In a blender, combine the chickpeas with the yogurt and the other ingredients, pulse well, divide into small cups and serve as an appetizer.

**Nutrition:** calories 143, fat 8, fiber 3, carbs 15, protein 5

# Hummus

*Prep Time: 10 minutes | Cook Time: 5 minutes | Servings: 16*

## Ingredients:

- 16 ounces chickpeas hummus
- 12 ounces lamb meat, ground
- A drizzle of olive oil
- ½ cup pomegranate
- seeds
- ¼ cup parsley, chopped
- A pinch of salt and black pepper

## Directions:

Heat up a pan with the oil over medium-high heat, add the ground meat and brown for 5 minutes. Spread the hummus on a platter, add the meat and the other ingredients on top and serve as an appetizer.

**Nutrition:** calories 154, fat 7, fiber 6, carbs 12, protein 6

# Cucumber Cups

*Prep Time: 10 minutes | Cook Time: 0 minutes | Servings: 20*

## Ingredients:

- 2 big cucumbers, cut into ½ inch thick slices and seeds scooped out
- 2 cups canned chickpeas, drained
- 7 ounces canned red peppers, roasted, drained and chopped
- ¼ cup lemon juice
- 1/3 cup tahini paste
- 1 garlic clove, minced
- Salt and black pepper to taste
- ¼ teaspoon cumin, ground
- 3 tablespoons olive oil
- 1 tablespoon hot water

## Directions:

In a food processor, mix red peppers with chickpeas with the oil and the other ingredients except the cucumber cups and pulse well. Arrange cucumber cups on a platter, fill each with chickpeas mix and serve right away as an appetizer.

**Nutrition:** calories 182, fat 1, fiber 3, carbs 4, protein 2

# Salmon Platter

*Prep Time: 7 minutes | Cook Time: 0 minutes | Servings: 44*

## Ingredients:

- 1 big long cucumber, sliced into 44 pieces
- 2 teaspoons lemon juice
- 4 ounces sour cream
- 1 teaspoon lemon zest, finely grated
- Salt and black pepper to taste
- 2 teaspoons dill, chopped
- 4 ounces smoked salmon, cut into 44 strips

## Directions:

In a bowl, mix lemon juice with lemon zest and the other ingredients except the cucumber and salmon strips and stir. Arrange cucumber and salmon stirps on a platter, add ½ teaspoon cream mix on each and serve.

**Nutrition:** calories 142, fat 3, fiber 1, carbs 3, protein 3

# Eggplant Meatballs

*Prep Time:* 15 minutes | *Cook Time:* 1 hour | *Servings:* 6

## Ingredients:

- 4 cups eggplants, cubed
- 3 tablespoons olive oil
- 3 garlic cloves, minced
- 1 tablespoon water
- 2 eggs, whisked
- Salt and black pepper to taste
- 1 cup parsley, chopped
- ½ cup parmesan cheese, finely grated
- ¾ cups breadcrumbs

## Directions:

Heat a pan with the oil over medium high heat, add garlic and eggplant, stir and brown it for a few minutes. Add water, stir, reduce heat to low, cover pan, cook for 20 minutes and transfer them to a bowl. Add the rest of the ingredients except the parmesan, stir well, shape medium balls and arrange them on a lined baking sheet. Place them in oven at 350 degrees F and bake for 30 minutes. Sprinkle parmesan, arrange on a platter and serve as an appetizer.

**Nutrition:** calories 142, fat 1, fiber 3, carbs 2, protein 3

# Eggplant Platter

*Prep Time:* 10 minutes | *Cook Time:* 15 minutes | *Servings:* 8

## Ingredients:

- 2 eggplants, cut into 20 slices

*For the tapenade:*

- 2 tablespoons olive oil
- ½ cup bottled roasted peppers, chopped
- ½ cup kalamata and black olives, pitted and chopped
- 1 tablespoon lemon juice

*For serving:*

- 2 tablespoons pine nuts, toasted
- 4 tablespoons feta
- A drizzle of olive oil

- 1 teaspoon red pepper flakes, crushed
- Salt and black pepper to the taste
- 2 tablespoons mixed mint, parsley, oregano and basil, chopped

cheese, crumbled
- A drizzle of olive oil

## Directions:

In a bowl, mix roasted peppers with 2 tablespoons oil and the other ingredients for the tapenade, stir well and keep in the fridge. Brush eggplant slices with a drizzle of olive oil on both sides, place them on preheated grill pan over medium high heat, cook for 7 minutes on each side and transfer them to a platter. Top each eggplant slice with the tapenade mix, also sprinkle the rest of the ingredients and serve.

**Nutrition:** calories 132, fat 2, fiber 3, carbs 4, protein 4

# Turmeric Veggie Chips

*Prep Time:* 10 minutes | *Cook Time:* 1 hour | *Servings:* 2

**Ingredients:**

- A drizzle of olive oil
- 2 eggplants, sliced
- ½ tablespoon garlic powder
- ½ tablespoon smoked paprika
- 1 teaspoon oregano, dried
- Salt and black pepper to taste
- ½ teaspoon turmeric, ground
- ½ teaspoon thyme, dried
- ½ teaspoon onion powder
- A pinch of cayenne pepper
- ¼ teaspoon sage, dried and ground

**Directions:**

Arrange eggplant slices on a lined baking sheet, season with salt and pepper, drizzle some olive oil and rub well. Add the rest of the ingredients, toss to coat, introduce in the oven and bake at 250 degrees F for 1 hour. Transfer them to bowls and serve as a snack.

**Nutrition:** calories 110, fat 1, fiber 2, carbs 2, protein 4

# Eggplant Salsa

*Prep Time:* 10 minutes | *Cook Time:* 20 minutes | *Servings:* 4

**Ingredients:**

- 1 tomato, diced
- 1 eggplant, pricked
- Salt and black pepper to taste
- 1 and ½ teaspoons red wine vinegar
- ½ teaspoon oregano, chopped
- 3 tablespoons olive oil
- 2 garlic cloves, minced
- 3 tablespoons parsley, chopped
- Capers, chopped for serving

**Directions:**

Heat a grill pan over medium high heat, add eggplant, cook for 15 minutes, turning from time to time, cool down, scoop flesh, chop and put in a bowl. Add the rest of the ingredients, toss well, divide into smaller cups and serve as an appetizer.

**Nutrition:** calories 132, fat 1, fiber 2, carbs 2, protein 4

# Veggie Salad

*Prep Time:* 10 minutes | *Cook Time:* 10 minutes | *Servings:* 4

**Ingredients:**

- 1 eggplant, sliced
- 1 red onion, sliced
- A drizzle of olive oil
- 1 avocado, pitted and chopped
- 1 teaspoon mustard
- 1 tablespoon red wine vinegar
- 1 tablespoon oregano, chopped
- 1 teaspoon honey
- Salt and black pepper to taste
- Zest from 1 lemon
- Some parsley sprigs, chopped for serving

**Directions:**

Brush red onion and eggplant slices with a drizzle of olive oil, place on preheated grill pan, cook for a few minutes on each side, cool down, chop and put in a bowl. Add all the other ingredients, toss, divide into smaller bowls and serve as an appetizer.

**Nutrition:** calories 142, fat 2, fiber 1, carbs 5, protein 2

# Eggplant Salad

*Prep Time:* 2 hours and 10 minutes | *Cook Time:* 1 hour and 30 minutes | *Servings:* 12

**Ingredients:**

- 1 garlic clove, minced
- 6 eggplants, pricked with a fork
- 1 teaspoon parsley, dried
- 1 teaspoon oregano, dried
- ¼ teaspoon basil, dried
- 3 tablespoons olive oil
- 2 tablespoons sugar
- 1 tablespoon balsamic vinegar
- Salt and black pepper to taste

**Directions:**

Arrange eggplants on a lined baking sheet, place in the oven at 350 degrees F, bake for 1 hour and 30 minutes, peel, chop and transfer to a salad bowl. Add the rest of the ingredients, toss to coat, keep in the fridge for 2 hours and serve as an appetizer.

**Nutrition:** calories 200, fat 3, fiber 1, carbs 3, protein 3

# Eggplant Bowls

*Prep Time:* 30 minutes | *Cook Time:* 10 minutes | *Servings:* 4

### Ingredients:

- 1 eggplant, cut in half lengthwise and sliced
- 1 small red onion, chopped
- Juice of 1 lemon
- Zest from 1 lemon
- A drizzle of olive oil
- 28 ounces canned chickpeas, drained
- 1 bunch parsley, chopped
- 2 tomatoes, chopped
- A pinch of cayenne pepper
- 2 teaspoons garlic infused olive oil
- Some silver almonds for serving
- Salt to taste

### Directions:

Put the onion in a bowl, add water to cover and leave aside for 30 minutes. Arrange eggplant slices on a lined baking sheet, brush with a drizzle of olive oil, place under a preheated broiler for 5 minutes, brush them again with some olive oil and with half of the lemon juice, broil for 5 minutes more and transfer to a salad bowl. Spread chickpeas on the same baking sheet, broil for a few minutes and add them to the bowl with the eggplant pieces. Add all the other ingredients, toss to coat, divide into small bowls and serve as an appetizer.

**Nutrition:** calories 154, fat 3, fiber 2, carbs 2, protein 4

# Egg Salad

*Prep Time:* 10 minutes | *Cook Time:* 35 minutes | *Servings:* 4

### Ingredients:

- 1 large eggplant, cubed
- ¼ cup olive oil
- 12 eggs, hard-boiled, peeled and chopped
- Juice of 1 lemon
- 14 ounces feta cheese, crumbled
- Salt and black
- pepper to taste
- 1/3 cup pine nuts
- ¼ cup mustard
- ¾ cup sun dried tomatoes, marinade and chopped
- 1 cup walnuts, halved

### Directions:

Arrange eggplant cubes on a lined baking sheet, add salt, pepper, oil and half of the lemon juice, toss and bake at 400 degrees F for 30 minutes. In a food processor, mix cheese with the rest of the lemon juice, sun dried tomatoes, walnuts, pine nuts, mustard, salt and pepper and blend. Put chopped eggs in a bowl, crush them with a fork, add eggplant cubes and cheese mix, toss to coat well and serve.

**Nutrition:** calories 153, fat 3, fiber 3, carbs 2, protein 2

# Cheese Stuffed Eggplant

*Prep Time:* 10 minutes | *Cook Time:* 45 minutes | *Servings:* 6

### Ingredients:

- 6 baby eggplants, sliced in halves
- 2 garlic cloves, minced
- 12 oregano sprigs
- 1 lemon, sliced
- Juice from 2 lemons
- Salt and black pepper to taste
- ¾ cup olive oil
- 8 ounces feta cheese, sliced

### Directions:

Arrange eggplant pieces in a baking pan, insert lemon slices, garlic and oregano into each, season them with salt and pepper, drizzle the oil and the lemon juice all over, cover with tin foil and bake at 450 degrees F for 40 minutes. Uncover pan, bake for 5 minutes, leave aside to cool down for 3-4 minutes. Transfer to plates, top with feta cheese slices and pan juices and serve.

**Nutrition:** calories 200, fat 1, fiber 1, carbs 4, protein 3

# Parsley Eggplant Mix

*Prep Time:* 6 hours and 30 minutes | *Cook Time:* 10 minutes | *Servings:* 4

### Ingredients:

- 1 ½ pounds eggplants, sliced
- ½ jalapeno pepper, chopped
- ¾ cup olive oil
- 1 red bell pepper, roasted and chopped
- 1 ½ teaspoons
- capers, drained and chopped
- 1 big garlic clove, minced
- 1 bunch parsley, chopped
- Salt and black pepper to taste

### Directions:

Sprinkle eggplant slices with salt on both sides, leave them aside for 30 minutes, pat dry and brush them with ¼ cup olive oil. Heat a pan over medium high heat, add eggplant slices, cook for 5 minutes on each side and arrange in a baking dish. In a bowl, mix chili pepper with roasted pepper and the other ingredients and toss. Pour this over eggplants, cover and leave in the fridge for 6 hours. Divide on plates and serve as an appetizer.

**Nutrition:** calories 168, fat 2, fiber 1, carbs 5, protein 4

# Eggplant and Pomegranate Platter

*Prep Time: 8 hours | Cook Time: 30 minutes | Servings: 6*

## Ingredients:

- 2 large eggplants, peeled and sliced
- 3 tablespoons lemon juice
- Salt to taste
- 3 garlic cloves
- 1/8 teaspoon cumin
- 6 tablespoons cold
- water
- ½ cup tahini paste
- Olive oil for frying
- ½ cup pomegranate seeds
- ¼ cup pistachios, halved

## Directions:

Arrange eggplant slices on a lined baking sheet, season with salt on both sides and transfer to the fridge for 8 hours. In a blender, mix lemon juice with salt to taste, garlic, cumin, water and tahini and pulse well. Heat up a pan with some olive oil over medium-high heat. Pat dry the eggplant slices, add to the pan, cook for 5 minutes on each side, drain away excess grease and arrange eggplant pieces on a platter. Drizzle with ¼ cup of tahini sauce, sprinkle the rest of the ingredients on top and serve as an appetizer.

**Nutrition:** calories 142, fat 12, fiber 3, carbs 9, protein 4

# Lentil Spread

*Prep Time: 1 hour and 10 minutes | Cook Time: 10 minutes | Servings: 6*

## Ingredients:

- 1 cup red lentils, soaked overnight
- Salt and black pepper to taste
- 1 bay leaf
- 2 tablespoons lemon juice
- 1 garlic clove, finely chopped
- 1 tablespoon tomato paste
- 2 tablespoon cilantro, finely chopped
- 2 teaspoons cumin
- 2 teaspoons harissa
- 2 tablespoons extra virgin olive oil

## Directions:

Put lentils in a saucepan, add salt, bay leaf and water to cover, bring to a boil over medium high heat, reduce temperature to medium and cook for 10 minutes. Drain lentils, leave aside for 10 minutes to cool down, transfer to a blender, add the rest of the ingredients, pulse well, transfer to a bowl and leave aside for 1 hour before serving.

**Nutrition:** calories 132, fat 1, fiber 2, carbs 3, protein 3

# Stuffed Potato Platter

*Prep Time: 10 minutes | Cook Time: 40 minutes | Servings: 36*

## Ingredients:

- 18 baby potatoes
- ½ cup goats cheese, crumbled
- ¾ cup red lentils, cooked and drained
- 2 tablespoons butter, melted
- 1 garlic clove,
- minced
- 1 tablespoon chives, chopped
- ½ teaspoon Sriracha sauce
- Salt and black pepper to taste

## Directions:

Put potatoes in a saucepan, add water to cover, bring to a boil over medium low heat, simmer for 15 minutes, drain, rinse, cool down, cut in halves, remove almost all the flesh and transfer it to a blender. Add the rest of the ingredients, pulse well and stuff the potato skins with this. Arrange potatoes on a lined baking sheet, place them in the oven at 375 degrees F and bake for 15 minutes. Divide between plates and serve right away as an appetizer.

**Nutrition:** calories 210, fat 2, fiber 3, carbs 3, protein 1

# Bulgur Balls

*Prep Time: 10 minutes | Cook Time: 45 minutes | Servings: 4*

## Ingredients:

- 1 cup red lentils
- 3 cups water
- 2 cups bulgur
- Some sea salt
- 3 teaspoons cumin, ground
- 1 tablespoon tomato paste
- 1 teaspoon red pepper flakes
- 1 ½ tablespoons
- olive oil
- 3 scallions, chopped
- 1 yellow onion, chopped
- ½ bunch parsley, chopped
- Lemon slices for serving
- Lettuce leaves for serving

## Directions:

Put lentils in a large saucepan, add 3 cups water and some salt, stir, heat over medium high heat, cook for 20 minutes and take off heat. Add bulgur, stir, cover pan, leave aside for 15 minutes, transfer the whole mix to a bowl and leave aside to cool down. Heat pan with the oil over medium high heat, add onion, tomato paste, pepper flakes and cumin, stir and cook for 7-8 minutes. Transfer to lentils and bulgur mix, add some more salt, parsley and scallions, knead well for 10 minutes. Shape balls out of mix, arrange them all on a platter and serve with lemon slices on the side.

**Nutrition:** calories 167, fat 3, fiber 4, carbs 3, protein 2

# Tomato and Okra Bowls

*Prep Time: 40 minutes | Cook Time: 0 minutes | Servings: 4*

## Ingredients:

- 1 pound okra, cut into medium pieces
- A pinch of sea salt
- Black pepper to taste
- 15 ounces canned black beans, drained
- 1 cup corn
- 1 pound cherry
- tomatoes, halved
- 1 white onion, chopped
- 3 tablespoons olive oil
- 1 avocado, pitted, peeled and chopped

## Directions:

In a bowl, mix the okra with the tomatoes and the other ingredients, toss to coat and keep in the fridge for 30 minutes before you serve it.

**Nutrition:** calories 120, fat 1, fiber 1, carbs 0, protein 7

# Tuna and Cream Cheese Roll

*Prep Time: 10 minutes | Cook Time: 0 minutes | Servings: 12*

## Ingredients:

- 6 ounces canned tuna, drained and flaked
- 3 teaspoons lemon juice
- 1 teaspoon onion salt
- 8 ounces cream cheese
- 4 drops hot pepper sauce
- ¼ cup parsley, chopped

## Directions:

In a bowl, mix tuna with cream cheese and the other ingredients except the parsley and stir well. Shape a big ball, roll in chopped parsley and keep in the fridge until you serve.

**Nutrition:** calories 132, fat 2, fiber 3, carbs 2, protein 4

# Spinach Muffins

*Prep Time: 10 minutes | Cook Time: 30 minutes | Servings: 4*

## Ingredients:

- 12 ounces spinach
- ½ cup ricotta cheese
- 2 eggs, whisked
- ½ cup parmesan, grated
- Salt and black pepper to taste
- 1 garlic clove, minced
- Olive oil spray

## Directions:

Put spinach in a food processor, pulse well and transfer to a bowl. Add the rest of the ingredients except the spray and whisk well. Spray a muffin pan with some olive oil, divide spinach into cups, place in the oven at 400 degrees F and bake for 20 minutes. Take spinach muffins out of the oven, transfer them to a platter and serve.

**Nutrition:** calories 141, fat 4, fiber 2, carbs 6, protein 13

# Meat Recipes

## Mustard Pork Chops

*Prep Time:* 1 day | **Cook Time:** 20 minutes | **Servings:** 6

### Ingredients:

- 2 pork chops
- ¼ cup olive oil
- 2 yellow onions, sliced
- 2 garlic cloves, minced
- 2 teaspoons mustard
- 1 teaspoon sweet paprika
- Salt and black pepper to taste
- ½ teaspoon oregano, dried
- ½ teaspoon thyme, dried
- A pinch of cayenne pepper

### Directions:

In a small bowl, mix oil with garlic and the other ingredients except the meat and toss. Add pork chops, toss to coat, cover and keep in the fridge for 1 day. Place meat on preheated grill pan over medium high heat, season with salt and cook for 10 minutes on each side. Meanwhile, heat a pan over medium heat, add marinated onions, stir and sauté for 4 minutes. Divide pork chops and onions on plates and serve.

**Nutrition:** calories 284, fat 4, fiber 4, carbs 7, protein 12

## Pork Salad

*Prep Time:* 3 hours and 10 minutes | **Cook Time:** 0 minutes | **Servings:** 10

### Ingredients:

- 1 green cabbage head, shredded
- 1 ½ cups brown rice, already cooked
- 2 cups pork roast, already cooked
- 3 ounces water chestnuts, drained and sliced
- ½ cup sour cream
- ½ cup mayonnaise
- A pinch of salt

### Directions:

In a bowl, mix the pork with the rice and the other ingredients, toss and keep in the fridge for 3 hours before serving.

**Nutrition:** calories 285, fat 14, fiber 3, carbs 7, protein 11

## Paprika Pork Mix

*Prep Time:* 10 minutes | **Cook Time:** 40 minutes | **Servings:** 6

### Ingredients:

- 2 pounds pork meat, boneless and cubed
- 2 yellow onions, chopped
- 1 tablespoon olive oil
- 1 garlic clove, minced
- 3 cups chicken stock
- 2 tablespoons paprika
- 1 teaspoon caraway seeds
- Salt and black pepper to taste
- ¼ cup water
- 2 tablespoons white flour
- 1 and ½ cups sour cream
- 2 tablespoons dill, chopped

### Directions:

Heat a pot with the oil over medium heat, add the pork and brown it for a few minutes. Add onions and garlic, stir and cook for 3 minutes. Add stock and the other ingredients except the flour mixed with the water and dill stir, bring to a boil, reduce temperature, cover and cook for 30 minutes. Add flour mixed with water, stir and boil 2 minutes more. Take off heat, add dill weed, stir well, divide into bowls and serve.

**Nutrition:** calories 300, fat 12, fiber 4, carbs 9, protein 12

# Mushroom and Pork Stir Fry

*Prep Time:* 10 minutes | *Cook Time:* 15 minutes | *Servings:* 4

## Ingredients:

- 4 ounces bacon, chopped
- 4 ounces snow peas
- 2 tablespoons butter
- 1 pound pork loin, cut into thin strips
- 2 cups mushrooms, sliced
- ¾ cup white wine
- ½ cup yellow onion, chopped
- 3 tablespoons sour cream
- Salt and white pepper to taste

## Directions:

Put snow peas and some salt in a saucepan, add water to cover, bring to a boil over medium heat, cook until they are soft, drain and leave aside. Heat a pan over medium high heat, add bacon, cook for a few minutes, drain grease, transfer to a bowl and also leave aside. Heat a pan with 1 tablespoon butter over medium heat, add pork strips, salt and pepper to taste, brown for a few minutes and transfer to a plate as well. Return pan to medium heat, add remaining butter, melt it, add the onions and mushrooms and brown for 5 minutes. Add the wine, cream, peas, pork, salt and pepper, stir and reduce it for a couple more minutes. Divide between plates, top with bacon and serve.

**Nutrition:** calories 310, fat 4, fiber 6, carbs 9, protein 10

# Pork Soup

*Prep Time:* 10 minutes | *Cook Time:* 1 hour | *Servings:* 6

## Ingredients:

- 1 small yellow onion, chopped
- 1 tablespoon olive oil
- 1 and ½ teaspoons basil, chopped
- 1 and ½ teaspoons ginger, grated
- 3 garlic cloves, chopped
- Salt and black pepper to taste
- ½ teaspoon cumin, ground
- 1 carrot, chopped
- 1 pound pork chops, bone-in
- 3 ounces brown lentils, rinsed
- 3 cups chicken stock
- 2 tablespoons tomato paste
- 2 tablespoons lime juice
- 1 teaspoon red chili flakes, crushed

## Directions:

Heat a pot with the oil over medium heat, add garlic, onion, basil, ginger, salt, pepper and cumin, stir well and cook for 6 minutes. Add carrots and pork, stir and cook 5 more minutes. Add lentils and the rest of the ingredients, stir, bring to a boil, cover pan and simmer for 50 minutes. Transfer pork to a plate, discard bones, shred it and return to pot. Stir, ladle into bowls and serve.

**Nutrition:** calories 263, fat 4, fiber 6, carbs 8, protein 10

# Butter Pork

*Prep Time: 40 minutes | Cook Time: 1 hour | Servings: 4*

## Ingredients:

- 2 pounds pork loin roast, boneless and cubed
- 5 tablespoons butter
- Salt and black pepper to taste
- 2 cups chicken stock
- ½ cup dry white wine
- 2 garlic cloves, minced
- 1 teaspoon thyme, chopped
- 1 thyme spring
- 1 bay leaf
- ½ yellow onion, chopped
- 2 tablespoons white flour
- ¾ pound pearl onions
- ½ pound red grapes

## Directions:

Heat a pan with 2 tablespoons butter over high heat, add pork loin, some salt and pepper, stir, brown for 10 minutes and transfer to a plate. Add wine to the pan, bring to a boil over high heat and cook for 3 minutes. Add stock, garlic, thyme spring, bay leaf, yellow onion and the meat, bring to a boil, cover, reduce heat to low, cook for 1 hour, strain liquid into another saucepan and transfer pork to a plate. Put pearl onions in a small saucepan, add water to cover, bring to a boil over medium high heat, boil them for 5 minutes, drain, peel them and leave aside for now. In a bowl, mix 2 tablespoons butter with flour and 1/2 cup of the cooking liquid, whisk well, pour this into the strained liquid from the pan, whisk, and simmer over medium heat for 5 minutes. Add salt and pepper, chopped thyme, pork and pearl onions, cover and simmer for a few minutes. Heat up another pan with the rest of the butter, add grapes, stir and cook them for 1-2 minutes. Divide pork meat on plates, drizzle the sauce all over, top with the grapes and onions and serve.

**Nutrition:** calories 320, fat 4, fiber 5, carbs 9, protein 18

# Pork and Tomato Mix

*Prep Time: 20 minutes | Cook Time: 8 hours | Servings: 4*

## Ingredients:

- 2 tablespoons white flour
- ½ cup chicken stock
- 1 tablespoon ginger, grated
- 1 teaspoon coriander, ground
- 2 teaspoons cumin, ground
- Salt and black pepper to taste
- 2 and ½ pounds pork butt, cubed
- 28 ounces canned tomatoes, drained and chopped
- 4 ounces carrots, chopped
- 1 red onion cut in wedges
- 4 garlic cloves, minced
- ½ cup apricots, cut in quarters
- 1 cup couscous, cooked
- 15 ounces canned chickpeas, drained
- Cilantro, chopped for serving

## Directions:

Put stock in your slow cooker. Add the meat and the other ingredients except the chickpeas, couscous and cilantro, stir, cover cooker and cook on Low for 7 hours and 50 minutes. Add chickpeas and couscous, cover and cook for 10 more minutes. Divide on plates, sprinkle cilantro and serve right away.

**Nutrition:** calories 216, fat 6, fiber 8, carbs 10, protein 20

# Italian Pork Salad

*Prep Time: 10 minutes | Cook Time: 15 minutes | Servings: 4*

**Ingredients:**

- 1 pound pork chops, boneless and cut into strips
- 8 ounces white mushrooms, sliced
- ½ cup Italian dressing
- 6 cups mixed salad greens
- 6 ounces jarred artichoke hearts, drained
- Salt and black pepper to the taste
- ½ cup basil, chopped
- 1 tablespoon olive oil

**Directions:**

Heat a pan with the oil over medium-high heat, add the pork and the mushrooms and brown for 10 minutes. Add the dressing, and the other ingredients, cook for 4-5 minutes, divide everything into bowls and serve.

**Nutrition:** calories 235, fat 6, fiber 4, carbs 14, protein 11

# Pork with Beans and Rice

*Prep Time: 10 minutes | Cook Time: 25 minutes | Servings: 4*

**Ingredients:**

- ½ pound pork loin, cut into strips
- Salt and black pepper to taste
- 2 tablespoons olive oil
- 2 carrots, chopped
- 1 red bell pepper, chopped
- 3 garlic cloves,
- minced
- 2 cups veggie stock
- 1 cup basmati rice
- ½ cup garbanzo beans
- 10 black olives, pitted and sliced
- 1 tablespoon parsley, chopped

**Directions:**

Heat a pan with the oil over medium high heat, add the meat, brown for 5 minutes and transfer to a plate. Add the carrots, bell pepper and the garlic, stir and cook for 5 more minutes. Add the rice and the rest of the ingredients, stir, cook for 15 minutes, divide between plates next to the meat, sprinkle the parsley on top and serve.

**Nutrition:** calories 220, fat 12, fiber 4, carbs 7, protein 11

# Lemon Pork

*Prep Time: 20 hours and 10 minutes | Cook Time: 8 hours | Servings: 6*

**Ingredients:**

- 3 pounds pork shoulder - boneless
- ¼ cup olive oil
- 2 teaspoons oregano, dried
- ¼ cup lemon juice
- 2 teaspoons mustard
- 2 teaspoons mint,
- chopped
- 3 garlic cloves, minced
- 2 teaspoons pesto sauce
- Salt and black pepper to taste

**Directions:**

In a bowl, mix the pork with the olive oil with lemon juice, oregano, mint, mustard, garlic, pesto, salt and pepper, toss and keep in the fridge for 10 hours. Flip pork shoulder and leave aside for 10 more hours. Transfer to your slow cooker along with the marinade juices, cover, cook on low for 8 hours, slice, divide between plates and serve.

**Nutrition:** calories 300, fat 4, fiber 6, carbs 7, protein 12

# Orange Pork and Potatoes

*Prep Time: 10 minutes | Cook Time: 4 hours | Servings: 8*

**Ingredients:**

- 1 pound small potatoes, chopped
- 2 medium carrots, chopped
- 15 ounces stewed tomatoes, drained
- 1 yellow onion, chopped
- Zest and juice from 1 orange
- 4 garlic cloves, minced
- 3 and ½ pounds pork roast, trimmed
- 3 bay leaves
- Salt and black pepper to taste
- ½ cup kalamata olives, pitted

**Directions:**

Put potatoes in your slow cooker. Add the meat and the rest of the ingredients, cover and cook on High for 4 hours. Transfer meat to a cutting board, slice it and divide among plates. Discard bay leaves, add veggies to a bowl, crush them a bit with a fork, divide this next to pork and serve.

**Nutrition:** calories 240, fat 4, fiber 7, carbs 9, protein 12

# Pork and Zucchinis Mix

*Prep Time:* 20 minutes | *Cook Time:* 4 hours | *Servings:* 4

## Ingredients:

- 2 pounds pork neck
- 1 tablespoon white flour
- 1 and ½ tablespoons olive oil
- 2 eggplants, chopped
- 1 brown onion, chopped
- 1 red bell pepper, chopped
- 3 garlic cloves, minced
- 1 tablespoon thyme, dried
- 2 teaspoons sage, dried
- 4 ounces canned white beans, drained
- 1 cup chicken stock
- 12 ounces zucchinis, chopped
- Salt and pepper to taste
- 2 tablespoons tomato paste

## Directions:

In a bowl, mix flour with salt, pepper, pork neck and toss. Heat a pan with 2 teaspoons oil over medium high heat, add pork, cook for 3 minutes on each side and transfer to a slow cooker. Heat the remaining oil in the same pan over medium heat, add eggplant, onion, bell pepper, thyme, sage and garlic, stir and cook for 5 minutes. Add reserved flour, stir and cook for 1 more minute. Add to pork, also add the rest of the ingredients, cover and cook on High for 4 hours. Uncover, transfer to plates and serve.

**Nutrition:** calories 310, fat 3, fiber 5, carbs 8, protein 12

# Pork and Herbed Couscous Mix

*Prep Time:* 10 minutes | *Cook Time:* 7 hours | *Servings:* 6

## Ingredients:

- 2 and ½ pounds pork loin boneless and trimmed
- ¾ cup chicken stock
- 2 tablespoons olive oil
- ½ tablespoon sweet paprika
- 2 and ¼ teaspoon sage, dried
- ½ tablespoon garlic powder
- ¼ teaspoon rosemary, dried
- ¼ teaspoon marjoram, dried
- 1 teaspoon basil, dried
- 1 teaspoon oregano, dried
- Salt and black pepper to taste
- 2 cups couscous, cooked

## Directions:

In a bowl, mix the pork with oil with stock, paprika, garlic powder, sage, rosemary, thyme, marjoram, oregano, salt and pepper to taste, toss well and transfer to the slow cooker. Add the rest of the ingredients, stir, cover and cook on Low for 7 hours. Divide between plates and serve with couscous on the side.

**Nutrition:** calories 310, fat 4, fiber 6, carbs 7, protein 14

# Pork Roast

*Prep Time:* 30 minutes | *Cook Time:* 4 hours | *Servings:* 6

## Ingredients:

- 3 tablespoons garlic, minced
- 3 tablespoons olive oil
- 4 pounds pork shoulder
- Salt and black pepper to taste

## Directions:

In a bowl, mix the pork with the oil and the other ingredients and rub well. Arrange in a baking dish and place in the oven at 425 degrees for 20 minutes. Reduce heat to 325 degrees F and bake for 4 hours. Take pork shoulder out of the oven, slice, arrange on a platter and serve.

**Nutrition:** calories 221, fat 4, fiber 4, carbs 7, protein 10

# Herbed Pork Mix

*Prep Time: 20 minutes | Cook Time: 2 hours | Servings: 10*

**Ingredients:**

- 5 and ½ pounds pork loin roast, trimmed, chine bone removed
- Salt and black pepper to taste
- 3 garlic cloves, minced
- 2 tablespoons
- rosemary, chopped
- 1 teaspoon fennel, ground
- 1 tablespoon fennel seeds
- 2 teaspoons red pepper, crushed
- ¼ cup olive oil

**Directions:**

In a food processor mix garlic with fennel seeds and the other ingredients except the meat and pulse well. Place pork roast in a roasting pan, spread 2 tablespoons of the garlic mix all over and rub well. Season with salt and pepper, place in the oven at 400 degrees F and bake for 1 hour. Reduce heat to 325 degrees F and bake for another 35 minutes. Carve roast into chops, divide between plates and serve right away.

**Nutrition:** calories 300, fat 4, fiber 2, carbs 6, protein 15

# Rosemary Beef

*Prep Time: 10 minutes | Cook Time: 9 hours | Servings: 8*

**Ingredients:**

- 6 pounds beef brisket
- 2 tablespoons cumin, ground
- 3 tablespoons rosemary, chopped
- 2 tablespoons coriander, dried
- 1 tablespoon oregano, dried
- 2 teaspoons cinnamon powder
- 1 cup beef stock
- A pinch of salt and black pepper

**Directions:**

In a slow cooker, combine the meat with the rosemary, cumin and the other ingredients, and toss well. Cover and cook on low for 9 hours. Slice and serve.

**Nutrition:** calories 400, fat 12, fiber 4, carbs 15, protein 17

# Ground Beef and Zucchinis

*Prep Time: 10 minutes | Cook Time: 15 minutes | Servings: 6*

**Ingredients:**

- 1 pound beef, ground
- 2 cups zucchinis, chopped
- ½ cup yellow onion, chopped
- Salt and black pepper to taste
- 15 ounces canned roasted tomatoes and garlic
- 1 cup water
- ¾ cup cheddar cheese, shredded
- 1 and ½ cups white rice

**Directions:**

Heat a pan over medium high heat, add beef, onion, salt, pepper and zucchini, stir and cook for 7 minutes. Add the rice, water and the other ingredients except the cheese, toss and cook for 8 minutes more. Divide between plates and serve with cheddar cheese on top.

**Nutrition:** calories 380, fat 9, fiber 4, carbs 16, protein 20

# Tartar Platter

*Prep Time: 10 minutes | Cook Time: 0 minutes | Servings: 1*

**Ingredients:**

- 1 shallot, chopped
- 4 ounces beef fillet, minced
- 5 small cucumbers, chopped
- 1 egg yolk
- A pinch of salt and
- black pepper
- 2 teaspoons mustard
- 1 tablespoon parsley, chopped
- 1 parsley spring, roughly chopped for serving

**Directions:**

In a bowl, mix the meat with the cucumbers and the other ingredients and stir well. Arrange on a platter and serve.

**Nutrition:** calories 210, fat 3, fiber 1, carbs 5, protein 8

# Beef Balls and Greek Sauce

*Prep Time: 5 minutes | Cook Time: 8 minutes | Servings: 4*

## Ingredients:

- 1 egg, whisked
- 1 teaspoon cumin, ground
- 1 teaspoon allspice, ground
- ¼ cup cilantro, chopped
- A pinch of salt and

*For the sauce:*

- 1 cucumber, chopped
- 1 cup Greek yogurt
- 2 tablespoons lemon

- black pepper
- 2 pounds beef, ground
- 1/3 cup bread crumbs
- Vegetable oil for frying

- juice
- 1 tablespoon dill, chopped

## Directions:

In a bowl, mix the beef with the bread crumbs and the other ingredients except the ones for the sauce and the oil, stir well and shape medium balls out of this mix. Heat a pan with oil over medium heat. Add the meatballs and cook for 4 minutes each side. In a bowl, mix the yogurt with the and the other ingredients for the sauce and whisk. Serve the meatballs with the yogurt sauce.

**Nutrition:** calories 263, fat 14, fiber 4, carbs 12, protein 9

# Beef Spaghetti

*Prep Time: 10 minutes | Cook Time: 20 minutes | Servings: 4*

## Ingredients:

- 12 ounces spaghetti
- Zest and juice from 1 lemon
- 2 garlic cloves, minced
- 2 tablespoons olive oil
- 1 pound beef, ground
- Salt and black pepper to taste

- 1-pint cherry tomatoes, chopped
- 1 small red onion, chopped
- ½ cup white wine
- 2 tablespoons tomato paste
- Some basil leaves, chopped for serving
- Some parmesan, grated for serving

## Directions:

Put water in a large saucepan, add a pinch of salt, bring to a boil over medium high heat, add spaghetti, cook according to instructions, drain and return pasta to pan. Add lemon zest and juice and 1 tablespoon oil to pasta, toss to coat, divide between plates and serv. Heat up a pan with remaining oil over medium heat, add garlic, the meat and the rest of the ingredients except the parmesan, stir and cook for 10 minutes. Divide beef on plates over the pasta, sprinkle the parmesan on top and serve.

**Nutrition:** calories 284, fat 2, fiber 1, carbs 5, protein 15

# Beef Salad

*Prep Time: 5 minutes | Cook Time: 10 minutes | Servings: 4*

## Ingredients:

- 1 pound beef steaks, boneless and cut into strips
- 1 teaspoon pepper seasoning
- 2 tablespoons olive oil
- 12 figs, cut into quarters

- ½ cup canned chickpeas, drained
- 6 cups baby spinach
- ½ cup pistachios, chopped
- ½ cup goat cheese, crumbled
- ½ cup red onion, sliced

## Directions:

Heat a pan with the oil over medium-high heat, add the meat and the other ingredients, toss, cook for 10 minutes, divide into bowls and serve.

**Nutrition:** calories 221, fat 12, fiber 4, carbs 8, protein 9

# Beef and Eggplant Soup

*Prep Time:* 10 minutes | *Cook Time:* 30 minutes | *Servings:* 8

## Ingredients:

- 1 yellow onion, chopped
- 1 tablespoon olive oil
- 1 garlic clove, minced
- 1 pound beef, ground
- 1 pound eggplant, chopped
- ¾ cup celery, chopped
- ¾ cup carrots, chopped
- Salt and black pepper to taste
- 29 ounces canned tomatoes, drained and chopped
- 28 ounces beef stock
- ½ teaspoon nutmeg, ground
- ½ cup macaroni
- 2 teaspoons parsley, chopped
- ½ cup parmesan cheese, grated

## Directions:

Heat a large saucepan with the oil over medium heat, add onion, garlic and meat, stir and brown for 5 minutes. Add celery, carrots and the other ingredients except the macaroni and the cheese, stir, bring to a simmer and cook for 20 minutes. Add macaroni, stir and cook for 12 minutes. Ladle into soup bowls, top with grated cheese and serve.

**Nutrition:** calories 241, fat 3, fiber 5, carbs 7, protein 10

# Beef and Tomato Soup

*Prep Time:* 10 minutes | *Cook Time:* 1 hour and 40 minutes | *Servings:* 8

## Ingredients:

- 1 pound beef chuck, cubed
- 2 tablespoons olive oil
- 2 celery stalks, chopped
- 2 carrots, chopped
- 1 yellow onion, chopped
- Salt and black pepper to taste
- 3 garlic cloves, chopped
- 2 cups lentils
- 32 ounces canned chicken stock
- 1 ½ teaspoons cilantro, dried
- 1 teaspoon oregano, dried
- 28 ounces canned tomatoes, chopped
- ¼ cup parsley, chopped
- ½ cup parmesan, grated

## Directions:

Heat a saucepan with the oil over medium high heat, add beef, salt and pepper to taste, stir, brown for 8 minutes, transfer to a plate and keep warm. Return saucepan to medium heat, add carrots, celery, garlic, onion, oregano and cilantro, stir and cook for 8 more minutes. Return beef to saucepan, add the rest of the ingredients except the lentils and parmesan, stir, bring to a boil, cover pan and cook for 1 hour. Add lentils, stir and simmer for 40 more minutes. Ladle into bowls, sprinkle parmesan on top and serve.

**Nutrition:** calories 210, fat 4, fiber 6, carbs 8, protein 10

# Beef Casserole

*Prep Time:* 15 minutes | *Cook Time:* 2 hours and 45 minutes | *Servings:* 6

## Ingredients:

- 4 tablespoons olive oil
- 3 pounds beef meat, cubed
- 6 ounces smoked bacon, chopped
- 1 pound carrots, cut into chunks
- 3 garlic cloves, chopped
- 2 yellow onions, chopped
- 3 cups beef stock
- 2 cups dry red wine
- 2 tablespoons
- tomato paste
- 4 tablespoons butter
- 1 teaspoon thyme, chopped
- 1 pound pearl onions
- 3 tablespoons white flour
- 3 bay leaves
- 1 pound button mushrooms, sliced
- Salt and black pepper to taste
- Some chopped parsley for serving

## Directions:

Heat a Dutch oven with 2 tablespoons oil over medium heat, add bacon, stir, brown for 3 minutes and transfer to a plate. Return Dutch oven to medium heat, add beef, salt and pepper, stir, brown meat for 4 minutes, transfer to the same plate as the bacon and leave aside. Heat up the pot with the rest of the oil over medium-high heat, add garlic, onions, carrots, salt and pepper to taste, stir and cook for 5 minutes. Return beef and bacon to pot, also add the rest of the ingredients except the butter, flour, parsley and mushrooms, stir, bring to a boil, cover pot, place in the oven at 350 degrees and cook the stew for 2 hours. In a bowl, mix half of the butter with the flour, stir well and leave aside. Heat a pan with the rest of the butter over medium heat, add mushrooms, stir and cook them for 3 minutes. Take stew out of the oven, add flour and butter mix, mushrooms and parsley, heat over medium heat, reduce to a simmer, cover and cook for 30 minutes. Discard bay leaves, transfer to bowls and serve.

**Nutrition:** calories 253, fat 4, fiber 2, carbs 6, protein 12

# Steak and Tomato Salad

*Prep Time:* 10 minutes | *Cook Time:* 20 minutes | *Servings:* 4

## Ingredients:

- 1 pound beef sirloin steaks
- A pinch of salt and black pepper
- 4 cups romaine lettuce, torn
- 1 cucumber, sliced
- ½ cup red onion, sliced
- 1 cup cherry tomatoes, halved
- ¼ cup olive oil
- 1 tablespoon oregano
- 2 garlic cloves, minced
- ½ cup feta cheese, crumbled

## Directions:

Place the steaks in a preheated broiler and cook over medium heat for 10 minutes on each side. Cool the meat then cut into thin strips and place in a salad bowl. Add the rest of the ingredients, toss and serve.

**Nutrition:** calories 277, fat 14, fiber 3, carbs 8, protein 14

# Beef and Mushroom Stew

*Prep Time:* 20 minutes | *Cook Time:* 7 hours | *Servings:* 4

## Ingredients:

- 2 pounds beef, cubed
- Salt and black pepper to taste
- 2 cups beef stock
- 2 tablespoons olive oil
- 2 bay leaves
- ¼ cup white flour
- 1 yellow onion, chopped
- 2 tablespoons thyme, chopped
- 4 garlic cloves, minced
- 16 ounces mushrooms, chopped
- 3 carrots, chopped
- 3 celery stalks, chopped
- 28 ounces canned tomatoes, crushed
- ½ cup parsley, chopped
- ½ pound orzo

## Directions:

Heat a pan with the oil over medium high heat, add the meat mixed with flour, salt and pepper, brown it for a few minutes and transfer to slow cooker. Add stock, thyme and the rest of the ingredients except the orzo and parsley, cover and cook on Low for 7 hours. When the stew is almost done, put water in a saucepan, add salt, bring to a boil, add orzo and cook according to instructions. Divide beef stew on plates, discard bay leaves, arrange orzo on the side and sprinkle parsley all over. Serve right away.

**Nutrition:** calories 240, fat 5, fiber 3, carbs 7, protein 11

## Beef and Beets Mix

*Prep Time: 10 minutes | Cook Time: 5 minutes | Servings: 4*

### Ingredients:

- 2 apples, cored, peeled and sliced
- 3 red beetroot, peeled and sliced
- Juice of 1 lemon
- 2 sirloin steaks
- 1 tablespoon olive oil
- 1 small bunch dill weed, chopped
- 3 ounces low fat buttermilk
- 2 tablespoon olive oil
- Salt and pepper to taste

### Directions:

In a salad bowl, mix beetroot with apple pieces and some of the lemon juice, toss to coat and leave aside for now. Heat your kitchen grill pan over medium high heat, place the steaks on grill after you seasoned them with salt, pepper and rubbed with half of the oil and cook for 2-3 minutes on each side. Slice steak and put in a bowl. Add the beets and apples but also the rest of the ingredients, toss and serve.

**Nutrition:** calories 210, fat 3, fiber 3, carbs 5, protein 8

## Tarragon Beef and Tomatoes

*Prep Time: 10 minutes | Cook Time: 5 minutes | Servings: 4*

### Ingredients:

- 4 medium sirloin steaks
- Salt and black pepper to taste
- 1 tablespoon olive oil
- 1 tablespoon butter
- 8 cherry tomatoes, halved
- A small handful tarragon, chopped

### Directions:

Heat a pan with the oil and the butter over medium high heat, add steaks, season with salt and pepper, cook them for 1 minute on each side, transfer them to heated grill at 400 degrees F and cook them for 4 more minutes. Divide steaks on plates, add the tomatoes on the side and serve with the tarragon sprinkled on top

**Nutrition:** calories 213, fat 4, fiber 2, carbs 6, protein 9

## Ginger Meatballs

*Prep Time: 10 minutes | Cook Time: 20 minutes | Servings: 4*

### Ingredients:

*For the meatballs:*

- 1 pound beef, ground
- 1/3 cup cilantro, chopped
- 1 cup red onion, chopped
- 4 garlic cloves, minced
- 1 tablespoon ginger, grated
- ½ tablespoon honey
- 1 red chili pepper, chopped
- 2 tablespoons olive oil

### Directions:

In a bowl, combine the meat with onion and the other ingredients except the oil, stir and shape medium meatballs out of this mix. Heat a pan with the oil over medium high heat, shape meatballs, add them to the pan, and cook for 5 minutes on each side. Drain using paper towels, arrange them on a platter and serve.

**Nutrition:** calories 200, fat 7, fiber 4, carbs 5, protein 9

## Beef and Peppers Mix

*Prep Time: 10 minutes | Cook Time: 20 minutes | Servings: 4*

### Ingredients:

- 2 yellow bell peppers, cut into strips
- 2 zucchinis, cut into rounds
- 8 white mushrooms, sliced
- 2 tomatoes, cubed
- 1 yellow onion, chopped
- 2 garlic cloves, minced
- 1 pound beef sirloin, cut into strips
- 2 tablespoons olive oil
- A pinch of salt and black pepper

### Directions:

Heat a pan with half the oil over medium-high heat, add the meat, cook for 5 minutes and transfer to a plate. Heat the pan with the rest of the oil over medium heat, add the onion, stir and sauté for 2 minutes. Add the rest of the ingredients, also return the meat to the pan, toss and cook everything for 10 minutes more. Divide the mix between plates and serve.

**Nutrition:** calories 273, fat 4, fiber 5, carbs 7, protein 12

# Flavored Beef Mix

*Prep Time: 40 minutes | Cook Time: 15 minutes | Servings: 4*

### Ingredients:

- 11 ounces steak fillets, sliced
- 4 garlic cloves, minced
- 2 tablespoons olive oil
- 1 red bell pepper, cut into strips
- Black pepper to taste
- 1 tablespoon sugar
- 2 teaspoons corn flour
- ½ cup beef stock
- 4 green onions, sliced

### Directions:

In a bowl, mix beef with oil, garlic, black pepper and bell pepper, toss and keep in the fridge for 30 minutes. Heat a pan over medium high heat, add the beef mixture, stir and cook for 1-2 minutes. Add the rest of the ingredients except the green onions, stir and cook for 10 minutes more. Add green onions, cook for 1-2 minutes, take off heat, transfer to plates and serve right away!

**Nutrition:** calories 243, fat 3, fiber 3, carbs 6, protein 9

# Beef with Beans and Tomato Sauce

*Prep Time: 10 minutes | Cook Time: 30 minutes | Servings: 6*

### Ingredients:

- 1 tablespoon olive oil
- 1 tablespoon butter, melted
- 1 yellow onion, chopped
- 3 garlic cloves, minced
- 1 pound beef, ground
- 1 pound green beans, trimmed
- 28 ounces tomato sauce
- 2 tablespoons red wine
- A pinch of salt and black pepper

### Directions:

Heat a pan with the oil and butter over medium heat, add the onions and saute for 5 minutes. Add the garlic and beef, stir and cook for 5 minutes. Add the rest of the ingredients except the green beans, stir and cook for 10 minutes. Add green beans and cook for a further 10 minutes. Divide everything into bowls and serve.

**Nutrition:** calories 234, fat 11, fiber 6, carbs 15, protein 9

# Beef Soup

*Prep Time: 20 minutes | Cook Time: 8 hours | Servings: 8*

### Ingredients:

- 2 tablespoons olive oil
- 2/3 cup barley soaked overnight, drained and rinsed
- 1 pound beef, cubed
- 2 yellow onions, chopped
- 4 ounces shitake mushrooms, quartered
- 5 ounces Portobello mushrooms, quartered
- 4 garlic cloves, minced
- 3 carrots, chopped
- 2 bay leaves
- 4 celery stalks, chopped
- 6 tablespoons dill, chopped
- 2 tablespoons tomato paste
- 90 ounces beef broth
- A pinch of salt and black pepper

### Directions:

Heat a pan with the oil over medium high heat, add beef, cook for 6 minutes and transfer to the slow cooker. Heat the same pan over medium heat, add onions, stir and cook for 10 minutes. Add mushrooms, stir and cook for 5 more minutes. Add garlic, cook for 5 minutes and transfer everything to the slow cooker. Add the rest of the ingredients, stir, cover and cook on Low for 8 hours. Discard bay leaves, ladle soup into bowls and serve.

**Nutrition:** calories 293, fat 4, fiber 2, carbs 7, protein 10

# Cabbage and Meat Soup

*Prep Time: 10 minutes | Cook Time: 9 hours | Servings: 12*

## Ingredients:

*For the stock:*

- 4 pounds beef shank, bone-in
- 3 carrots, cut into thirds
- 2 cups water
- 3 yellow onions
- 1 bay leaf
- 4 celery stalks
- 16 peppercorns

*For the soup:*

- 2 tablespoons olive oil
- 1 yellow onion, chopped
- 2 garlic cloves, minced
- 1 tablespoon sweet paprika
- 1 head cabbage, shredded
- 6 ounces canned diced tomatoes, juice reserved
- Juice of 1 lemon
- Salt and black pepper to taste
- ¼ cup white sugar
- ¼ cup dill weed, chopped

## Directions:

Put beef shanks and water in a large pot, mix with carrot, onions, celery, bay leaf and peppercorns, bring to a boil, cook over medium heat for 4 hours, discard veggies, strain the stock and cool it down. Heat a pan with the oil over medium heat, add garlic and 1 chopped onion, stir and cook for a few minutes. Transfer this to your slow cooker, add cabbage, the stock and the other ingredients except the lemon juice, cover pot and cook on LOW for 5 hours. Uncover pot, add lemon juice, stir well, ladle into bowls and serve.

**Nutrition:** calories 239, fat 6, fiber 8, carbs 9, protein 12

# Lamb with Prunes and Rice

*Prep Time: 1 hour | Cook Time: 1 hour and 30 minutes | Servings: 6*

## Ingredients:

- 2 ounces raisins
- 4 ounces prunes, pitted
- 1 tablespoon lemon juice
- 1 yellow onion, chopped
- 1 pound lamb, boneless and cubed
- 1 ounce butter
- 3 ounces lamb meat, ground
- 2 garlic cloves, minced
- Salt and black pepper to taste
- 2 ½ cups veggie stock
- 2 cups white rice
- A handful parsley, chopped
- A pinch of saffron

## Directions:

In a bowl, mix raisins with prunes and lemon juice, add water to cover, leave everything aside for 1 hour, drain and chop prunes. Heat up a pan with the butter over medium high heat, add onion, stir and cook for 5 minutes. Add the rest of the ingredients except the rice and saffron, stir, bring to a boil, cover and cook for 1 hour over medium heat. Add rice, stir and cook for 15 minutes more. Add prunes and raisins, stir, divide between plates and serve.

**Nutrition:** calories 210, fat 3, fiber 6, carbs 8, protein 10

# Garlic Lamb Chops

*Prep Time: 4 hours and 5 minutes | Cook Time: 8 minutes |*
*Servings: 4*

## Ingredients:

- 1 teaspoon garlic paste
- 1 teaspoon allspice
- ½ teaspoon green cardamom, ground
- ½ teaspoon hot paprika
- ½ teaspoon nutmeg, ground
- 1 tablespoon mint, chopped
- A drizzle of olive oil
- 2 racks of lamb
- Juice of 1 lemon
- 1 red onion, sliced
- A pinch of salt and black pepper

## Directions:

In a bowl, mix the racks of lamb with garlic paste and the rest of the ingredients, toss and marinate for 4 hours. Place the lamb on a preheated grill and cook over medium-high heat for 4 minutes on each side. Divide the lamb between plates and serve.

**Nutrition:** calories 265, fat 13, fiber 7, carbs 8, protein 11

# Herbed Lamb Roast

*Prep Time: 1 day | Cook Time: 2 hours and 15 minutes |*
*Servings: 8*

## Ingredients:

- 5 pounds leg of lamb
- 2 cups low fat buttermilk
- 2 tablespoons mustard
- ½ cup butter
- 2 tablespoons basil and rosemary, chopped
- 2 tablespoons tomato paste
- 2 garlic cloves, minced
- Salt and black pepper to taste
- 1 cup white wine
- 1 tablespoon cornstarch mixed with 1 tablespoon water
- ½ cup sour cream

## Directions:

Put lamb roast in a big dish, add buttermilk, toss to coat, cover and keep in the fridge for 24 hours. Pat dry lamb and put in a baking dish. Add the rest of the ingredients except the wine, cornstarch and sour cream, toss, place in the oven at 160 degrees F and bake for 2 hours. Transfer cooking juices to a pan and heat over medium heat. Add wine and the remaining ingredients, whisk well and take off heat. Slice lamb, divide between plates, top with gravy and serve.

**Nutrition:** calories 287, fat 4, fiber 7, carbs 9, protein 12

# Mint Lamb and Potatoes Bake

*Prep Time: 10 minutes | Cook Time: 1 hour and 30 minutes |*
*Servings: 4*

## Ingredients:

- 1 red bell pepper, sliced
- 4 medium potatoes, chopped
- 1 green bell pepper, sliced
- 1 eggplant, chopped
- 2 tablespoons olive oil
- 1/3 cup mint jelly
- 1 garlic head, cut in half
- 1 and ½ tablespoon lemon juice
- 4 lamb chops
- 1 tablespoon thyme, chopped
- Salt flakes to the taste

## Directions:

Put potatoes in a roasting pan, add red, green bell pepper, the garlic and half of the oil, toss and bake at 400 degrees F for 45 minutes. In a bowl, mix lemon juice with mint jelly and thyme and whisk well. Heat a pan with the remaining oil over medium high heat, add lamb chops, cook for 2 minutes on each side and brush them on both sides with half of the jelly mix. Take veggies out of oven, put lamb chops on top, and bake for 15 minutes. Brush with the rest of the jelly mix, bake for 10 minutes more, divide everything between plates and serve.

**Nutrition:** calories 310, fat 4, fiber 6, carbs 7, protein 10

# Lamb, Cabbage and Cauliflower Soup

*Prep Time:* 20 minutes | *Cook Time:* 1 hour and 10 minutes | *Servings:* 8

## Ingredients:

- 3 pounds lamb
- 2 tablespoons olive oil
- 1 teaspoon garlic, minced
- 1 yellow onion, chopped
- 1/3 cup brown rice
- ½ teaspoon thyme, dried
- 3 cups water
- ½ teaspoon oregano, dried
- 3 carrots, chopped
- ½ cabbage head, chopped
- 1 cup cauliflower florets
- 4 potatoes, chopped
- Salt and pepper to taste

## Directions:

Heat a large saucepan with the oil over medium high heat, add garlic, stir and sauté for 2 minutes. Add lamb and brown for a few minutes more. Add the rest of the ingredients, toss, and simmer everything over medium heat for 1 hour stirring from time to time. Remove meat from saucepan, discard bones, chop it and return to pan again. Cook for 5 more minutes, ladle into soup bowls and serve right away!

**Nutrition:** calories 273, fat 3, fiber 6, carbs 9, protein 12

# Meat and Onions Stew

*Prep Time:* 10 minutes | *Cook Time:* 8 hours | *Servings:* 6

## Ingredients:

- 1 pound pork, cubed
- 1 pound lamb meat, cubed
- 1 tablespoon olive oil
- Salt to taste
- 2 yellow onions,
- chopped
- 2 teaspoon peppercorns
- A pinch of whole allspice
- 3 cups water
- 2 bay leaves

## Directions:

Heat a pan over medium high heat, add the meat, brown it on all sides and transfer to your slow cooker. Add the rest of the ingredients, stir, cover slow cooker and cook on low for 8 hours. Divide plates and serve right away.

**Nutrition:** calories 300, fat 3, fiber 2, carbs 6, protein 10

# Herbed Leg of Lamb

*Prep Time:* 10 minutes | *Cook Time:* 20 minutes | *Servings:* 6

## Ingredients:

- 1 cup parsley leaves
- ½ cup mint leaves
- 1 red onion, chopped
- 3 garlic cloves, minced
- 1 teaspoon sumac spice
- 1 teaspoon coriander, ground
- 1 and ½ teaspoons
- allspice, ground
- ½ teaspoon cardamom, ground
- Juice of 1 lemon
- ¼ cup olive oil
- 1 leg of lamb, boneless
- A pinch of salt and black pepper

## Directions:

In a blender, mix the parsley, mint and the other ingredients except the meat and pulse well. In a bowl, mix the leg of lamb with the herbed marinade, toss and leave aside for 10 minutes. Place the leg of lamb on a preheated grill and cook over medium-high heat for 10 minutes on each side. Serve with a side salad.

**Nutrition:** calories 231, fat 13, fiber 5, carbs 12, protein 11

# Lemon Lamb and Potatoes Mix

*Prep Time:* 1 hour | *Cook Time:* 1 hour and 10 minutes | *Servings:* 6

- **Ingredients:** 1-4 pounds leg of lamb, trimmed
- 8 gold potatoes, cut into wedges
- 4 garlic cloves, minced
- A drizzle of olive oil
- A pinch of salt and black pepper
- 1 yellow onion, chopped
- 1 teaspoon sweet paprika
- 2 tablespoons oregano, dried
- 2 tablespoons mint flakes
- ½ tablespoon nutmeg, ground
- Juice of 2 lemons
- 1 teaspoon garlic powder

## Directions:

In a bowl, mix the leg of lamb with the garlic, oil and the other ingredients except the potatoes, toss and keep in the fridge for 1 hour. Transfer the lamb to a roasting pan, add the potatoes, toss and bake at 375 degrees F for 1 hour and 10 minutes. Divide everything between plates and serve.

**Nutrition:** calories 232, fat 13, fiber 4, carbs 15, protein 9

# Lamb and Raisins

*Prep Time: 20 minutes | Cook Time: 6 hours | Servings: 4*

**Ingredients:**

- 4 and ½ pounds shoulder lamb steak, diced
- 2 tomatoes, chopped
- 1 garlic clove, minced
- 1 tablespoon cinnamon powder
- 2 teaspoons sugar
- Salt and white pepper to taste
- ½ cup water
- ¾ cup raisins
- 1 bunch coriander, chopped

**Directions:**

Put lamb in your slow cooker. Add the rest of the ingredients, toss, cover and cook on Low for 6 hours. Divide between plates and serve hot!

**Nutrition:** calories 283, fat 4, fiber 5, carbs 8, protein 10

# Sherry Lamb Mix

*Prep Time: 15 minutes | Cook Time: 6 hours | Servings: 4*

**Ingredients:**

- 4 lamb shanks
- 1 yellow onion, chopped
- 1 tablespoon olive oil
- 4 teaspoons coriander seeds, crushed
- 2 tablespoons white
- flour
- 4 bay leaves
- 2 teaspoons honey
- 5 ounces dry sherry
- 2 and ½ cups chicken stock
- Salt and pepper to taste

**Directions:**

Heat a pan with the oil over medium high heat, add lamb shanks, brown them on all sides and transfer to slow cooker. Heat the same pan over medium high heat, add onion, stir and cook for 5 minutes. Add coriander, and the other ingredients, stir and bring to a boil. Pour this over lamb, cover and cook on High for 6 hours turning meat once. Divide everything between plates and serve.

**Nutrition:** calories 283, fat 4, fiber 2, carbs 7, protein 10

# Garlic Lamb Roast

*Prep Time: 15 minutes | Cook Time: 6 hours | Servings: 6*

**Ingredients:**

- 4 pounds lamb roast
- 1 spring rosemary
- 3 garlic cloves, minced
- 6 potatoes, halved
- ½ cup lamb stock
- 4 bay leaves
- Salt and black pepper to taste

**Directions:**

Put potatoes in a slow cooker. Add and the rest of the ingredients, toss, cook on High for 6 hours. Divide the mix between plates and serve with cooking juices on top.

**Nutrition:** calories 273, fat 4, fiber 2, carbs 5, protein 12

# Herbed Roast and Baby Potatoes

*Prep Time: 15 minutes | Cook Time: 8 hours and 10 minutes | Servings: 6*

**Ingredients:**

- 4 pounds lamb leg
- 2 tablespoons olive oil
- 2 sprigs rosemary, chopped
- 2 tablespoons parsley, chopped
- 2 tablespoons oregano, chopped
- 1 tablespoon lemon rind, grated
- 3 garlic cloves, minced
- 2 tablespoons lemon juice
- 2 pounds baby potatoes
- 1 cup beef stock

**Directions:**

Make small cuts all over the lamb, insert rosemary, season with salt and pepper and leave aside. In a bowl mix 1 tablespoon oil with oregano, parsley, garlic, lemon juice and rind, whisk and rub the lamb with this mix. Heat a pan with remaining oil over medium high heat, add potatoes, stir, cook for 3 minutes and transfer to a slow cooker. Add the meat to the slow cooker, also add the stock, cover and cook on High for 2 hours and on Low for 6 hours. Divide everything between plates and serve.

**Nutrition:** calories 264, fat 4, fiber 2, carbs 7, protein 12

# Lamb and Artichokes Stew

*Prep Time: 10 minutes | Cook Time: 8 hours | Servings: 8*

## Ingredients:

- 3 pounds lamb shoulder, boneless and trimmed
- 3 white onions, chopped
- 1 tablespoon olive oil
- 1 tablespoon oregano, dried
- 3 garlic cloves, minced
- 1 tablespoon lemon rind, grated
- Salt and black pepper to taste
- A pinch of allspice
- 2 tablespoons white flour
- 1 ½ cups beef stock
- 6 ounces artichoke hearts
- ¼ cup tomato paste
- ½ cup feta cheese
- 2 tablespoons parsley, chopped

## Directions:

Heat a pan with the olive oil over medium high heat, add lamb, brown for a few minutes and add to your slow cooker. Heat the pan again over medium heat, add onion, rind, garlic, salt, pepper, oregano and allspice, stir and cook for 5 minutes. Add flour, stir and cook for 1 minute. Transfer to the slow cooker, return the meat as well, also add the parsley, cover cooker and cook on Low for 7 hours and 45 minutes. Add feta, stir gently, transfer to plates and serve right away.

**Nutrition:** calories 310, fat 2, fiber 3, carbs 5, protein 9

# Meatballs and Greek Sauce

*Prep Time: 30 minutes | Cook Time: 1 hour | Servings: 42 meatballs*

## Ingredients:

*For the pomegranate sauce:*

- 2 cups Greek yogurt
- 1 cup pomegranate juice
- 2 tablespoons pomegranate seeds

*For the meatballs:*

- 2 slices whole wheat bread
- 1 yellow onion, chopped
- 1/3 cup parsley, chopped
- 1 pound ground lamb meat
- ¾ teaspoon allspice
- ½ teaspoon red pepper flakes
- Salt to taste
- 2 tablespoons olive oil
- ¼ teaspoon cinnamon powder
- 2 tablespoons canola oil

## Directions:

Put bread slices in a bowl, add water to cover, soak for a few minutes, squeeze them and leave aside for now. In a bowl, mix the meat with the bread and the other ingredients except the pomegranate seeds, canola and olive oil, stir and shape medium meatballs out of this mix. Heat a pan with the olive and canola oil over medium high heat, add meatballs and cook for 2 minutes on each side. Transfer to a lined baking pan, place in the oven at 350 degrees F, bake for 15 minutes, drain excess grease and arrange on a platter. In a bowl, mix yogurt with warm pomegranate juice, pomegranate seeds and whisk. Serve meatballs with the sauce on the side.

**Nutrition:** calories 265, fat 4, fiber 6, carbs 8, protein 12

# Lamb and Cabbage Pitas

*Prep Time:* 10 minutes | *Cook Time:* 10 minutes | *Servings:* 4

Ingredients:

- 4 lamb leg steaks
- 1 teaspoon cumin, ground
- 2 teaspoons olive oil
- 1 tablespoon sugar
- 2 carrots, grated
- 3 tablespoons wine vinegar
- 2 spring onions, chopped
- 4 ounces white cabbage, shredded
- 5 sweet peppers
- 4 pita bread
- 3 tablespoons mayonnaise
- Salt and black pepper to taste

Directions:

Rub lamb with olive oil, cumin, salt and pepper, place on preheated grill pan over medium high heat, cook for 4 minutes on each side, transfer to a plate and leave aside for now. In a bowl, mix sugar with vinegar and the rest of the ingredients except the pitas and mayonnaise. Divide this mix on each flatbread, add sliced lamb on top, drizzle mayonnaise, roll up flatbreads and serve right away.

Nutrition: calories 264, fat 4, fiber 2, carbs 5, protein 9

# Lamb with Tomatoes and Eggplants

*Prep Time:* 15 minutes | *Cook Time:* 1 hour | *Servings:* 6

Ingredients:

- 4 eggplants, cut into halves lengthwise
- 4 ounces olive oil
- 2 yellow onions, chopped
- 4 ounces lamb meat, ground
- 2 green bell peppers, chopped
- 1 pound tomatoes, chopped
- 4 tomato slices
- 2 tablespoons tomato paste
- ½ cup parsley, chopped
- 4 garlic cloves, minced
- ½ cup hot water
- Greek yogurt for serving
- Salt and pepper to taste

Directions:

Heat a pan with the olive oil over medium high heat, add eggplant halves, cook for 5 minutes, flipping once and transfer to a plate. Heat the same pan over medium high heat, add onion and peppers stir and cook for 5 minutes. Add lamb, tomato paste, salt, pepper and chopped tomatoes and stir again. Add parsley and cook for 5 more minutes. Place eggplant halves on a baking tray, open them up, divide meat filling and garlic top with a tomato slice. Pour water over them, cover tray with foil, bake in the oven at 350 degrees F for 40 minutes, divide between plates and serve with the yogurt on top.

Nutrition: calories 253, fat 3, fiber 2, carbs 5, protein 10

# Harissa Chicken

*Prep Time:* 10 minutes | *Cook Time:* 25 minutes | *Servings:* 4

## Ingredients:

- 1 and ½ pounds chicken thighs, boneless and skinless
- 2 tablespoons harissa paste
- ½ cup Greek yogurt
- Salt and black pepper to taste
- 1 tablespoon lemon juice
- 1 tablespoon mint, finely chopped

## Directions:

Put chicken thighs in a lined baking dish, add salt, pepper and the other ingredients except the mint, toss, place in the oven and cook at 365 degrees F for 25 minutes. Divide chicken on plates, sprinkle mint on top and serve.

**Nutrition:** calories 250, fat 12, fiber 0, carbs 2, protein 31

# Chicken and Olives

*Prep Time:* 10 minutes | *Cook Time:* 10 minutes | *Servings:* 4

## Ingredients:

- 2 tablespoon vegetable oil
- 4 chicken breast halves, skinless and boneless
- Salt and black pepper to taste
- 1 tablespoon shallot, chopped
- 1 tablespoon vinegar
- ½ teaspoon sugar
- ½ teaspoon mustard
- 6 tablespoons olive oil
- 2 tablespoons parsley chopped
- 2 tablespoons kalamata olives, pitted and chopped

## Directions:

Place each chicken piece between 2 parchment paper pieces, brush meat with the vegetable oil, season with salt and pepper, place on preheated grill pan, cook for 10 minutes turning once, transfer to a cutting board, cool down, slice and arrange on a platter. In a bowl, mix shallot with vinegar and the other ingredients, whisk, drizzle over the chicken and serve.

**Nutrition:** calories 400, fat 32, fiber 0, carbs 2, protein 24

# Rabbit Stew

*Prep Time:* 10 minutes | *Cook Time:* 1 hour and 30 minutes | *Servings:* 4

## Ingredients:

- 1-2 pounds rabbit, cut into 8 pieces
- 1 whole rabbit, cut into 12 pieces
- Salt and black pepper to taste
- 3 garlic cloves, minced
- 3 tablespoons olive oil
- 1 yellow onion, chopped
- 3 tomatoes, seeded, peeled and grated
- ¼ cup dry white wine
- 3 carrots, chopped
- 1 thyme spring
- 1 cup chicken stock
- 12 almonds, toasted
- 1 tablespoon parsley, chopped
- Crusty bread

## Directions:

Heat a pan with the oil over medium-high heat, add the meat, salt and pepper, cook for 10 minutes and transfer to a bowl. Heat the pan again over medium heat, add the garlic and onion, stir and cook for 5 minutes. Add tomatoes, stir, reduce heat to low and cook for 15 minutes. Return rabbit pieces to the pan, add wine, stock, thyme and carrots, stir and cook for 45 minutes over medium heat. In a mortar and pestle, mix liver with garlic, parsley, almonds and water and stir until you obtain a paste, add over the rabbit, cook for another 10 minutes, divide into bowls and serve with the bread on the side.

**Nutrition:** calories 500, fat 28, fiber 4, carbs 12, protein 56

# Smoked Lamb Chops

*Prep Time:* 10 minutes | *Cook Time:* 6 minutes | *Servings:* 2

**Ingredients:**

- 1 red onion, thinly sliced
- Salt and black pepper to taste
- 2 teaspoons brown sugar
- 6 lamb chops
- 1 teaspoon smoked paprika
- 6 mint leaves, chopped
- 1 tablespoons olive oil

**Directions:**

In a bowl, mix the lamb chops with the onion and the other ingredients, toss and leave aside for 10 minutes. Heat your kitchen grill pan over medium high heat, place lamb chops, grill them for 3 minutes on each side and transfer to a platter. Serve with a side salad.

**Nutrition:** calories 460, fat 31, fiber 1, carbs 18, protein 34

# Spicy Beef

*Prep Time:* 10 minutes | *Cook Time:* 15 minutes | *Servings:* 4

**Ingredients:**

- 2 teaspoons chili powder
- 2 and ½ tablespoons olive oil
- Salt and black pepper to taste
- 1 ½ teaspoons onion powder
- 1 ½ teaspoons garlic powder
- 1 tablespoon smoked paprika
- 1 red bell pepper, cut in halves
- 2 tomatoes, cut in halved
- 1 small red onion, cut into 6 wedges
- 4 beef steaks
- 2 teaspoons sherry vinegar
- 1 tablespoon oregano, chopped
- Hot sauce to taste
- A pinch of cumin, ground
- 1/3 cup black olives, pitted and sliced

**Directions:**

In a bowl, mix chili powder with paprika, salt, pepper, garlic and onion powder. In another bowl, mix bell pepper with onion, tomatoes, 1 tablespoon spice mixture and ½ tablespoon oil then toss to coat. Mix steaks with remaining spice mix and toss to coat. Heat your kitchen grill pan over medium high heat, add pepper and onion, cook for 4 minutes on each side and transfer to a plate. Add tomatoes, grill for 2 minutes and also transfer to the plate with the rest of the veggies. Place steaks on the grill, cook for 4 minutes on each side and transfer to a platter. In a blender, mix grilled veggies with cumin, remaining oil and the remaining ingredients pulse well and drizzle over the steaks. Sprinkle the olives on top and serve.

**Nutrition:** calories 450, fat 23, fiber 2, carbs 8, protein 43

# Kebabs with Sauce

*Prep Time: 1 hour | Cook Time: 13 minutes | Servings: 6*

## Ingredients:

- 1 yellow onion, chopped
- 1 pound ground pork
- 3 tablespoons parsley, chopped
- 1 tablespoon lemon juice
- 1 garlic clove,

*For the sauce:*

- 2 tablespoons olive oil
- ¼ cup tahini sauce
- ¼ cup water
- 1 tablespoon lemon

- minced
- 1 teaspoon oregano, dried
- 1 teaspoon mint, dried
- Salt and black pepper to taste
- Vegetable oil

  juice
- 1 garlic clove, minced
- Salt and cayenne pepper to taste

## Directions:

In a bowl, mix ground pork with onion, and the other ingredients except the ones for the sauce stir well, divide into 6 portions, shape the kebabs by squeezing each portion on a skewer, cover and keep them in the fridge for 1 hour. Heat your kitchen grill pan over medium high heat, place kebabs on it, cook them for 13 minutes, turning from time to time and transfer to plates. In a food processor, mix tahini with olive oil and the other ingredients for the sauce and pulse well. Serve your kebabs with this sauce all over.

**Nutrition:** calories 250, fat 23, fiber 1, carbs 4, protein 14

# Lamb with Artichokes

*Prep Time: 4 hours | Cook Time: 35 minutes | Servings: 8*

## Ingredients:

- 6 tablespoons olive oil
- 2 racks of lamb, boneless and trimmed
- Zest from 1 lemon
- 10 garlic cloves, crushed
- Juice of 1 lemon
- 2 rosemary sprigs
- ¼ teaspoon red pepper flakes, crushed
- 10 ounces shiitake mushrooms, sliced
- 2 tablespoons olive

- oil
- 1 tablespoon thyme, chopped
- 6 ounces jarred artichokes, drained
- 1 cup fava beans
- ½ cup chicken stock
- 6 tablespoons vermouth
- 2 teaspoons lemon zest, grated
- 1 tablespoon butter
- 2 cups Greek yogurts for serving
- 1 jar hot peppers in oil

## Directions:

Put the lamb in a heatproof dish, add the oil, garlic, lemon juice, lemon zest, rosemary, pepper flakes, salt and pepper, toss and keep in the fridge for 4 hours. Discard lemon zest, rosemary and garlic, transfer meat to a pan heated over medium/high, sear for 2 minutes on each side, return to baking dish, place in the oven at 400 degrees F, bake for 20 minutes, transfer to a cutting board, cool down, cut into separated chops and leave aside. Heat a pan with butter over medium high heat, add artichokes, mushrooms, salt and pepper, stir and cook for 2 minutes. Add the rest of the ingredients except the yogurt and hot peppers, stir and cook for 3 minutes more. Divide yogurt on serving plates and spread. Top yogurt with jarred peppers, add ¼ cup veggie mix on each plate on top of yogurt and peppers, place 2 lamb chops on each plate and serve.

**Nutrition:** calories 500, fat 23, fiber 3, carbs 23, protein 41

# Grilled Lamb

*Prep Time: 1 hour | Cook Time: 15 minutes | Servings: 8*

## Ingredients:

- 4 and ½ pounds butterflied lamb leg
- 1 cup black olives, pitted
- ½ cup olive oil
- Salt and black pepper to taste
- ½ cup mixed parsley
- with thyme and rosemary, finely chopped
- Salt and black pepper to taste
- 4 garlic cloves, minced
- Juice of ½ lemon

## Directions:

Mash olives with a fork until you obtain a paste, add 1 tablespoon mixed herbs, half of the olive oil, some salt and pepper and stir well. In a bowl, mix remaining oil with the rest of the herb mix and garlic, stir and rub the lamb with this. Place lamb on heated grill pan over medium high heat, add salt and pepper to taste, cook for 18 minutes flipping once, cool down, slice, arrange on a platter, drizzle the lemon juice all over and serve with the olives puree.

**Nutrition:** calories 450, fat 23, fiber 1, carbs 3, protein 44

# Pork and Mayo Sandwiches

*Prep Time: 10 minutes | Cook Time: 20 minutes | Servings: 4*

## Ingredients:

- 1 pork tenderloin, cut in half crosswise
- Salt and black pepper to taste
- 3 tablespoons fennel seeds, crushed
- ¼ teaspoon allspice
- 1 tablespoon olive oil
- 4 sandwich rolls, toasted and cut in half
- 1/3 cup mayonnaise
- ½ cup cucumber, sliced
- ½ cup dill weed, chopped

## Directions:

In a bowl, mix half of the fennel seeds with half of the allspice, salt, pepper and the oil, whisk well and rub the pork with this. Place pork on preheated grill pan over medium high heat, cook for 20 minutes, turning a few times, transfer to a cutting board, slice and leave aside for now. In a bowl, mix mayo with remaining fennel seeds, allspice, salt and pepper. Spread this on sandwich rolls, divide the pork, cucumber slices and dill and serve.

**Nutrition:** calories 430, fat 21, fiber 2, carbs 23, protein 32

# Spiced Meatballs

*Prep Time: 10 minutes | Cook Time: 20 minutes | Servings: 4*

## Ingredients:

- 1 pound lamb shoulder, ground
- 1 tablespoon pine nuts
- 1 tablespoon ras el hanout
- 2 garlic cloves,
- minced
- Salt and black pepper to taste
- 2 cups Greek yogurt
- ½ cup olive oil
- ¼ cup parsley, finely chopped

## Directions:

Heat a pan over medium heat, add pine nuts, toast for 4 minutes, transfer to a plate, cool them down and chop them. In a bowl, mix the meat with all the ingredients except the yogurt, oil and parsley, stir well, shape 8 large meatballs, arrange them on a lined baking sheet and bake at 425 degrees F for 16 minutes. Meanwhile, in a bowl, mix yogurt with salt, pepper, oil and parsley and whisk well. Serve your meatballs with yogurt sauce.

**Nutrition:** calories 96, fat 6, fiber 1, carbs 5, protein 6

# Turkey and Couscous

*Prep Time:* 10 minutes | *Cook Time:* 25 minutes | *Servings:* 4

## Ingredients:

- 1 ½ cups couscous
- ½ cup vegetable oil
- 1 cup breadcrumbs
- 2 cups chicken stock
- 1 tablespoons sesame seeds
- Salt and black pepper to taste
- A pinch of paprika
- A pinch of cayenne pepper
- 2 eggs
- 4 turkey breast cutlets
- ¼ cup parsley, chopped
- 4 ounces feta cheese, crumbled
- ¼ cup red onion, chopped
- ½ cup white flour
- 4 lemon wedges

## Directions:

Heat a pan with 2 tablespoon oil over medium high heat, add couscous, stir, cook for 7 minutes, add the stock, bring to a boil, cook for 10 more minutes and then cool down for a few minutes. In a bowl, mix breadcrumbs with sesame seeds, cayenne, paprika, salt and pepper. Whisk eggs well in another bowl and put the flour in a third one. Dredge turkey in flour, eggs and breadcrumbs. Heat a pan with remaining oil over medium high heat, add cutlets, cook for 6 minutes flipping once and transfer them to paper towels in order to drain excess grease. Mix couscous with parsley and the remaining ingredients except the lemon, stir, divide between plates, also divide the turkey and serve with lemon wedges.

**Nutrition:** calories 760, fat 20, fiber 4, carbs 34, protein 40

# Chicken and Carrots Mix

*Prep Time:* 10 minutes | *Cook Time:* 6 hours and 15 minutes | *Servings:* 4

## Ingredients:

- 1 pound carrots, roughly chopped
- Zest from 1 lemon
- 30 apricots, dried
- ¼ cup white flour
- ¼ teaspoon cinnamon, ground
- A pinch of ginger, ground
- ¼ teaspoon coriander, ground
- A pinch of cardamom, ground
- Salt and black pepper to taste
- A pinch of cayenne pepper
- 8 chicken thighs, bone-in and skinless
- 2 tablespoons vegetable oil
- 2 and ¼ cups yellow onion, chopped
- 2 tablespoons tomato paste
- 1 tablespoon butter
- 1 and ½ tablespoons garlic, minced
- ¼ cup lemon juice
- 1 cup apricot juice
- ½ cup chicken stock
- ¼ cup cilantro, chopped
- ¼ cup pine nuts, toasted

## Directions:

In a bowl, mix the chicken with flour with salt, pepper, cayenne pepper, cinnamon, coriander, ginger and cardamom and toss. Heat a pan with the oil and butter over medium-high heat, add chicken pieces, brown for 11 minutes and transfer to the slow cooker. Add the rest of the ingredients except the pine nuts and cilantro, toss, cover and cook for 6 hours on High. Cook everything for 6 hours on High, transfer to plates, garnish with nuts and cilantro on top.

**Nutrition:** calories 340, fat 3, fiber 4, carbs 12, protein 20

# Lamb Meatloaf

**Prep Time:** *10 minutes* | **Cook Time:** *1 hour and 20 minutes* | *Servings: 8*

## Ingredients:

- 1 yellow onion, chopped
- 2 tablespoons olive oil
- 2 garlic cloves, minced
- ¾ cup red wine
- 4 ounces white bread, chopped
- 2 pounds lamb, ground
- 1 cup milk
- ¼ cup feta cheese, crumbled
- 2 eggs
- 1/3 cup kalamata olives, pitted and chopped
- 4 tablespoons oregano, chopped
- Salt and black pepper to taste
- 2 tablespoons honey
- 1 tablespoon Worcestershire sauce
- 2 teaspoons lemon zest, grated

## Directions:

Heat a pan with the oil over medium heat, add garlic and onion, stir and cook for 8 minutes. Add wine, stir, simmer for 5 minutes and transfer everything to a bowl. Put bread pieces in a bowl, add milk, leave aside for 10 minutes, squeeze bread a bit, chop and add it to onions mix. Add lamb, eggs, onions mix and the other ingredients except the honey, stir and shape your meatloaf. Transfer meatloaf mix to a baking dish, spread honey all over, place in the oven at 375 degrees F and bake for 50 minutes. Take meatloaf out of the oven, leave aside for 5 minutes, slice and arrange on a platter.

**Nutrition:** calories 350, fat 23. fiber 1, carbs 17, protein 24

# Minty Beef Short Ribs

**Prep Time:** *30 minutes* | **Cook Time:** *3 hours and 30 minutes* | *Servings: 6*

## Ingredients:

*For the ribs:*
- 6 beef short ribs
- 1 tablespoon thyme, chopped
- Salt and black pepper to taste
- 3 tablespoons olive oil
- 1 carrot, chopped
- 1 yellow onion, chopped
- 1 celery stalk, chopped
- 1 and ½ cups ruby port
- 2 bay leaves
- 2 and ½ cups red wine
- 2 tablespoons

- balsamic vinegar
- 6 cups beef stock
- 4 parsley sprigs
- 1 cup parsley, chopped
- 1 teaspoons marjoram, chopped
- ¼ cup mint, chopped
- 1 garlic clove, minced
- 1 tablespoons capers, drained
- 1 anchovy
- ¾ cup olive oil
- Salt and black pepper to taste
- ½ cup feta cheese, crumbled

## Directions:

In a bowl, mix thyme with salt and pepper, add short ribs, toss to coat and leave aside for 30 minutes. Heat a large saucepan with 3 tablespoons oil over high heat, add short ribs, sear for 3 minutes on each side and transfer to a bowl. Heat the pan again over medium heat, add celery, onion, carrot and bay leaves, stir and cook for 8 minutes. Add port and the rest of the ingredients except the mint, garlic, capers, anchovy, ¾ cup oil and cheese, toss, introduce everything in the oven and cook at 325 degrees F for 3 hours and 30 minutes. In a food processor, mix 1 cup parsley with all the remaining ingredients and pulse. Divide short ribs into bowls, toss with the salsa and serve.

**Nutrition:** calories 450, fat 45, fiber 2, carbs 18, protein 43

## Oregano Spareribs

*Prep Time: 3 hours and 10 minutes | Cook Time: 1 hour | Servings: 4*

### Ingredients:

- 1 rack of baby back pork ribs, trimmed
- 2 garlic cloves, minced
- 1 teaspoon Spanish paprika
- 3 tablespoons red
- wine vinegar
- ¼ cup olive oil
- 1 tablespoon oregano, dried
- Salt and black pepper to the taste

### Directions:

In a bowl, mix the pork ribs with the garlic and the other ingredients, toss and keep in the fridge for 3 hours. Place the ribs on your preheated BBQ and cook over medium heat for 30 minutes on each side. Serve the ribs with a side salad.

**Nutrition:** calories 450, fat 34, fiber 1, carbs 2, protein 35

## Short Ribs and Figs Mix

*Prep Time: 10 minutes | Cook Time: 3 hours | Servings: 6*

### Ingredients:

- 3 tablespoons vegetable oil
- 12 beef short ribs
- Salt and black pepper to taste
- 1 cup onions, chopped
- 1 cup carrots, chopped
- 1 cup figs, dried and chopped
- 1 tablespoon ginger, grated
- 3-star anise
- 1 tablespoon garlic, minced
- 2 cinnamon sticks
- 1 cup canned tomatoes, crushed
- 1 cup red wine
- 1 cup chicken stock
- ¼ cup soy sauce
- 2 tablespoons mint, chopped
- 2 tablespoons parsley, chopped

### Directions:

Heat a saucepan with 2 tablespoons oil over medium high heat, add short ribs, salt and pepper, cook for 5 minutes on each side and transfer to a bowl. Add remaining oil to your saucepan, heat over medium high heat, add onions, carrots, figs, garlic, ginger, cinnamon, star anise, salt and pepper and cook for 8 minutes. Add the wine, toss and cook for 2 more minutes. Return ribs to the pan, add tomatoes and the remaining ingredients, stir, bring to a simmer, cover, place in the oven at 325 degrees F and cook for 2 hours and 50 minutes, tossing the mix every 40 minutes. Divide into plates and serve.

**Nutrition:** calories 300, fat 23, fiber 4, carbs 23, protein 35

## Chicken and Pomegranate Mix

*Prep Time: 10 minutes | Cook Time: 1 hour | Servings: 4*

### Ingredients:

- 8 chicken pieces, trimmed
- Salt and black pepper to taste
- Zest and juice from 1 orange
- ¼ teaspoon cinnamon powder
- 1 and ½ teaspoons thyme, dried
- 1 cup pomegranate
- juice
- 6 teaspoons olive oil
- 2 sweet potatoes, cubed
- ¼ cup chicken stock
- 2 parsnips, chopped
- 1 red onion, cut into medium wedges
- 1 cup walnuts, chopped

### Directions:

Heat a pan with the pomegranate juice, stock, the orange juice, thyme, orange zest, cinnamon, salt and pepper, bring to a simmer, cook over medium heat for 15 minutes and take off the heat. Arrange the chicken pieces in a roasting pan, add the rest of the ingredients, also add the pomegranate sauce, toss bake at 400 degrees F for 30 minutes, divide everything between plates and serve.

**Nutrition:** calories 246, fat 13, fiber 5, carbs 14, protein 11

## Simple Chorizo Mix

*Prep Time: 10 minutes | Cook Time: 13 minutes | Servings: 4*

### Ingredients:

- 1 and 1.2 cups soft chorizo, sliced
- 3 tablespoons olive oil
- 1/3 cup dry red wine
- White bread, cubed

### Directions:

Heat a pan with the olive oil over medium high heat, add chorizo, stir and cook for 4 minutes. Add the wine, toss and cook for 9 more minutes. Pour this into bowls and serve with cubed bread on top.

**Nutrition:** calories 340, fat 23, fiber 0, carbs 2, protein 21

# Pork Roast and Baby Carrots

*Prep Time: 10 minutes | Cook Time: 3 hours | Servings: 6*

## Ingredients:

- 2 ½ pounds pork shoulder roast, boneless
- 1 tablespoon olive oil
- Salt and black pepper to taste
- 4 shallots, chopped
- 2 cups beef stock
- 1 and ½ cups red wine
- 2 teaspoons herbs de provender
- 1 red onion, cut into wedges
- 2/3 cup black olives, pitted
- 12 baby carrots
- 1 cup cherry tomatoes
- 1 zucchini, chopped

## Directions:

Heat a large saucepan with the oil over medium high heat; add the pork shoulder, season with salt and pepper, brown for 10 minutes and transfer to a plate. Add shallots and wine to the pan, stir and sauté for 8 minutes. Add the herbs, stock and return the pork roast, cover, reduce heat to medium-low and cook for 2 hours and 30 minutes, turning the pork from time to time. Take roast out of the pan, transfer to a platter, cover and keep warm. Add carrots, onion, tomatoes, zucchinis and olives to the saucepan, cover and cook for 20 minutes. Bring cooking liquid to a boil, cook for 5 minutes, and take off the heat. Slice roast and divide between plates and drizzle the sauce on top.

**Nutrition:** calories 432, fat 12, fiber 2, carbs 13, protein 42

# Simple Grilled Pork Chops

*Prep Time: 30 minutes | Cook Time: 7 minutes | Servings: 4*

## Ingredients:

- 8 pork loin chops
- Salt and black pepper to taste
- 1 tablespoon olive oil
- ¼ cup red wine
- vinegar
- 1 teaspoon oregano, dried
- 1 tablespoon garlic, minced
- ¼ cup sweet paprika

## Directions:

In a bowl mix the pork chops with the rest of the ingredients rub well and leave aside for 30 minutes. Heat your kitchen grill pan over medium high heat, place pork chops on it, cook for 3 minutes on each side, transfer to a platter and leave aside for 5 minutes. Serve right away with your favorite side salad.

**Nutrition:** calories 430, fat 23, fiber 2, carbs 4, protein 45

# Fish and Seafood Recipes

## Shrimp Pasta

*Prep Time:* 10 minutes | *Cook Time:* 15 minutes | *Servings:* 4

### Ingredients:

- 3 tablespoons extra virgin olive oil
- 12 ounces linguine
- 1 tablespoon garlic, minced
- 30 large shrimp, peeled and deveined
- A pinch of red pepper flakes, crushed
- 1 cup green olives, pitted and chopped
- 3 tablespoons lemon juice
- 1 teaspoon lemon zest, grated
- ¼ cup parsley, chopped

### Directions:

Put some water in a large saucepan, add water, bring to a boil over medium high heat, add linguine, cook according to instructions, take off heat, drain and put in a bowl and reserve ½ cup cooking liquid. Heat a pan with the oil over medium high heat, add shrimp, pepper flakes, garlic, lemon juice and zest, stir and cook for 4 minutes. Add pasta and olives, reserved cooking liquid and parsley, stir, cook for 2 minutes more, take off heat, divide between plates and serve.

**Nutrition:** calories 500, fat 20, fiber 5, carbs 45, protein 34

## Mussels and Chorizo

*Prep Time:* 10 minutes | *Cook Time:* 25 minutes | *Servings:* 4

### Ingredients:

- 1 tablespoon white wine vinegar
- 1 potato, chopped
- 5 ounces chorizo, chopped
- Salt and black pepper to taste
- 2 tablespoons olive oil
- 1/3 cup parsley, finely chopped
- 1 tablespoon parsley, finely chopped
- 1 garlic clove, minced
- 1 sweet onion, chopped
- 4-pound mussels, scrubbed and debearded
- 1 cup white wine

### Directions:

Put the potato in a large saucepan, add some water to cover, vinegar and salt, bring to a boil over high heat, cook for 4 minutes, drain and transfer to a plate. Heat a saucepan with the oil over medium high heat, add potato and chorizo and cook for 12 minutes. Add 1/3 cup parsley, salt and pepper, stir and transfer to a plate. Add onion to the pan, stir and cook for 3 minutes. Add mussels, chorizo, the potato mix, the rest of the parsley and the wine, stir, cover and cook for 5 minutes. Divide into bowls and serve.

**Nutrition:** calories 345, fat 5, fiber 2, carbs 23, protein 27

# Seafood Platter

*Prep Time: 10 minutes | Cook Time: 35 minutes | Servings: 4*

**Ingredients:**

- 12 clams, scrubbed and cleaned
- 3 dried chilies, soaked in hot water for 30 minutes, drained and chopped
- 1 lobster, tail separated and cut in half lengthwise
- ¼ cup water
- ¼ cup flour
- 3 tablespoons olive oil
- 1 and ½ pounds monkfish, skinless, boneless and cut in thin fillets
- Salt and black
- pepper to taste
- 35 shrimp, unpeeled
- 1 onion, chopped
- 4 garlic cloves, minced
- 4 tomatoes, grated
- 1 baguette slice, toasted
- 30 hazelnuts, skinned
- 2 tablespoons parsley, chopped
- 1 cup fish stock
- ¼ teaspoon smoked paprika
- Lemon wedges for serving
- Crusty bread slices for serving

**Directions:**

Put the water in a large saucepan, bring to a boil over high heat, add clams, cover, cook for 4 minutes, take off heat, discard unopened ones and keep warm for now. Heat a saucepan with the oil over medium high heat. Mix the fish with flour, salt and pepper, put it in the pan, cook for 4 minutes on each side and transfer to a plate. Add shrimp to the pan, cook for 2 minutes on each side and also transfer to a plate. Reduce heat to medium-low, add garlic, onion and tomatoes to the pan, stir, cook for 15 minutes and transfer to a blender. In a blender, mix sautéed garlic and tomatoes with baguette slice, nuts, parsley, 2 tablespoons liquid from the clams, chili peppers, pulse well and return to the pan. Add fish, lobster, shrimp, clams, stock, salt and pepper, stir, bring to a boil and cook for 2 minutes. Divided into bowls and serve with lemon wedges and crusty bread on the side.

**Nutrition:** calories 344, fat 14, fiber 4, carbs 14, protein 23

# Saffron Oysters

*Prep Time: 10 minutes | Cook Time: 0 minutes | Servings: 4*

**Ingredients:**

- 2 tablespoons shallots, finely chopped
- ½ cup sherry vinegar
- A pinch of saffron threads
- ½ cup olive oil
- 1 tablespoon olive oil
- Salt and black pepper to taste
- 1 pound chorizo sausage, cooked and chopped
- 1 pound fennel bulbs, thinly sliced lengthwise
- 24 oysters, shucked

**Directions:**

In a bowl, mix shallots with vinegar, saffron, salt, pepper and ½ cup olive oil and stir well. Spoon the vinaigrette into each oyster, also divide the fennel and sausage, place them on the platter and serve.

**Nutrition:** calories 113, fat 1, fiber 3, carbs 10, protein 7

# Shrimp with Endives

*Prep Time: 10 minutes | Cook Time: 4 minutes | Servings: 4*

**Ingredients:**

- 30 big shrimp, peeled and deveined
- Salt and black pepper to taste
- A pinch of cayenne pepper
- ¼ cup olive oil
- 2 tablespoons shallots, chopped
- 1 teaspoon lime zest
- 4 teaspoons lime juice
- ½ pound frisee or curly endive, torn into small pieces
- 1 honeydew melon, peeled, seeded and chopped
- ¼ cup mint, chopped
- 8 ounces feta cheese, crumbled
- 1 tablespoon coriander seeds

**Directions:**

Heat a pan with 2 tablespoons oil over medium high heat add shrimp, lime zest, 1 teaspoon lime juice, shallots salt and pepper, stir cook for 2 minutes and take off the heat. In a bowl, mix the remaining oil with the rest of the lime juice, salt and pepper to taste, honeydew and endives, toss and divide between plates. Add shrimp coriander seeds, mint and feta on top and serve.

**Nutrition:** calories 245, fat 23, fiber 3, carbs 23, protein 45

# Shrimp, Mussels and Tomatoes Mix

*Prep Time:* 10 minutes | *Cook Time:* 22 minutes | *Servings: 4*

**Ingredients:**

- 2 tablespoons olive oil
- 12 cherry tomatoes
- 2 tablespoons butter, melted
- ½ cup fennel, sliced
- 1 cup escarole leaves, sliced
- 3 garlic cloves, minced
- 1 cup fish stock
- 1 tablespoon amontillado sherry
- 16 clams, scrubbed
- 16 mussels, scrubbed
- 1 cup shrimp, peeled and deveined
- ¼ cup parsley, chopped
- A pinch of red pepper flakes, crushed
- 2 teaspoons lemon zest, grated
- ½ teaspoon rosemary, chopped
- Salt and black pepper to taste
- 1 teaspoon lemon juice

**Directions:**

Heat up a pan with the oil over medium high heat, add tomatoes, garlic, fennel, escarole and sherry, stir and cook for 8 minutes. Add fish stock, stir and simmer for 4 minutes. Add clams, stir, cover and cook for 2 minutes. Add mussels, stir and cook for 2 minutes more. Add shrimp, stir, cook for 1 minute more and transfer all these to a bowl. Add pepper flakes and kale to the pan with the stock, stir and cook for 1 minute. Take off heat, add melted butter, parsley, rosemary, lemon juice, lemon zest, salt and pepper and stir well. Divide shellfish and shrimp on plates, add veggies and stock mix on top and serve.

**Nutrition:** calories 250, fat 5, fiber 2, carbs 10, protein 27

# Shrimp with Scallops and Rice

*Prep Time:* 10 minutes | *Cook Time:* 25 minutes | *Servings: 4*

**Ingredients:**

- 1 yellow onion, chopped
- 1 teaspoon smoked paprika
- 1 teaspoon thyme, dried
- 3 tablespoons sherry
- 1 tablespoon extra-virgin olive oil
- 10 ounces risotto rice
- 12 ounces mixed shrimp and sea scallops, cooked and frozen
- 14 ounces canned tomatoes, chopped
- 1-quart chicken stock
- Juice of ½ lemon
- ½ lemon cut into wedges
- A handful parsley, chopped
- Salt and black pepper to taste

**Directions:**

Heat a pan with the oil over medium high heat, add onion, stir and cook for 5 minutes. Add thyme, rice, paprika, sherry, tomatoes and stock, stir and cook for 16 minutes. Add salt and pepper to taste, seafood mix, parsley and lemon juice, stir and cook for 5 minutes more. Divide bowls and serve with lemon wedges on the side.

**Nutrition:** calories 430, fat 4, fiber 2, carbs 33, protein 25

# Scallops and Grapes Mix

*Prep Time:* 10 minutes | *Cook Time:* 15 minutes | *Servings:* 4

**Ingredients:**

- 1 and ½ cups green grapes, cut in quarters
- Zest from 1 lemon, chopped
- Juice of 1 lemon
- Salt and black pepper to taste
- 2 scallions, chopped
- ¼ cup olive oil
- 2 tablespoons mint, chopped
- 2 tablespoons
- cilantro, chopped
- 1 teaspoon cumin, ground
- 1 teaspoon paprika
- ½ teaspoon ginger, ground
- ¼ teaspoon cinnamon, ground
- 1 teaspoon turmeric, ground
- ½ cup water
- 1 and ½ pounds sea scallops

**Directions:**

Heat a pan with the water, some salt and the lemon zest over medium high heat, simmer for 10 minutes, drain the zest, transfer to a bowl, add grapes, 2 tablespoons oil, mint, scallions and cilantro and stir. In another bowl, mix cumin with turmeric, paprika, cinnamon and ginger and stir. Add scallops, salt and pepper and toss. Heat a pan with remaining oil over medium high heat, add scallops, cook for 2 minutes on each side and transfer to a plate. Divide scallops on 4 plates, pour lemon juice over them and serve with grape relish.

**Nutrition:** calories 320, fat 12, fiber 2, carbs 18, protein 28

# Lemon Shrimp

*Prep Time:* 10 minutes | *Cook Time:* 3 minutes | *Servings:* 4

**Ingredients:**

- 40 big shrimp, peeled and deveined
- 6 garlic cloves, minced
- Salt and black pepper to taste
- 3 tablespoons olive oil
- ¼ teaspoon sweet paprika
- A pinch of red pepper flakes, crushed
- ¼ teaspoon lemon zest, grated
- 3 tablespoons sherry
- 1 and ½ tablespoons chives, sliced
- Juice of 1 lemon

**Directions:**

Heat a pan with the oil over medium high heat, add shrimp, season with salt and pepper and cook for 1 minute. Add the rest of the ingredients, toss, cook for 2-3 minutes more, divide between plates and serve.

**Nutrition:** calories 140, fat 1, fiber 0, carbs 1, protein 18

# Shrimp with Orzo and Spinach

*Prep Time:* 10 minutes | *Cook Time:* 25 minutes | *Servings:* 6

**Ingredients:**

- 1 pound shrimp, peeled and deveined
- 1 pound orzo
- 5 tablespoons olive oil
- Salt and black pepper to taste
- 1 garlic clove, minced
- 5 ounces baby spinach
- 2 teaspoons thyme, chopped
- ¾ cup panko
- 6 ounces feta cheese, crumbled
- Zest from 1 lemon, grated

**Directions:**

Heat a pan with 2 tablespoons oil over medium high heat, add shrimp, garlic, spinach, season with salt and pepper, stir, cook for 4 minutes and take off the heat. Put water in a large saucepan, add salt, bring to a boil over medium high heat, add orzo, stir, cook according to package instructions, drain and add over shrimp mix. Also add cheese, 2 tablespoons oil, half of the thyme and lemon juice, stir and pour this into a greased baking dish. In a bowl, mix panko with the remaining oil, remaining thyme, salt and pepper and stir. Spread this over orzo and shrimp mix, bake at 425 degrees F for 20 minutes, divide between plates and serve.

**Nutrition:** calories 345, fat 13, fiber 4, carbs 33, protein 22

# Salmon with Lentils and Apricots

*Prep Time:* 10 minutes | *Cook Time:* 1 hour | *Servings:* 4

## Ingredients:

- 3 cups water
- 1 cup French lentils, rinsed
- Salt and black pepper to taste
- 2 tablespoons olive oil
- 1/3 cup apricots, dried and chopped
- 1 yellow onion, chopped
- 1 tablespoon capers
- 1 tablespoon lemon juice
- ½ teaspoon lemon zest, grated
- ½ teaspoon paprika
- ½ teaspoon cumin, ground
- ¼ teaspoon cinnamon, ground
- A pinch of allspice, ground
- ¼ teaspoon ginger, ground
- ¼ teaspoon turmeric
- A pinch of cayenne pepper
- 4 salmon fillets, skinless
- Lemon wedges

## Directions:

Put the water in a saucepan, add salt, bring to a boil over medium high heat, add lentils and apricots, stir, simmer for 45 minutes and drain. Heat a pan with 1 tablespoons oil over medium high heat, add the onion, lentils, apricots, lemon juice and zest, salt, pepper, capers and parsley, stir and cook for 8 minutes. In a bowl, mix the salmon with paprika with cumin, ginger, cinnamon, turmeric, cayenne, salt, pepper and allspice and stir. Heat a pan with remaining oil, add salmon, cook for 4 minutes, flip and cook for 3 minutes more, divide between plates and serve with the lentils and lemon wedges on the side

**Nutrition:** calories 450, fat 12, fiber 15, carbs 40, protein 42

# Fish and Tomatoes Mix

*Prep Time:* 10 minutes | *Cook Time:* 45 minutes | *Servings:* 4

## Ingredients:

- 1 cup water
- 4 medium sea bass fillets, skin on
- 2 tablespoons olive oil
- 2 teaspoons olive oil
- Salt and black pepper to taste
- 1 yellow onion, sliced
- 2 red bell peppers, chopped
- 3 garlic cloves, minced
- 15 ounces canned tomatoes, chopped
- 2 bay leaves
- 1 cup white wine
- 1-pint cherry tomatoes, cut in halves
- ¼ cup parsley, chopped

## Directions:

Season fish with salt, pepper and 2 teaspoons oil, rub well, place on a plate and leave aside. Heat a saucepan with remaining oil over medium high heat, add onion, garlic and bell peppers, some salt and pepper, stir and cook for 5 minutes. Add wine and the other ingredients except the fish and parsley, stir and cook for 10 minutes more. Add fish fillets, place everything in the oven at 350 degrees F and bake for 25 minutes. Take braised fish out of the oven, divide into plates, sprinkle parsley on top and serve.

**Nutrition:** calories 345, fat 12, fiber 4, carbs 15, protein 16

## Cod with Pancetta and Tomatoes

*Prep Time: 10 minutes | Cook Time: 15 minutes | Servings: 4*

**Ingredients:**

- 4 cod fillets
- 2 tablespoons oil
- Salt and black pepper to taste
- 2 ounces pancetta, chopped
- 1 teaspoon thyme, chopped
- 1 yellow onion, chopped
- ½ cup dry white wine
- ¼ teaspoon red pepper flakes, crushed
- 15 ounces canned tomatoes, chopped
- ½ cup green olives, pitted and chopped
- 1 cup artichoke hearts, marinated and chopped

**Directions:**

Heat a pan with the oil over medium high heat, add pancetta, stir, cook for 3 minutes, drain excess grease on paper towels and leave aside for now. Heat the pan again, add fish, season with salt and pepper to taste, cook for 4 minutes, flip and transfer to a plate with the seared side up. Add onion, wine, tomatoes, olives, artichokes, pepper flakes and thyme, stir and cook for 6 minutes. Return fish to pan, cover and cook for 3 minutes over medium heat. Divide into bowls, sprinkle pancetta all over and serve.

**Nutrition:** calories 340, fat 3, fiber 2, carbs 13, protein 32

## Salmon and Pistachio Mix

*Prep Time: 10 minutes | Cook Time: 40 minutes | Servings: 4*

**Ingredients:**

- 2 fennel bulbs, sliced into medium wedges
- 3 tablespoons extra virgin olive oil
- 1 small red onion, sliced
- Salt and black pepper to taste
- 4 salmon fillets, skinless
- ½ cup pistachios, chopped
- ½ cup parsley, chopped
- 1 tablespoon lemon zest, grated
- 1 tablespoon garlic, minced

**Directions:**

In a bowl, mix fennel and onion with salt, pepper and oil, toss to coat, spread into a baking dish, place in the oven at 400 degrees F and bake for 25 minutes. Add the fish, place in the oven again and bake for 15 minutes more. In a bowl, mix parsley with the rest of the ingredients and toss. Divide salmon and fennel on plates, top with parsley mixture and serve.

**Nutrition:** calories 430, fat 13, fiber 8, carbs 22, protein 45

## Trout and Green Beans Mix

*Prep Time: 10 minutes | Cook Time: 5 minutes | Servings: 4*

**Ingredients:**

- 12 ounces green beans
- ½ cup sunflower oil
- 2 cucumbers, chopped
- 4 cups cannellini beans, already cooked
- 1 cup black olives, pitted and chopped
- ¼ cup parsley, chopped
- ½ cup sunflower seeds, toasted
- ½ cup red onion, chopped
- 3 tablespoons lemon juice
- ¼ cup dill weed, chopped
- 3 tablespoons red wine vinegar
- 2 tablespoon marjoram, chopped
- 2 garlic cloves, minced
- 1 tablespoon water
- 1 tablespoon lemon zest, grated
- Salt and black pepper to taste
- 10 ounces smoked trout fillet, skinless
- 1 cup Greek yogurt

**Directions:**

Heat a pan with the oil over medium heat, add green beans and water, stir, cook for 5 minutes, transfer to a bowl and leave aside for 10 minutes. Add the rest of the ingredients except the trout and yogurt, toss and divide between plates. Top each serving with the trout and yogurt and serve.

**Nutrition:** calories 300, fat 12, fiber 8, carbs 21, protein 14

## Creamy Swordfish

*Prep Time: 10 minutes | Cook Time: 2 hours and 30 minutes | Servings: 6*

**Ingredients:**

- 28 ounces canned tomatoes, chopped
- 1 shallot, chopped
- 1 small fennel bulb, chopped
- 2 tablespoons tomato paste
- 1 tablespoon rosemary
- 1 teaspoon fennel seeds
- Salt and black pepper to taste
- 1 teaspoon garlic, minced
- ¼ cup heavy cream
- 1 and ½ pounds swordfish steaks

**Directions:**

In a slow cooker, mix fennel with and the other ingredients except the fish, stir, cover and cook on High for 2 hours. Add fish, cover it with some sauce and cook on High for 30 minutes more. Divide into bowls and serve.

**Nutrition:** calories 340, fat 14, fiber 5, carbs 15, protein 32

# Buttery Fish and Polenta

*Prep Time: 10 minutes | Cook Time: 40 minutes | Servings: 4*

## Ingredients:

- ½ teaspoon lemon zest
- 1 and ½ teaspoons coriander seeds, toasted
- 2 tablespoons lemon juice
- 1 lemon cut in wedges
- 1 cup cornmeal
- 4 cod pieces
- 3 ounces butter, melted
- 3 cups water
- Salt and black pepper to the taste
- 2 tablespoons harissa paste
- 2 teaspoons cilantro, chopped

## Directions:

In a pot, mix the water with lemon zest, salt and pepper, bring to a boil, add the cornmeal, stir, cook for 20 minutes stirring often and take off the heat. Place fish in a baking dish, season with salt and pepper, add harissa, lemon juice and melted butter, stir, place in the oven at 400 degrees F and bake for 15 minutes. Take fish out of the oven, divide it between plates, top with cilantro and serve with the polenta and with lemon wedges on the side.

**Nutrition:** calories 450, fat 23, fiber 2, carbs 30, protein 30

# Tuna with Tomatoes

*Prep Time: 10 minutes | Cook Time: 6 minutes | Servings: 4*

## Ingredients:

- 4 tuna steaks, boneless and skinless
- 2 tablespoons extra virgin olive oil
- Salt and black pepper to taste
- 2 cups cherry tomatoes, yellow
- and red, cut in halves
- 1 shallot, chopped
- ½ cup green olives, pitted and chopped
- ½ tablespoon lemon juice
- 2 tablespoons basil, chopped

## Directions:

Heat a pan with the oil over medium high heat, add tuna steaks, salt and pepper, cook for about 4 minutes and transfer to a platter. Heat the pan again over medium heat, add shallots, olives and the rest of the ingredients, stir, cook for 3 minutes and take off the heat. Divide this mix into serving plates, add tuna on the side and serve.

**Nutrition:** calories 300, fat 14, fiber 1, carbs 4, protein 42

# Mahi Mahi and Olives

*Prep Time: 10 minutes | Cook Time: 20 minutes | Servings: 4*

## Ingredients:

- 4 mahi-mahi fillets, skinless
- 2 tablespoons olive oil
- 1 yellow onion, chopped
- Salt and black pepper to taste
- ¾ cup dry white wine
- 1 garlic clove,
- crushed
- 1 teaspoon oregano, dried
- ½ cup green olives, pitted and chopped
- 14 ounces canned tomatoes, chopped
- 1 tablespoon capers, drained
- ¼ cup parsley, chopped

## Directions:

Heat a pan with 1 tablespoon oil over medium high heat, add fish fillets, salt and pepper to taste, cook for 5 minutes on each side and transfer to a platter. Heat up the pan again with the rest of the oil, add the onion, garlic, oregano and wine, stir and cook for 7 minutes. Add tomatoes, olives, capers, salt and pepper, stir, cook for 5 minutes and drizzle over fish. Sprinkle parsley at the end and serve.

**Nutrition:** calories 300, fat 11, fiber 2, carbs 7, protein 22

# Artic Char and Potatoes

*Prep Time: 10 minutes | Cook Time: 15 minutes | Servings: 4*

## Ingredients:

- 4 red potatoes, sliced
- 4 Arctic char fillets
- Salt and black pepper to taste
- 3 tablespoons olive oil
- ½ cup kalamata
- olives, pitted
- 2 rosemary sprigs
- 3 tablespoons parsley, chopped
- 4 lemon wedges
- 1 tablespoon balsamic vinegar

## Directions:

Put water in a saucepan, add potatoes and salt, bring to a boil over medium heat, cook for 5 minutes, drain and leave aside. Heat a pan with 1 ½ tablespoons oil over medium high heat, add fish, salt and pepper, cook for 3 minutes on each side and transfer to a plate. Add remaining oil to the pan, heat over medium high heat as well, add potatoes and rosemary and cook for 5 minutes. Add the rest of the ingredients except the lemon wedges, stir gently and cook for 2 minutes more. Add this next to fish and serve with lemon wedges on the side.

**Nutrition:** calories 340, fat 21, fiber 2, carbs 13, protein 23

# Honey Salmon Mix

*Prep Time: 20 minutes | Cook Time: 10 minutes | Servings: 6*

## Ingredients:

- 3 tablespoons soft butter
- 3 tablespoons mustard
- 5 teaspoons honey
- ½ cup breadcrumbs
- ½ cup pecans, chopped
- 6 salmon fillets
- 3 teaspoons parsley, chopped
- Salt and pepper to taste
- 6 lemon wedges

## Directions:

In a bowl, mix mustard with honey and butter and whisk. In another bowl, mix pecans with parsley, bread crumbs and stir well. Season salmon fillets with salt and pepper to taste, place on a baking sheet, brush with honey mix, top with breadcrumbs and bake at 400 degrees F for 10 minutes/inch. Take out of the oven, transfer to serving plates and serve with lemon wedges.

**Nutrition:** calories 200, fat 4, fiber 2, carbs 5, protein 12

# Balsamic Salmon

*Prep Time: 10 minutes | Cook Time: 15 minutes | Servings: 4*

## Ingredients:

- ½ cup olive oil
- ¼ cup balsamic vinegar
- 4 garlic cloves, minced
- 4 salmon fillets, skinless
- 2 tablespoons cilantro, chopped
- Sea salt and black pepper to taste

## Directions:

In a bowl, mix the salmon fillets with the oil, vinegar, garlic, cilantro, salt and pepper, toss and leave aside for 10 minutes. Transfer to a roasting pan, put in the preheated broiler and broil over medium heat for 15 minutes, flipping the fillets once. Serve the fish with a side salad.

**Nutrition:** calories 230, fat 13, fiber 7, carbs 12, protein 7

# Garlic Salmon and Herbs

*Prep Time: 10 minutes | Cook Time: 25 minutes | Servings: 4*

## Ingredients:

- 1 cup balsamic vinegar
- ¼ cup honey
- 5 garlic cloves, minced
- 3 tablespoons mustard
- 2 tablespoons olive oil
- ¼ cup dill, chopped
- ¼ cup parsley, chopped
- 4 salmon fillets, boneless
- A pinch of salt and black pepper

## Directions:

Heat a saucepan with the vinegar over medium heat, add the honey, whisk well, simmer for 15 minutes, cool down, add oil, mustard and garlic, stir and leave aside for 10 minutes. Arrange the salmon on a lined baking sheet, brush it well with garlic mix, add salt and pepper, sprinkle the dill and parsley on top, bake at 400 degrees F for 10 minutes, divide between plates and serve.

**Nutrition:** calories 240, fat 12, fiber 5, carbs 14, protein 9

# Salmon Meatballs with Rice

*Prep Time: 10 minutes | Cook Time: 30 minutes | Servings: 4*

## Ingredients:

- 28 ounces canned pink salmon, drained, skinless and boneless
- 1 ¼ cup breadcrumbs
- ¼ cup mayonnaise
- 1 large egg, whisked
- 1 tablespoon Worcestershire sauce
- ¼ cup capers, drained
- 1 ½ teaspoons tarragon, dried
- Sea salt and black pepper to taste
- 2 cups instant brown rice, cooked
- 4 tablespoons olive oil
- 2 tablespoons parsley, chopped
- 1 tablespoon olive oil
- 1 tablespoon lemon juice
- 1 lemon cut in quarters

## Directions:

In a bowl, mix the salmon with mayonnaise, egg, ½ cup bread crumbs, Worcestershire sauce, tarragon, capers, salt and pepper to taste, stir, shape 12 meatballs, coat them in the rest of the breadcrumbs and arrange them on a plate. Heat a large pan with the olive oil over medium high heat, add the meatballs, cook for 3 minutes on each side, drain excess grease, arrange on serving plates and leave aside. Serve with brown rice and lemon wedges, sprinkle parsley and drizzle olive oil and lemon juice on top.

**Nutrition:** Calories 142, fat 3, fiber 2, carbs 3, protein 3

# Lime and Garlic Salmon Fillets

*Prep Time: 30 minutes | Cook Time: 8 minutes | Servings: 4*

## Ingredients:

- 4 salmon fillets, boneless
- 4 tablespoons olive oil
- 2 teaspoons lime
- zest, grated
- 3 tablespoons lime juice
- 4 garlic cloves, minced

## Directions:

In a bowl, mix the salmon with the oil with lime zest, lime juice and garlic, toss and leave aside for 30 minutes. Place the salmon fillets on a preheated kitchen grill and cook over medium heat for 4 minutes on each side. Serve with a side salad.

**Nutrition:** calories 220, fat 11, fiber 8, carbs 15, protein 7

# Watercress and Salmon Salad

*Prep Time: 10 minutes | Cook Time: 0 minutes | Servings: 6*

## Ingredients:

- 2 bunches watercress
- 1 pound smoked salmon, flaked
- 2 tablespoons jarred horseradish
- 2 teaspoons mustard
- ¼ cup lemon juice
- ½ cup sour cream
- Salt and black pepper to taste
- 1 big cucumber, sliced
- 2 tablespoons dill, chopped
- 1 lemon wedges

## Directions:

In a bowl, mix the salmon with the watercress, horseradish and the other ingredients except the lemon wedge, toss and divide into bowls. Serve with the lemon wedge on the side.

**Nutrition:** calories 132, fat 2, fiber 3, carbs 4, protein 3

# Mustard Salmon with Pecans and Asparagus

*Prep Time: 10 minutes | Cook Time: 10 minutes | Servings: 8*

## Ingredients:

- 1 pound fresh asparagus, chopped
- ½ cup pecans
- 2 red lettuce heads, torn
- ½ cup peas
- ¼ pound smoked salmon, cut into
- small chunks
- ¼ cup olive oil
- 1 teaspoon Dijon mustard
- 2 tablespoon lemon juice
- Sea salt and black pepper to taste

## Directions:

Put some water in a saucepan, bring to a boil over medium heat, add asparagus, cook for 5 minutes, drain and leave aside for now. Heat a pan over medium heat, add pecans, toast for 5 minutes and take off heat. In a large bowl, mix asparagus with the pecans, lettuce and the other ingredients, toss and serve.

**Nutrition:** calories 253, fat 3, fiber 2, carbs 5, protein 3

## Salmon and Mushroom Salad

*Prep Time:* 10 minutes | *Cook Time:* 20 minutes | *Servings: 4*

**Ingredients:**

- 2 medium salmon fillets
- ¼ cup melted butter
- 4 ounces mushrooms, sliced
- Sea salt and black pepper to taste
- 12 cherry tomatoes, halved
- 2 tablespoons olive oil
- 8 ounces lettuce
- leaves, torn
- 1 avocado, pitted, peeled and cubed
- 1 jalapeno pepper, chopped
- 5 cilantro sprigs, chopped
- 2 tablespoons white wine vinegar
- 1 ounce feta cheese, crumbled

**Directions:**

Place salmon on a lined baking sheet, brush with 2 tablespoons melted butter, season with salt and pepper, and broil for 15 minutes under medium heat. Heat up a pan with remaining butter over medium heat, add mushrooms, stir. cook for a few minutes and transfer to a bowl. Add the salmon and the rest of the ingredients, toss and serve.

**Nutrition:** calories 315, fat 8, fiber 2, carbs 4, protein 7

## Parsley Salmon Mix

*Prep Time:* 10 minutes | *Cook Time:* 25 minutes | *Servings: 4*

**Ingredients:**

- 4 salmon fillets, boneless
- 1 cup mayonnaise
- A drizzle of olive oil
- 1 cup parsley,
- chopped
- 1 tablespoon lemon juice
- A pinch of salt and black pepper

**Directions:**

In a baking dish, combine the salmon with mayonnaise, lemon juice and the other ingredients, bake at 350 degrees F for 25 minutes, divide between plates and serve.

**Nutrition:** calories 233, fat 12, fiber 5, carbs 8, protein 9

## Salmon and Sauce

*Prep Time:* 10 minutes | *Cook Time:* 20 minutes | *Servings: 2*

**Ingredients:**

- 2 medium salmon fillets
- 1 tablespoon basil, chopped
- 6 lemon slices
- Sea salt and black pepper to taste
- 1 cup Greek yogurt
- 2 teaspoons curry
- powder
- A pinch of cayenne pepper
- 1 garlic clove, minced
- ½ teaspoon cilantro, chopped
- ½ teaspoon mint, chopped

**Directions:**

Place each salmon fillet on parchment paper, do 3 splits in each. stuff them with basil, add salt and pepper, top each fillet with 3 lemon slices, fold parchment, seal edges, place in the oven at 400 degrees F and bake for 20 minutes. Meanwhile, in a bowl, mix yogurt with the rest of the ingredients and whisk. Transfer fish to plates, drizzle the yogurt sauce and serve right away!

**Nutrition:** calories 242, fat 1, fiber 2, carbs 3, protein 3

## Salmon and Couscous

*Prep Time:* 20 minutes | *Cook Time:* 10 minutes | *Servings: 4*

**Ingredients:**

- ½ cup couscous
- 1 and ½ cups water
- 1 tablespoon olive oil
- 4 salmon fillets, skinless and boneless
- 4 tablespoons tahini paste
- Juice of 1 lemon
- 1 lemon, cut into wedges
- ½ cucumber, chopped
- Seeds from 1 pomegranate
- A small bunch of parsley, chopped

**Directions:**

Put couscous in a bowl, add water, cover and leave aside for 8 minutes. Heat up a with the oil over medium heat, add salmon, cook for 5 minutes on one side, flip, cook for 2 more minutes, remove from heat and leave aside. In a bowl, mix tahini with lemon juice and a splash of water and whisk well. Drain couscous, the remaining ingredients except the lemon wedges, toss and divide between plates. Add the salmon next to the couscous and serve with lemon wedges on the side.

**Nutrition:** calories 254, fat 3, fiber 1, carbs 3, protein 4

# Salmon and Onions

*Prep Time:* 10 minutes | *Cook Time:* 30 minutes | *Servings:* 6

## Ingredients:

- 2 cups whole bread croutons
- 3 red onions, cut into wedges
- ¾ cup green olives, pitted
- 3 red bell peppers, cut into 6 pieces
- ½ teaspoon smoked paprika
- Salt and black pepper to taste
- 5 tablespoons olive oil
- 6 - 6 ounce salmon fillets, skinless and boneless
- 2 tablespoons parsley, chopped

## Directions:

Arrange croutons, paprika, salt, pepper, 3 tablespoons oil, peppers, onions and olives on a lined baking sheet, toss, place in the oven at 375 degrees F, bake for 15 minutes and leave aside for now. Rub salmon fillets with remaining olive oil, add croutons, bake for 12 more minutes, divide between plates, sprinkle the parsley on top and serve.

**Nutrition:** calories 321, fat 2, fiber 3, carbs 5, protein 8

# Salmon and Salsa

*Prep Time:* 10 minutes | *Cook Time:* 30 minutes | *Servings:* 6

## Ingredients:

- 6 salmon fillets, boneless
- Cooking spray
- Juice of ½ lemon
- 2 garlic cloves, minced
- Salt and black pepper to taste
- 4 tomatoes, cubed
- 1 cup kalamata
- olives, pitted and chopped
- ½ cup feta cheese, crumbled
- A drizzle of olive oil
- 3 tablespoons basil, chopped
- ½ teaspoon balsamic vinegar

## Directions:

Put the salmon fillets, garlic, salt, pepper and lemon juice in a baking dish greased with cooking spray and bake at 375 degrees F for 30 minutes. In a bowl, mix the tomatoes with the rest of the ingredients and toss. Divide the salmon between plates, spread the tomato mix over each fillet and serve.

**Nutrition:** calories 220, fat 13, fiber 6, carbs 12, protein 8

# Salmon and Yogurt Sauce

*Prep Time:* 10 minutes | *Cook Time:* 15 minutes | *Servings:* 4

## Ingredients:

- 4 medium salmon fillets, skinless and boneless
- 1 fennel bulb, chopped
- Salt and black pepper to taste
- ¼ cup dry white wine
- ¼ cup water
- 1 cup Greek yogurt
- ¼ cup green olives pitted and chopped
- ¼ cup fresh chives, chopped
- 1 tablespoon olive oil
- 1 tablespoon lemon juice

## Directions:

Arrange the fennel in a baking dish, add salmon fillets, season with salt and black pepper, add wine and water, place in the microwave, cook on High for 8 minutes, drain the grease and arrange on a platter. In a bowl, mix yogurt with chives and the rest of the ingredients and toss. Transfer salmon to plates, top with the baked fennel and pour olives and yogurt sauce on top.

**Nutrition:** calories 342, fat 2, fiber 2, carbs 2, protein 3

# Salmon and Fettucine

*Prep Time:* 10 minutes | *Cook Time:* 10 minutes | *Servings:* 6

## Ingredients:

- 1 tablespoon lemon zest
- 1 tablespoon lemon juice
- 1 lemon cut in wedges
- Salt and black pepper to taste
- 1 cup low fat cream
- 1 pound asparagus
- 18 ounces fresh fettuccine
- Water for boiling
- 20 ounces salmon, skinless and boneless
- 1 ounce parmesan cheese, grated

## Directions:

Put water in a saucepan, add a pinch of salt, bring to a boil over medium heat, add asparagus, cook for 1 minute, drain and transfer to a plate. Add pasta to the same pot, cook according to instruction, drain and put in a bowl. Heat the saucepan with the water again over medium heat, add salmon, cook for 5 minutes and also drain. In a bowl, mix lemon peel with cream and lemon juice and whisk. Heat a pan over medium high heat, add pasta, salmon, asparagus, cream mix, salt and pepper, cook for 1 more minute, divide between plates, and serve with grated parmesan and lemon wedges.

**Nutrition:** calories 354, fat 2, fiber 2, carbs 2, protein 4

# Salmon with Zucchini

*Prep Time:* 10 minutes | *Cook Time:* 20 minutes | *Servings:* 4

## Ingredients:

- 4 medium salmon fillets, skinless and boneless
- 1 tablespoon olive oil
- 8 ounces canned tomatoes, chopped with ¼ cup juice reserved
- 1 yellow onion, chopped
- ¼ cup kalamata olives, pitted and chopped
- 1 tablespoon capers
- 3 zucchinis, sliced
- 2 tablespoons water
- 1 tablespoon lemon juice
- Salt and black pepper to taste

## Directions:

Heat a pan with the oil over medium high heat, add salmon, salt and pepper, cook for 3 minutes on each side and transfer to a plate. Heat the same pan over medium heat, add onion, stir and cook for 5 minutes stirring all the time. Add tomatoes, reserved tomato juice and the rest of the ingredients, toss, bring to a boil and cook for 5 minutes. Divide salmon on plates, add zucchini mix on the side and serve.

**Nutrition:** calories 275, fat 2, fiber 2, carbs 1, protein 3

# Salmon with Paprika Sprouts

*Prep Time:* 10 minutes | *Cook Time:* 20 minutes | *Servings:* 6

## Ingredients:

- 2 tablespoons brown sugar
- 1 teaspoon onion powder
- 1 teaspoon garlic powder
- 1 teaspoon smoked paprika
- 3 tablespoons olive oil
- 1 ¼ pounds Brussels sprouts, halved
- 10 medium salmon fillets
- Chopped chives for serving

## Directions:

In a baking sheet, mix the sprouts with the salmon and the other ingredients except the chives, toss, place in the oven at 450 degrees F and bake for 20 minutes. Transfer salmon and sprouts to plates, sprinkle chives on top and serve right away!

**Nutrition:** calories 312, fat 3, fiber 3, carbs 5, protein 4

# Salmon with Herbed Beets

*Prep Time:* 10 minutes | *Cook Time:* 25 minutes | *Servings:* 4

## Ingredients:

- 1 pound medium beets, sliced
- 6 tablespoons olive oil
- 1 and ½ pounds salmon fillets, skinless and boneless
- Salt and pepper to taste
- 1 tablespoon chives, chopped
- 1 tablespoon parsley, chopped
- 1 tablespoon fresh tarragon, chopped
- 3 tablespoon shallots, chopped
- 1 tablespoon grated lemon zest
- ¼ cup lemon juice
- 4 cups mixed baby greens

## Directions:

In a bowl, mix beets with ½ tablespoon oil, salt and pepper, toss, arrange on a baking sheet and bake at 450 degrees F for 20 minutes. Add salmon on top, brush with remaining oil, and season with salt and pepper. In a bowl, mix chives with parsley and tarragon, sprinkle 1 tablespoon of this mix over salmon and bake everything for 15 minutes more. In mix shallots with lemon peel, salt, pepper and lemon juice and the rest of the herbs mixture and stir gently. Combine 2 tablespoons of shallots dressing with mixed greens and toss gently. Arrange the fish between plates, add beets and greens on the side, drizzle the rest of the shallot dressing on top and serve.

**Nutrition:** calories 312, fat 2, fiber 2, carbs 2, protein 4

# Salmon Pitas and Tzatziki

*Prep Time:* 10 minutes | *Cook Time:* 0 minutes | *Servings:* 4

## Ingredients:

- 1 pound smoked salmon, boneless, skinless and flaked
- 1 red onion, sliced
- ½ cup feta cheese, crumbled

*For the tzatziki:*
- 1 and ½ cups Greek yogurt
- 1 tablespoon dill, chopped
- 1 teaspoon lemon juice
- ½ cup kalamata olives, pitted and chopped
- 4 pita breads
- ½ cup beet tzatziki

- 1 garlic clove, minced
- 2 roasted beets, cooled, peeled and grated

## Directions:

In a bowl, mix the yogurt with dill, and the other ingredients for the tzatziki and whisk. Arrange the pita breads on a work surface, divide the salmon, onion, olives, cheese in each, top with the sauce, roll the breads and serve.

**Nutrition:** calories 200, fat 14, fiber 6, carbs 15, protein 8

# Salmon with Feta Mix

*Prep Time:* 2 minutes | *Cook Time:* 6 minutes | *Servings:* 4

## Ingredients:

- 1 tablespoon red wine vinegar
- 1 tablespoon lemon juice
- 2 garlic cloves, minced
- ½ teaspoon oregano, dried
- A pinch of salt and black pepper
- ¼ cup olive oil
- 1 tablespoon feta cheese, crumbled
- 4 salmon fillets, boneless

## Directions:

In the instant pot, mix the salmon with the vinegar and the other ingredients except the cheese, cover and cook on high for 6 minutes. Release the pressure quick for 2 minutes, divide the salmon and cooking juices between plates and serve with feta cheese crumbled on top.

**Nutrition:** calories 270, fat 14, fiber 6, carbs 9, protein 11

## Shrimp with Basil and Spinach

*Prep Time: 3 minutes | Cook Time: 8 minutes | Servings: 4*

**Ingredients:**

- 2 pounds shrimp, peeled and deveined
- 2 teaspoons olive oil
- 3 garlic cloves, minced
- A pinch of salt and black pepper
- 1 cup chicken stock
- 2 tablespoons lemon juice
- 4 cups spinach, chopped
- ¼ cup basil, chopped
- ½ cup feta cheese, crumbled

**Directions:**

Heat a pan with the oil over medium heat, add the shrimp and cook for 2 minutes. Add the garlic and the rest of the ingredients except the cheese, toss, bring to a simmer and cook over medium heat for 4-5 minutes. Divide the shrimp and spinach between 4 bowls, top each serving with the cheese and serve.

**Nutrition:** calories 229, fat 7, fiber 2, carbs 16, protein 11

## Shrimp with Lemon Sauce

*Prep Time: 10 minutes | Cook Time: 15 minutes | Servings: 4*

**Ingredients:**

- 1 pound shrimp, deveined and peeled
- 2 teaspoons extra virgin olive oil
- 6 tablespoons lemon juice
- 3 tablespoons dill, chopped
- 1 tablespoon oregano, chopped
- 2 garlic cloves, chopped
- Salt and black pepper to taste
- ¾ cup Greek yogurt
- ½ pounds cherry tomatoes
- 2 cucumbers, sliced
- 1 red onion, sliced
- lettuce leaves

**Directions:**

In a bowl, mix the shrimp with 2 tablespoons lemon juice, 1 tablespoon dill, 1 tablespoon oregano and 1 teaspoon oil, toss and leave aside for 10 minutes. In another bowl, mix ¼ cup yogurt with 1 tablespoon dill, half of the garlic, 2 tablespoons lemon juice, cucumber, salt and pepper and whisk. In a third bowl, mix ½ cup yogurt with the rest of the lemon juice, remaining garlic and remaining dill and whisk well. In a bowl, mix tomatoes with onion and 1 teaspoon olive oil in a bowl. Heat a grill pan over medium high heat, grill tomatoes and shrimp for 5 minutes, divide between plates, add cucumber salad, onions, tomatoes, shrimp and lettuce leaves and serve.

**Nutrition:** calories 353, fat 6, fiber 6, carbs 10, protein 31

## Salmon with Potatoes and Horseradish Mix

*Prep Time: 10 minutes | Cook Time: 10 minutes | Servings: 4*

**Ingredients:**

- 1 and ½ pounds potatoes, chopped
- 1 tablespoon olive oil
- 4 ounces smoked salmon, chopped
- 1 tablespoon chives, chopped
- 2 teaspoons jarred horseradish
- ¼ cup sour cream
- Salt and black pepper to taste

**Directions:**

Heat a pan with the oil over medium heat, add potatoes and cook until they are tender enough and take off heat. In a bowl, mix sour cream with salt, pepper, horseradish, potatoes and salmon, toss and serve.

**Nutrition:** calories 233, fat 6, fiber 5, carbs 9, protein 12

## Cod and Cucumber Salad

*Prep Time: 10 minutes | Cook Time: 15 minutes | Servings: 4*

**Ingredients:**

- 4 medium cod fillets, skinless and boneless
- 2 tablespoons mustard
- 1 tablespoon tarragon, chopped
- 1 tablespoon capers, drained
- 4 tablespoons olive oil + 1 teaspoon
- Salt and black pepper to taste
- 2 cups lettuce leaves, torn
- 1 small red onion, sliced
- 1 small cucumber, sliced
- 2 tablespoons lemon juice
- 2 tablespoons water

**Directions:**

In a bowl, mix mustard with 2 tablespoons olive oil tarragon, capers and water, whisk well and leave aside Heat a pan with 1 teaspoon oil over medium high heat, add the fish, salt and pepper, toss and cook for 6 minutes on each side. In a bowl, mix cucumber with onion, lettuce, lemon juice, 2 tablespoons olive oil, salt and pepper to taste. Divide the cod between plates and serve with the mustard sauce and cucumber salad on the side.

**Nutrition:** calories 278, fat 12, fiber 1, carbs 5, protein 28

# Shrimp Bake

*Prep Time:* 10 minutes | *Cook Time:* 30 minutes | *Servings:* 20

## Ingredients:

- 2 ounces cream cheese, soft
- ½ pound shrimp, already cooked, peeled, deveined and chopped
- 1 cup mayonnaise
- ½ cup mozzarella cheese, shredded
- 3 garlic cloves,
- minced
- 1 tablespoon Worcestershire sauce
- ¼ teaspoon hot sauce
- 1 tablespoon lemon juice
- Olive oil spray
- ½ cup scallions, finely sliced

## Directions:

In a lightly greased baking dish, mix the shrimp with the cream cheese and the other ingredients, place in the oven at 350 degrees F and bake for 30 minutes. Transfer dip to bowls and serve.

**Nutrition:** calories 175, fat 3, fiber 2, carbs 2, protein 3

# Crab and Dill Spread

*Prep Time:* 10 minutes | *Cook Time:* 30 minutes | *Servings:* 10

## Ingredients:

- ½ pound crab meat, flaked
- ounces cream cheese, soft
- 1 tablespoon dill, chopped
- 1 teaspoon lemon juice

## Directions:

In a baking dish, mix the crab with the other ingredients, toss, place in the oven at 350 degrees F and bake for 30 minutes. Transfer to a bowl and serve right away.

**Nutrition:** calories 321, fat 2, fiber 3, carbs 5, protein 4

# Cheesy Salmon and Radish Spread

*Prep Time:* 1 hour and 5 minutes | *Cook Time:* 0 minutes | *Servings:* 8

## Ingredients:

- 2 ounces goat cheese
- 4 ounces cream cheese
- 3 tablespoons beet horseradish, already prepared
- 1 pound smoked salmon, skinless, boneless and flaked
- 2 teaspoons lemon
- zest, grated
- 2 radishes, chopped
- ½ cup capers, drained and chopped
- 1/3 cup red onion, chopped
- 3 tablespoons chives, chopped

## Directions:

In a bowl, mxi the horseradish with the cream cheese and the other ingredients except the salmon and whisk well. Spread a layer of salmon in a dish, add a layer of cream cheese and continue with the ingredients again. Cover this and keep in the fridge for 1 hour and serve.

**Nutrition:** calories 254, fat 2, fiber 1, carbs 2, protein 2

# Yogurt and Trout Spread

*Prep Time:* 6 minutes | *Cook Time:* 0 minutes | *Servings:* 8

## Ingredients:

- 4 ounces smoked trout, skinless, boneless and flaked
- ¼ cup sour cream
- 1 tablespoon lemon juice
- 1/3 cup Greek yogurt
- 1 ½ tablespoon dill weed, chopped
- 3 tablespoons chives, chopped
- Salt and black pepper to taste
- A drizzle of olive oil

## Directions:

In a bowl mix trout with yogurt and the other ingredients except the oil and stir well. Drizzle some olive oil on top before serving.

**Nutrition:** calories 254, fat 2, fiber 2, carbs 2, protein 3

# Anchovy and Garlic Spread

*Prep Time: 5 minutes | Cook Time: 0 minutes | Servings: 6*

## Ingredients:

- 8 ounces anchovies in oil, drained
- 1 tablespoon red wine vinegar
- ½ cup olive oil
- 2 garlic cloves, minced

## Directions:

In a food processor, mix anchovies with the vinegar, garlic and the oil gradually and pulse well,. Divide into bowls and serve right away!

**Nutrition:** calories 200, fat 2, fiber 3, carbs 2, protein 3

# Roasted Salmon and Green Beans Mix

*Prep Time: 10 minutes | Cook Time: 20 minutes | Servings: 4*

## Ingredients:

- 1-pint grape tomatoes, halved
- 2 tablespoon olive oil
- Salt and black pepper to taste
- 3 anchovy fillets
- ½ cup kalamata olives, pitted
- 1 pound green beans
- 2 garlic cloves, minced
- 1 salmon fillet, skinless

## Directions:

Arrange tomatoes, garlic, beans, olives and anchovies on a lined baking sheet, sprinkle pepper and 1 tablespoon oil, toss, place in the oven at 425 degrees F and roast for 15 minutes. Heat a pan with the rest of the oil over medium high heat, add salmon, salt and pepper, cook for 5 minutes on each side, divide between plates and serve with the green beans on the side.

**Nutrition:** calories 200, fat 2, fiber 3, carbs 5, protein 4

# Shrimp and Potatoes

*Prep Time: 10 minutes | Cook Time: 30 minutes | Servings: 4*

## Ingredients:

- 4 gold potatoes, cut into wedges
- 2 fennel bulbs, trimmed and cut into wedges
- 3 shallots, cut into wedges
- 2 garlic cloves, minced
- ½ cup kalamata olive, pitted and chopped
- 4 tablespoons olive
- oil
- 2 pounds shrimp, peeled and deveined
- A pinch of salt and black pepper
- 1 teaspoon lemon zest, grated
- 2 teaspoons oregano, dried
- 1 cup feta cheese, crumbled
- 2 tablespoons parsley, chopped

## Directions:

In a roasting pan, mix the potatoes with fennel, shallot and the other ingredients except the shrimp, toss and bake at 420 degrees F for 25 minutes. Add the shrimp, toss well, bake for 5 minutes more, divide everything between plates and serve.

**Nutrition:** calories 234, fat 13, fiber 7, carbs 9, protein 11

# Salmon and Cucumber Tartar

*Prep Time: 10 minutes | Cook Time: 0 minutes | Servings: 4*

## Ingredients:

- 14 ounces wild salmon fillet, boneless, skinless, minced
- 7 ounces smoked salmon, boneless, skinless and minced
- 3 tablespoons red onion, minced
- 2 tablespoons pickled cucumber, minced
- Salt and black pepper to taste
- Juice of 1 lemon
- Zest of 1 lemon, grated
- 2 garlic cloves, minced
- 2 tablespoons Dijon mustard
- 4 tablespoons olive oil
- 2 teaspoons oregano dried
- 2 tablespoons basil, minced
- 2 tablespoons mint, minced

## Directions:

In a bowl, mix the wild salmon with smoked salmon and the other ingredients, stir well and serve right away.

**Nutrition:** calories 220, fat 11, fiber 5, carbs 15, protein 7

# Balsamic Salmon and Veggie Mix

*Prep Time:* 10 minutes | *Cook Time:* 10 minutes | *Servings:* 4

## Ingredients:

*For the salad dressing:*

- 3 tablespoons balsamic vinegar
- tablespoons olive oil
- 1/3 cup kalamata olives, pitted and minced
- 1 garlic clove crushed and finely

*For the salad:*

- ½ pound green beans, chopped
- ¾ pound small red potatoes, cut into quarters
- ½ pound cherry tomatoes, halved
- Salt and black

  chopped
- Salt and black pepper to taste
- ½ teaspoons red pepper flakes, crushed
- ½ teaspoon lemon zest, grated

  pepper to taste
- ½ fennel bulb, sliced
- ½ red onion, sliced
- 2 cups baby arugula
- ¾ pound cedar planked salmon, skinless, boneless and cut into 4 pieces

## Directions:

In a bowl, mix vinegar with garlic, olives, oil, red pepper flakes, lemon zest, salt and pepper to taste, and whisk. Put potatoes in a large saucepan, add water to cover, add salt, bring to a boil over medium high heat, cook for 5 minutes, drain, reserve liquid and put in a bowl. Mix potatoes with 2 tablespoons salad dressing, add salt and pepper to taste and toss. Return reserved water to heat, bring to a boil over medium heat, add green beans, blanch for 2 minutes, drain and put them in a bowl filled with ice water. Drain beans again and add to potatoes. Add the onion, tomatoes, fennel, the rest of the dressing, arugula, salt and pepper and toss. Transfer salad to a platter, add salmon on top, and serve right away.

**Nutrition:** calories 312, fat 3, fiber 3, carbs 6, protein 4

# Shrimp and Clam Sauce

*Prep Time:* 10 minutes | *Cook Time:* 30 minutes | *Servings:* 4

## Ingredients:

- 1 teaspoon lemon juice
- Salt and black pepper to taste
- ½ cup mayo
- ½ teaspoon paprika
- A pinch of cayenne pepper
- 3 tablespoons olive oil
- 1 fennel bulb, chopped
- 1 yellow onion, chopped
- 3 thin strips orange

  zest
- garlic cloves, minced
- A pinch of cloves, ground
- ½ cup dry white wine
- 1 cup clam juice
- 1 cup water
- 1 cup canned tomatoes chopped
- 1 and ½ pounds big shrimp, peeled and deveined
- ¼ teaspoon saffron crumbled

## Directions:

Put 2 garlic cloves in a bowl, add salt, mayo, cayenne, pepper, lemon juice and 1 tablespoon oil and whisk well. Heat a pan with remaining oil over medium high heat, add onion and fennel, stir and cook for 7 minutes. Add 4 garlic cloves, ground cloves, wine and orange zest, stir and cook 6 minutes. Add clam juice, and the other ingredients except the shrimp, bring to a boil, add salt and pepper and simmer for 10 minutes. Add shrimp, stir gently and simmer for 4 more minutes. Discard orange zest, stir gently, divide between plates and serve.

**Nutrition:** calories 310, fat 2, fiber 1, carbs 3, protein 4

# Crab and Watermelon Soup

*Prep Time: 4 hours and 10 minutes | Cook Time: 0 minutes | Servings: 4*

## Ingredients:

- ¼ cup basil, chopped
- 2 pounds tomatoes
- 5 cups watermelon, cubed
- ¼ cup red wine vinegar
- 1/3 cup olive oil
- 2 garlic cloves, minced
- 1 zucchini, chopped
- Salt and black pepper to taste
- 1 cup crabmeat

## Directions:

In a food processor, combine the tomatoes with the watermelon and the other ingredients except the zucchini, crab and basil and pulse. Pour this into a bowl, cover and keep in the fridge for 4 hours. Divide soup into bowls, top with the rest of the watermelon, zucchini, crab and basil and serve.

**Nutrition:** calories 231, fat 3, fiber 3, carbs 6, protein 6

# Shrimp, Peas and Tomato Bake

*Prep Time: 10 minutes | Cook Time: 30 minutes | Servings: 4*

## Ingredients:

- 1 pound shrimp, peeled and deveined
- Salt and black pepper to taste
- 3 garlic cloves, minced
- 1 tablespoon olive oil
- ½ teaspoon oregano, dried
- 1 yellow onion,
- chopped
- 2 cups chicken stock
- 2 ounces orzo
- ½ cup water
- 4 ounces canned tomatoes, chopped
- Juice of 1 lemon
- ¼ cup parmesan, grated
- ½ cup peas

## Directions:

Put shrimp in a bowl, mix with salt and pepper to taste and leave aside for now. Heat a pan with the oil over medium high heat, add onion, garlic and oregano, stir and cook for 4 minutes. Add orzo, stock and ½ cups, stir and cook for 14 minutes over low heat. Add peas, lemon juice, tomatoes and shrimp, toss, sprinkle the parmesan on top and bake at 400 degrees F for 14 minutes. Take out of the oven and serve right away.

**Nutrition:** calories 298, fat 4, fiber 3, carbs 7, protein 8

# Shrimp Toast

*Prep Time: 1 hour | Cook Time: 25 minutes | Servings: 24*

## Ingredients:

- 24 medium shrimp, cooked, peeled and deveined
- 24 baguette slices, toasted
- ½ cup raisins
- 4 cups yellow onion, chopped
- 2 tablespoons olive oil
- 2 tablespoons capers, chopped
- 2 tablespoons dill, chopped
- Salt and black pepper to taste

## Directions:

Place raisins in a bowl, cover with boiling water and leave aside for 30 minutes. Heat up large pan with the oil over medium high heat, add onions, stir and cook for 10 minutes. Cover pan and cook for another 10-15 minutes. Add drained raisins, capers, dill, salt. Add pepper, stir, cook for 6 more minutes, transfer to a bowl and leave aside for 30 minutes. Scoop mixture on each baguette slice, add 1 shrimp on each and serve right away.

**Nutrition:** calories 200, fat 2, fiber 2, carbs 6, protein 4

# Sardine Sandwich

*Prep Time: 10 minutes | Cook Time: 15 minutes | Servings: 12*

## Ingredients:

- 4 ounces canned and smoked sardines in olive oil, skinless, boneless and crushed
- 2 teaspoons olive oil
- 2 tablespoons mint, chopped
- Salt to taste
- 3 slices whole grain baguette
- 1 small tomato, chopped
- 1 tablespoon yellow onion, sliced

## Directions:

In a bowl, mix sardines with olive oil, salt and mint and stir well. Cut each slice of bread into 4 triangles, place them all on a lined baking sheet, place in the oven at 350 degrees F, bake for 15 minutes, divide the sardine and tomato on each, top with onion slices and serve.

**Nutrition:** calories 200, fat 6, fiber 3, carbs 11, protein 6

# Salmon Crepes

*Prep Time:* 15 minutes | *Cook Time:* 0 minutes | *Servings: 16*

## Ingredients:

- 8 slices smoked salmon
- 1 cup cream cheese,
- 1 and ½ teaspoons lemon rind, grated
- 3 teaspoons dill weed, chopped
- 3 ounces Greek style crepes
- 1 small red onion, sliced
- Salt and pepper to taste

## Directions:

In a bowl, mix cream cheese with lemon rind, dill, salt and pepper and whisk. Place 1 crepe on a working surface, spread 1 tablespoon cream mixture, add 1 salmon slice and onion, roll, arrange on a platter, repeat with the other crepes and serve.

**Nutrition:** calories 200, fat 3, fiber 3, carbs 6, protein 3

# Wrapped Scallops

*Prep Time:* 10 minutes | *Cook Time:* 6 minutes | *Servings: 12*

## Ingredients:

- 2 pounds scallops
- 1 pound prosciutto, sliced and then cut into halves lengthwise
- A drizzle of olive oil
- 2 lemons, cut in wedges
- Salt and black pepper to taste

## Directions:

Wrap each scallop in a prosciutto slice, sprinkle salt and pepper, drizzle some oil, place on preheated grill pan over medium high heat, cook for 3 minutes on each side, arrange on a platter and serve with the lemon wedges.

**Nutrition:** calories 173, fat 2, fiber 5, carbs 4, protein 7

# Mussels and Tomatoes

*Prep Time:* 10 minutes | *Cook Time:* 30 minutes | *Servings: 4*

## Ingredients:

- 3 tablespoons olive oil
- 2 pounds mussels, scrubbed
- 4 ounces dried chorizo, chopped
- Salt and black pepper to taste
- 3 cups canned tomatoes, crushed
- 1 big shallot,
- chopped
- 2 garlic cloves, minced
- ¼ teaspoon red pepper flakes, crushed
- 2 cups dry white wine
- 1/3 cup parsley, chopped

## Directions:

Heat a large pan with the olive oil over medium high heat, add shallot, stir and cook for 3 minutes. Add garlic, salt, pepper, wine, crushed tomatoes, chorizo and red pepper flakes and cook for another 15 minutes. Add mussels, cover the pan and boil for another 10 minutes. Add parsley at the end, stir and serve.

**Nutrition:** calories 210, fat 2, fiber 3, carbs 5, protein 6

# Scallop, Quinoa and Peas Salad

*Prep Time:* 15 minutes | *Cook Time:* 35 minutes | *Servings:* 6

## Ingredients:

- 12 ounces dry sea scallops
- 4 tablespoons olive oil + 2 teaspoons
- 4 teaspoons soy sauce
- 1 ½ cup quinoa, rinsed
- 2 teaspoons garlic, minced
- A pinch of salt
- 3 cups water
- 1 cup snow peas, sliced
- 1 teaspoon sesame oil
- 1/3 cup rice vinegar
- 1 cup scallions, sliced
- 1/3 cup red bell pepper, chopped
- ¼ cup cilantro, chopped

## Directions:

In a bowl, mix scallops with 2 teaspoons soy sauce and toss. Heat a pan with 1 tablespoon olive oil over medium heat, add quinoa and garlic, stir and cook for 8 minutes. Add water and a pinch of salt, bring to a boil, stir, cover and cook for 15 minutes. Add snow peas, cover and leave for 5 more minutes. In a bowl, mix 3 tablespoons olive oil with 2 teaspoons soy sauce, quinoa, snow peas, scallions, bell pepper and vinegar and sesame oil and whisk well. Heat another pan with 2 teaspoons olive oil over medium high heat, add scallops and cook for 1 minute on each side. Add scallops to quinoa salad, stir gently and serve with chopped cilantro on top.

**Nutrition:** calories 201, fat 5, fiber 2, carbs 5, protein 8

# Kale, Beets and Salmon Mix

*Prep Time:* 7 minutes | *Cook Time:* 18 minutes | *Servings:* 4

## Ingredients:

- 2/3 cup cider vinegar+ 2 tablespoons
- ½ cup water
- 1 cup red onion, sliced
- 1 tablespoon honey
- 4 golden beets, trimmed
- 2 tablespoons olive oil
- Salt and black pepper to taste
- 1 teaspoon, mustard
- 4 cups curly kale,
- 10 ounces canned salmon, skinless, boneless and drained
- ¼ cup almonds, toasted

## Directions:

In a small pan, mix 2/3 cup vinegar with ½ cup water, onion and 2 teaspoons honey, stir, bring to a boil over medium heat, cook for 1-2 minutes, leave aside for 10 minutes and drain. Wrap beets in parchment paper, place in the microwave for 7 minutes, peel, cut into wedges and leave aside. In a bowl, mix 2 tablespoons vinegar with 1 teaspoon honey, oil, mustard, salt and pepper to taste and whisk well. Add kale and beets, stir gently, divide between plates, top each serving with salmon, almonds and onion and serve.

**Nutrition:** calories 242, fat 3, fiber 1, carbs 4, protein

# Shrimp, Spinach and Radish Salad

*Prep Time: 1 hour and 10 minutes | Cook Time: 0 minutes | Servings: 4*

## Ingredients:

- 4 cups shrimp, cooked, peeled, deveined and chopped
- 5 tablespoons rice vinegar
- 2 tablespoons garlic chili sauce
- 1 and ½ tablespoons olive oil
- 1 tablespoon lime rind, rind
- ¼ cup lime juice
- ½ teaspoon paprika
- ½ teaspoon cumin, ground
- 2 garlic cloves, minced
- A pinch of salt
- 4 cups baby spinach
- 1 cup radishes, sliced
- 1 cup mango, peeled and chopped
- ½ cup green onions, chopped
- 2 tablespoon pumpkin seeds
- ¼ cup avocado, pitted, peeled and sliced

## Directions:

In a large bowl, mix the shrimp with the vinegar, garlic sauce and the other ingredients, toss and keep in the fridge for 1 hour before serving.

**Nutrition:** calories 194, fat 3, fiber 2, carbs 4, protein 4

# Squid Salad

*Prep Time: 10 minutes | Cook Time: 15 minutes | Servings: 4*

## Ingredients:

- ounces squid, cut into medium pieces
- ounces shrimp, peeled and deveined
- 1 red onion, sliced
- 1 cucumber, chopped
- 2 tomatoes, cut into medium wedges
- 2 tablespoons
- cilantro, chopped
- 1 hot jalapeno pepper, cut in rounds
- 3 tablespoons rice vinegar
- 3 tablespoons olive oil
- 1 teaspoon salt
- ¼ teaspoon pepper

## Directions:

In a bowl, mix onion with cucumber, tomatoes, pepper, cilantro, shrimp and squid, toss, divide this on parchment paper, fold, seal edges, place on a baking sheet and place in the oven at 400 degrees F for 15 minutes. In a small bowl mix olive oil with vinegar, salt and pepper and whisk very well. Unwrap parchment papers, divide seafood mix between plates, drizzle the dressing all over and serve.

**Nutrition:** calories 210, fat 2, fiber 3, carbs 5, protein 6

# Seafood and Greens Salad

*Prep Time: 2 hours | Cook Time: 1 hour and 30 minutes | Servings: 4*

## Ingredients:

- 1 large octopus, cleaned and head on
- 1 pound mussels
- 2 pounds clams
- 1 big squid, cut into rings
- 3 garlic cloves, minced
- 1 celery stalk, cut crosswise into thirds
- ½ cup celery stalk, sliced
- 1 carrot, cut crosswise into 3 pieces
- 1 small white onion, chopped
- 1 bay leaf
- ¾ cup white wine
- 2 cups radicchio, sliced
- 1 red onion, sliced
- 1 cup parsley, chopped
- 1 cup olive oil
- 1 cup red wine vinegar
- Salt and black pepper to taste

## Directions:

Place the octopus in a large pot with celery cut in thirds, garlic, carrot, bay leaf, white onion, water to cover and white wine, bring to a boil over high heat, reduce to medium-low, cook for 1 hour and 30 minutes, drain, reserve cooking liquid, slice into small pieces and leave it aside. Put ¼ cup octopus cooking liquid in another pot, add mussels, cook over medium heat until they open, transfer to a bowl and leave aside. Add clams to this pan, cover, cook over medium high heat until they open as well, transfer to the bowl with mussels and leave aside. Add squid to the pan, cover and cook over medium high heat for 3 minutes, transfer to the bowl with mussels and clams. Add the octopus, sliced celery, radicchio, red onion, vinegar, olive oil, parsley, salt and pepper, stir gently and leave aside for 2 hours. Serve.

**Nutrition:** calories 210, fat 3, fiber 3, carbs 6, protein 8

# Shrimp and Olives

*Prep Time: 5 minutes | Cook Time: 10 minutes | Servings: 4*

## Ingredients:

- 1 pound large shrimp, peeled and deveined
- A drizzle of olive oil
- 4 egg yolks
- 1/3 cup lemon juice
- 1 cup chicken stock
- A pinch of salt and black pepper
- 1 cup mixed olives, pitted and chopped
- 2 teaspoons thyme leaves, chopped

## Directions:

In a bowl, mix the egg yolks with the lemon juice and whisk well. Heat a pan with oil over medium heat, add the shrimp, cook them for 2 minutes on each side and transfer to a plate. Heat up the same pan over medium heat, add the stock and simmer for 2 minutes. Mix ½ cup of stock with the egg yolks mix, whisk well, pour into the pan, whisk, return the shrimp to the pan as well, also add olives and thyme, toss, cook for 2 more minutes, divide into bowls and serve.

**Nutrition:** calories 228, fat 14, fiber 5, carbs 15, protein 4

# Shrimp and Lettuce Salad

*Prep Time:* 25 minutes | *Cook Time:* 15 minutes | *Servings:* 4

## Ingredients:

- ¾ pound shrimp, peeled and deveined
- ½ pounds sea scallops, halved
- 1 celery stalk, quartered
- 2 celery stalks, sliced
- 3 garlic cloves, minced
- Salt and black pepper to taste
- Juice of 1 lemon
- 4 ounces baby

- carrots cut in halves
- 1 small avocado, peeled, pitted and chopped
- 2 romaine lettuces, shredded
- 1 tablespoon capers
- 1 tablespoon capers brine
- 1 tablespoon mayonnaise
- cups water

## Directions:

In a large pan, mix 1 celery stalk, 2 garlic cloves, 10 cups water, salt and pepper to taste and half of the lemon juice, whisk, bring to a boil, simmer over medium-high heat for 2 minutes, add the shrimp, cook for 4 minutes and transfer both the shrimp and carrots to a bowl Bring the water to a boil again over medium heat, add scallops, cook for 2 minutes, rinse with cold water and also leave aside. In a bowl, mix half of the avocado with chopped celery, lettuce, capers, scallops, shrimp and carrots and toss.. In a blender, mix remaining avocado with some of the cooking liquid, the rest of the lemon juice, caper brine, mayo, remaining garlic, salt and pepper to taste and blend again. Add this dressing to your seafood salad, toss and serve right away.

**Nutrition:** calories 214, fat 3, fiber 3, carbs 6, protein 4

# Citrus Squid Salad

*Prep Time:* 1 hour | *Cook Time:* 15 minutes | *Servings:* 8

## Ingredients:

- 1 pound baby squid, washed, body and tentacles chopped
- ½ teaspoon lemon zest, grated
- ½ teaspoon orange zest, grated
- ½ teaspoon lime zest, grated
- 1 cup olive oil
- 1 ¼ teaspoon red pepper flakes, crushed
- 2 cups parsley, chopped
- 2 anchovy fillets
- 4 garlic cloves,

- minced
- 1 shallot, chopped
- 2 tablespoons capers
- 2 tablespoons red wine vinegar
- Salt and black pepper to taste
- 2 tablespoons lemon juice
- 4 ounces baby arugula
- 3 cups cantaloupe, cubed
- 2 celery ribs, sliced
- 1 red-hot chili pepper, sliced

## Directions:

In a bowl, mix squid pieces with grated lemon zest, lime zest, orange zest, 1 teaspoon red pepper flakes and ¼ cup oil, toss and keep in the fridge for 1 hour. Meanwhile, in another bowl mix parsley with garlic, ¼ teaspoon pepper flakes, vinegar, anchovies, capers, shallots and ½ cup olive oil and whisk well. Place squid pieces on your preheated grill pan over medium high heat, season with some salt and cook for 5 minutes. Transfer squid to a bowl, add half of the dressing, and toss. In another bowl, mix ¼ cup olive oil with the lemon juice, salt, arugula, celery, chili pepper, lemon and toss. Divide the squid and arugula and divide between plates. Top with remaining salad dressing and serve right away!

**Nutrition:** calories 253, fat 3, fiber 1, carbs 5, protein 3

# Leeks and Salmon Soup

*Prep Time:* 15 minutes | *Cook Time:* 15 minutes | *Servings:* 6

## Ingredients:

- 2 tablespoon butter
- 1 leek, chopped
- 1 red onion, chopped
- Salt and white pepper to taste
- 3 potatoes, peeled and cubed
- 2 carrots, chopped
- 4 cups fish stock
- 4 ounces salmon skinless cut in cubes
- ½ cup heavy cream
- 1 tablespoon dill weed, chopped

## Directions:

Heat a pan with the butter over medium heat, add leek and onion, stir and cook for 7 minutes. Add salt and pepper, add carrots, potatoes and stock, stir, bring to a boil and cook for 8 more minutes. Add salmon, cream and dill, boil for 6 more minutes, divide into bowls and serve.

**Nutrition:** calories 132, fat 3, fiber 4, carbs 5, protein 5

## Duck and Sauce

*Prep Time:* 10 minutes  |  *Cook Time:* 4 hours and 50 minutes  |
*Servings:* 4

### Ingredients:

- 1 medium duck
- 1 celery stalk, chopped
- 2 yellow onions, chopped
- 2 teaspoons thyme, dried
- 8 garlic cloves,

*For the sauce:*

- 1 tablespoon tomato paste
- 1 yellow onion, chopped
- ½ teaspoon sugar
- ½ cup white wine
- 3 cups water

- minced
- 2 bay leaves
- ¼ cup parsley, chopped
- A pinch of salt and black pepper
- 1 teaspoon herbs de Provence

- 1 cup chicken stock
- 1 and ½ cups black olives, pitted and chopped
- ¼ teaspoon herbs de Provence

### Directions:

In a baking dish, arrange the duck, thyme, parsley, garlic, 2 onions, salt, pepper and 1 teaspoon herbs de Provence, toss and bake at 475 degrees F for 10 minutes. Cover the dish, reduce heat to 275 degrees F and roast duck for 3 hours and 30 minutes. Heat up a pan over medium heat, add 1 yellow onion, stir and cook for 10 minutes. Add tomato paste, stock, and the other ingredients, cover, reduce heat to low and cook for 1 hour. Transfer duck to a surface, carve, discard bones, divide between plates, drizzle the sauce on top and serve.

**Nutrition:** calories 254, fat 3, fiber 3, carbs 8, protein 13

## Cinnamon Duck and Sauce

*Prep Time:* 10 minutes  |  *Cook Time:* 20 minutes  |  *Servings:* 4

### Ingredients:

- 4 duck breasts, boneless
- Salt and black pepper to taste
- ¼ teaspoon cinnamon, ground
- ¼ teaspoon coriander, ground
- 5 tablespoons apricot preserves
- 3 tablespoons chives, chopped

- 2 tablespoons parsley, chopped
- A drizzle of olive oil
- 3 tablespoons apple cider vinegar
- 2 tablespoons red onions, chopped
- 1 cup apricots, chopped
- ¾ cup blackberries
- 

### Directions:

Season duck breasts with salt, pepper, coriander and cinnamon, place them on preheated grill pan over medium high heat, cook for 2 minutes, flip them, cook for 3 minutes more, flip again, brush with 3 tablespoons apricot preserves, cook for 1 more minute, transfer to a cutting board, cool down a bit and slice. Heat a pan over medium heat, add vinegar, onion and the remaining ingredients, stir and cook for 3 minutes. Divide sliced duck breasts between plates and serve with apricot sauce drizzled on top.

**Nutrition:** calories 275, fat 4, fiber 4, carbs 7, protein 12

# Duck and Orange Salad

*Prep Time:* 10 minutes | *Cook Time:* 20 minutes | *Servings:* 4

## Ingredients:

- 3 tablespoons white wine vinegar
- 2 tablespoons sugar
- 2 oranges, peeled and cut into segments
- 1 teaspoon orange zest, grated
- 1 tablespoons lemon juice
- 1 teaspoon lemon zest, grated
- 3 tablespoons shallot, minced
- 2 tablespoons canola oil
- Salt and black pepper to taste
- 2 duck breasts, boneless but skin on, cut into 4 pieces
- 1 head of frisee, torn
- 2 small lettuce heads washed, torn into small pieces
- 2 tablespoons chives, chopped

## Directions:

Heat a small saucepan with the oil over medium high heat, add vinegar and sugar, stir and boil for 5 minutes and take off heat. Add orange zest, shallot, salt, pepper, lemon zest and lemon juice, stir and leave aside. Pat dry duck pieces, score skin, trim and season with salt and pepper. Heat a pan over medium high heat for 1 minute, arrange duck breast pieces skin side down, brown for 8 minutes, reduce heat to medium, cook for 4 more minutes, flip the pieces, cook for 3 minutes more, transfer to a cutting board, cool down and slice. Put frisee and lettuce in a bowl, add duck slices, orange, chives and drizzle the vinaigrette on top.

**Nutrition:** calories 320, fat 4, fiber 4, carbs 6, protein 14

# Duck, Veggies and Orange Sauce

*Prep Time:* 10 minutes | *Cook Time:* 5 hours | *Servings:* 6

## Ingredients:

- 2 medium ducks, fat trimmed
- 1 tablespoon olive oil
- 1 cup water
- 2 tomatoes, chopped
- 2 carrots, chopped
- 2 celery stalks, chopped
- 1 leek, chopped
- 2 garlic cloves, minced
- 1 yellow onion, chopped
- 2 bay leaves
- 3 tablespoons white flour
- 1 teaspoon thyme, dried
- 2 tablespoons tomato paste
- 1-quart chicken stock
- Juice of 2 oranges
- 3 oranges, peeled and cut into segments
- 1/3 cup sugar
- 2 tablespoons currant jelly
- 1/3 cup cider vinegar
- 2 tablespoons cold butter

## Directions:

Pierce the duck skin, season all over with salt and pepper. Arrange them in a roasting pan, add the water, bake in the oven at 450 degrees F for 20 minutes, reduce heat to 350 degrees F, flip the ducks, cook for 30 minutes more, flip them again, cook for another 30 minutes, flip once more and cook for another 40 minutes. Meanwhile, heat a pan with the oil over high heat, add carrots, celery, leek, tomatoes, garlic, onion, thyme and bay leaves, stir and cook for 10 minutes. Add tomato paste, flour, the wine and the stock gradually, bring to a boil, reduce heat to medium low, simmer for 50 minutes, take off heat and strain the sauce into a bowl. Heat a small pan over medium high heat, add vinegar and sugar, stir and cook for 4 minutes. Add orange juice, currant jelly, strained sauce, salt and pepper, stir and cook for 8 minutes. Add butter gradually and stir well again. Take ducks out of the oven again, place them under preheated broiler and broil them for 3 minutes. Transfer ducks to a platter. Heat up juices from the pan in a saucepan over medium heat, take off heat and strain them into a bowl. Add this to orange sauce and stir. Arrange the orange segments next to the ducks, and serve with orange sauce on top.

**Nutrition:** calories 342, fat 13, fiber 4, carbs 17, protein 12

# Duck and Berries

*Prep Time: 10 minutes | Cook Time: 25 minutes | Servings: 4*

## Ingredients:

- 4 duck breasts
- 2 tablespoons balsamic vinegar
- 3 tablespoons sugar
- Salt and black pepper to taste
- 1 ½ cups water
- 4 ounces blackberries
- ¼ cup chicken stock
- 1 tablespoon butter
- 2 teaspoons corn flour

## Directions:

Pat dry duck breasts with paper towels, score the skin, season with salt and pepper to taste, and set aside for 30 minutes. Put breasts skin side down in a pan, heat over medium heat, cook for 8 minutes, flip, cook for 1 more minute, transfer to a baking dish and bake at 425 degrees F for 15 minutes. Take the meat out of the oven, cool down for 10 minutes, slice and leave aside for now. Meanwhile, put sugar in a pan, heat over medium heat, and melt it, stirring all the time. Take pan off heat, add the water, stock, balsamic vinegar and the blackberries. Heat this mix to medium temperature, cook until sauce is reduced to half, transfer it to another pan, add corn flour and water, heat up for another 4 minutes and take off the heat. Add salt and pepper, the butter and whisk really well. Slice the duck breasts, divide between plates and serve with the berries sauce on top.

**Nutrition:** calories 320, fat 15, fiber 5, carbs 16, protein 11

# Rosemary Duck and Wine Sauce

*Prep Time: 10 minutes | Cook Time: 1 hour and 30 minutes | Servings: 4*

## Ingredients:

- 4 duck legs, trimmed
- Salt and black pepper
- 1 teaspoon olive oil
- 2 shallots, chopped
- 1 carrot, chopped
- 1 and ½ cups red wine
- 2 teaspoons tomato paste
- ½ cup chicken stock
- 2 tablespoons sugar
- 1 tablespoon balsamic vinegar
- 1 teaspoon rosemary, dried

## Directions:

Heat a pan with the oil over medium-high heat, add the meat, salt and pepper, brown for 5 minutes and transfer to a plate. Heat up the same pan over medium heat, add the shallots and carrots, stir and cook for 2 minutes. Add the rest of the ingredients, stir and cook for another 5 minutes. Return the duck legs, toss, cook everything for 1 hour and 30 over medium-low heat stirring often, divide everything between plates and serve.

**Nutrition:** calories 257, fat 14, fiber 6, carbs 14, protein 8

# Parsley Duck Mix

*Prep Time: 10 minutes | Cook Time: 5 hours | Servings: 4*

## Ingredients:

- 1 duck, cut into pieces
- 2 yellow onions, chopped
- 1 celery rib, chopped
- 6 garlic cloves, minced
- 1 and ½ tablespoons thyme, chopped
- ¼ cup parsley, chopped
- A pinch of salt and black pepper
- ½ cup white wine
- ½ teaspoon sugar
- 1 cup chicken stock
- 1 and ½ cups black olives, pitted and sliced
- ¼ teaspoon Italian seasoning

## Directions:

In your slow cooker, mix the duck with the onions, celery and the other ingredients, toss and cook on High for 5 hours. Divide the duck pieces and the cooking juices between plates and serve.

**Nutrition:** calories 320, fat 14, fiber 4, carbs 15, protein 11

# Black Tea Turkey Mix

*Prep Time:* 10 minutes | *Cook Time:* 2 hours and 20 minutes | *Servings:* 8

## Ingredients:

- 1 cup hot water
- 12 black tea bags
- 2/3 cup brown sugar
- 2 tablespoons butter
- ½ cup cranberry sauce
- 1 large turkey
- 1 onion, cut into 4 wedges
- 1 lemon, cut into 4 wedges
- 2 tablespoons cornstarch
- 1 cup chicken stock
- Salt and black pepper to taste

## Directions:

Put the hot water in a bowl, add tea bags, leave aside covered for 5 minutes and discard bags. Heat a pan with the butter over medium high heat, add sugar, tea and cranberry, stir and cook for 15 minutes. Stuff turkey with lemon and onion pieces, place it in a roasting pan, brush it with the tea glaze and bake at 350 degrees F for 2 hours, flipping and basting the turkey with the glaze every 20 minutes. Put chicken stock in a saucepan, heat up over medium heat, add cornstarch, salt and pepper, cook for 1-2 minutes and take off the heat. Carve turkey and divide it between plates. Strain gravy and drizzle it over your turkey.

**Nutrition:** calories 500, fat 13, fiber 1, carbs 20, protein 7

# Herbed Turkey Mix

*Prep Time:* 30 minutes | *Cook Time:* 4 hours | *Servings:* 10

## Ingredients:

- 1 whole turkey, neck and giblets removed
- Zest and juice from 1 lemon
- ½ cup butter
- ½ shallot, chopped
- 2 sage leaves
- 1 tablespoon rosemary, dried
- 2 tablespoon thyme, chopped
- 1 garlic clove, minced
- 1 yellow onion, roughly chopped
- 2 carrots, roughly chopped
- 2 celery stalks, chopped
- 1 cup dry white wine
- 1 cup chicken stock
- ¼ cup whole wheat flour

## Directions:

In a food processor, mix the lemon zest, lemon juice, butter, shallot, sage, thyme, rosemary and garlic and pulse. Lift skin from turkey breast without detaching it, rub it with 3 tablespoons of the herb butter under the skin, secure with toothpicks, season the cavity and turkey with salt and pepper, put in a baking dish, add onions, celery and carrots, tie ends of turkey legs together, rub with the rest of the butter, add stock and wine as well, bake at 425 degrees F for 30 minutes, reduce heat to 325 F and bake for another 2 hours and 30 minutes. Transfer to a platter, pour veggie drippings through a strainer and reserve 2 ½ cups of drippings. Heat a pan with the reserved chilled herb butter over medium heat, add flour, stir well and cook for 2 minutes. Add reserved pan drippings, bring to a boil, reduce the temperature and cook for 5 minutes stirring occasionally. Cut turkey and serve with the gravy you've just prepared.

**Nutrition:** calories 287, fat 4, fiber 7, carbs 9, protein 12

## Cheesy Chicken

*Prep Time:* 10 minutes | *Cook Time:* 15 minutes | *Servings:* 6

### Ingredients:

- ¼ cup breadcrumbs
- ¼ teaspoon garlic powder
- ½ cup pecorino cheese, grated
- 1 teaspoon basil, dried
- 3 tablespoons olive oil
- A pinch of salt and black pepper
- 6 chicken breast halves, skinless and boneless

### Directions:

In a bowl, mix breadcrumbs with garlic powder, cheese, basil, salt and pepper and stir. Rub chicken with half of the oil and dip in breadcrumbs. Heat a pan with remaining oil over medium high heat, add the meat, cook for 7 minutes, flip, cook for 8 minutes more, divide between plates and serve. with a side salad.

**Nutrition:** calories 212, fat 2, fiber 1, carbs 3, protein 18

## Chicken and Wine Sauce

*Prep Time:* 10 minutes | *Cook Time:* 40 minutes | *Servings:* 6

### Ingredients:

- 6 chicken breast halves, skinless and boneless
- 2 teaspoons olive oil
- ½ cup white wine+ 2 tablespoons
- 1 tablespoon basil, chopped
- 2 teaspoons thyme, chopped
- ½ cup yellow onion, chopped
- 3 garlic cloves, minced
- ½ cup kalamata olives, pitted and sliced
- ¼ cup parsley, chopped
- 3 cups tomatoes, chopped

### Directions:

Heat a pan with the oil and 2 tablespoons wine over medium heat, add chicken, cook for 6 minutes on each side and transfer to a plate. Heat the same pan over medium heat, add garlic and onion, stir and cook for 5 minutes. Add tomatoes, remaining wine and the other ingredients except the parsley, stir, bring to a simmer and cook for 15 minutes. Add chicken, stir, cover pan and cook for 10 minutes more. Add parsley, stir, divide between plates and serve.

**Nutrition:** calories 221, fat 2, fiber 4, carbs 7, protein 19

## Chicken with Potatoes

*Prep Time:* 10 minutes | *Cook Time:* 50 minutes | *Servings:* 4

### Ingredients:

- 1 tablespoon olive oil
- 4 teaspoons garlic, minced
- A pinch of salt and black pepper
- ¼ teaspoon thyme, dried
- 12 small red potatoes, halved
- Olive oil cooking spray
- 2 pounds chicken breast, skinless, boneless and cubed
- 1 cup red onion, sliced
- ¾ cup white wine
- ¾ cup chicken stock
- ½ cup pepperoncini peppers, chopped
- 2 cups tomato, chopped
- ¼ cup kalamata olives, pitted and halved
- 2 tablespoons basil, chopped
- 14 ounces canned artichokes, chopped
- ½ cup parmesan, grated

### Directions:

In a baking dish, mix potatoes with 2 teaspoons garlic, olive oil, thyme, salt and pepper, toss and cook at 400 degrees F for 30 minutes. Heat a saucepan with cooking spray over medium high heat, add chicken, salt and black pepper, cook for 5 minutes on each side and transfer to a plate. Heat the saucepan again over medium heat, add onion, stir and cook for 5 minutes. Add wine, stir and cook for 2 minutes. Add stock, return chicken, add olives, pepperoncini, potatoes and the rest of the ingredients except the cheese, stir and cook for 6 more minutes. Divide between plates and serve with cheese sprinkled on top.

**Nutrition:** calories 271, fat 2, fiber 3, carbs 10, protein 17

# Chicken with Mushrooms and Tomatoes

*Prep Time: 10 minutes | Cook Time: 25 minutes | Servings: 4*

## Ingredients:

- 8 chicken breast halves, skinless and boneless
- 6 tablespoons olive oil
- 1 and ½ pounds oyster mushrooms
- 1 and ½ cups chicken stock
- A pinch of salt and black pepper
- 3 plum tomatoes, chopped
- 2/3 cup kalamata olives, pitted and sliced
- 1 tablespoon shallot, chopped
- 3 garlic cloves, minced
- 1 tablespoon capers
- 2 tablespoons butter
- 1 cup cherry tomatoes, red and yellow
- 3 tablespoons pine nuts
- 3 tablespoons parsley, chopped

## Directions:

Heat a pan with 3 tablespoons oil over medium high heat, add chicken, salt and pepper, cook for 3 minutes on each side and transfer to a plate. Add the remaining oil, heat over medium high heat, add mushrooms, stir and cook for 3 minutes. Add stock, tomatoes, shallots, garlic, olives and capers, stir and cook for 12 minutes more. Add a pinch of salt and black pepper, also add butter and cherry tomatoes, stir and cook for a few minutes more. Divide chicken on plates, add mushroom mix on the side, sprinkle parsley and pine nuts on top and serve.

**Nutrition:** calories 241, fat 4, fiber 5, carbs 6, protein 16

# Garlic Chicken

*Prep Time: 8 hours and 10 minutes | Cook Time: 30 minutes | Servings: 8*

## Ingredients:

- 1 whole chicken, cut into medium pieces
- A pinch of salt and black pepper
- ½ cup olive oil
- 1 tablespoon rosemary, chopped
- 3 garlic cloves, minced
- 1 tablespoon thyme, chopped
- 1 tablespoon oregano, chopped
- Juice from 2 lemons

## Directions:

In a bowl, mix the chicken with the oil with salt, pepper, garlic, rosemary, thyme, oregano and lemon juice, toss and keep in the fridge for 8 hours. Place chicken pieces on preheated grill pan over medium heat, cook for 15 minutes on each side, divide between plates and serve with a side salad.

**Nutrition:** calories 287, fat 3, fiber 1, carbs 4, protein 20

# Mustard Chicken

*Prep Time: 2 hours and 10 minutes | Cook Time: 30 minutes | Servings: 5*

## Ingredients:

- 1 and ½ pounds chicken breast, skinless and boneless
- ½ cup olive oil
- 1 tablespoon mustard
- ¼ cup red wine vinegar
- 2 garlic cloves, minced
- ½ teaspoon basil, dried
- ½ teaspoon oregano, dried
- ½ teaspoon onion powder
- A pinch of salt and black pepper
- 1 red onion, sliced
- 1-pint cherry tomatoes, halved
- Feta cheese, crumbled for serving
- Black olives, pitted and sliced for serving

## Directions:

In a bowl, mix the oil with vinegar, mustard, oregano, basil, garlic, salt, pepper and onion powder, whisk well, mix the chicken with half of this, cover and leave aside for 1 hour. In another bowl, mix onion and tomatoes with the rest of the marinade, toss and keep in the fridge for 1 more hour. Combine veggies and chicken in a baking dish, toss them gently, bake in the oven at 375 degrees F for 30 minutes, divide between plates and serve with the cheese and olives on top.

**Nutrition:** calories 300, fat 4, fiber 2, carbs 7, protein 30

# Chicken with Salad and Sauce

*Prep Time: 20 minutes | Cook Time: 10 minutes | Servings: 4*

## Ingredients:

*For the chicken:*

- ¼ cup olive oil
- 2 pounds chicken breasts, skinless and boneless
- 3 tablespoons garlic, minced
- 1/3 cup lemon juice
- 1 tablespoon oregano, dried
- 1 tablespoon red wine vinegar
- 1/3 cup Greek yogurt

*For the salad:*

- 2 cucumbers, sliced
- 2 tablespoons olive oil
- 1/3 cup lemon juice
- 1 tablespoon red wine vinegar
- ½ teaspoon oregano, dried
- ½ tablespoon garlic, minced

*For the sauce:*

- 1 tablespoon garlic, minced
- 1 cucumber, chopped
- 1 cup Greek yogurt
- ½ tablespoon dill, chopped
- ½ teaspoon mint, chopped
- 1 teaspoon lemon zest, grated
- 1 tablespoon lemon juice

*For serving:*

- ½ cup red onion, sliced
- 1 and ½ pounds cherry tomatoes, halved
- 3 cups brown rice, already cooked

## Directions:

In a bowl, mix chicken with 3 tablespoons garlic, 1/3 cup lemon juice, 1 tablespoon vinegar, 1 tablespoon oregano, 1/3 cup Greek yogurt, salt and pepper and ½ cup oil, toss really well, cover and keep in the fridge for 20 minutes. Heat a pan with ½ cup oil over medium high heat, add the meat, cook for 4 minutes on each side, transfer to a plate and keep warm for now. In a salad bowl, mix 2 cucumbers with 2 tablespoons oil, 1 tablespoon vinegar, 1/3 cup lemon juice, ½ teaspoon oregano and ½ teaspoon garlic and toss well. In a small bowl, mix 1 cucumber with 1 tablespoon garlic, ½ tablespoon dill, ½ teaspoon mint, 1 tablespoon lemon juice, 1 teaspoon lemon zest and 1 cup yogurt and whisk well. Divide brown rice into bowls, add onions, tomatoes, the salad on the side, the chicken on top and drizzle the cucumber sauce all over.

**Nutrition:** calories 298, fat 4, fiber 5, carbs 7, protein 18

# Chicken with Peppers and Potatoes

*Prep Time: 10 minutes | Cook Time: 1 hour | Servings: 8*

## Ingredients:

- 3 pounds potatoes, peeled and roughly chopped
- 2 green bell peppers, chopped
- 1 yellow onion, chopped
- 4 garlic cloves, minced
- ½ cup black olives, pitted and sliced
- 14 ounces canned tomatoes, chopped
- 16 chicken drumsticks, skinless
- 1 tablespoon mixed herbs, dried
- 3 ounces feta cheese, crumbled
- ½ cup parsley, chopped

## Directions:

Put potatoes in a large saucepan, add water to cover, bring to a boil over medium heat, cook for a couple of minutes, drain and transfer to a large roasting pan. Add the bell pepper and the other ingredients except the cheese, place in the oven at 400 degrees F and roast for 1 hour. Divide on plates, sprinkle feta on top and serve.

**Nutrition:** calories 298, fat 3, fiber 3, carbs 7, protein 16

# Chicken and Onion and Mustard Sauce

*Prep Time: 10 minutes | Cook Time: 30 minutes | Servings: 4*

## Ingredients:

- 8 bacon strips, cooked and chopped
- 1/3 cup mustard
- 1 cup yellow onion, chopped
- 1 tablespoon olive oil
- 1 and ½ cups chicken stock
- 4 chicken breasts, skinless and boneless
- ¼ teaspoon sweet paprika

## Directions:

In a bowl, mix the chicken with paprika with mustard, salt and pepper and stir well. Heat the a pan with the oil over medium high heat, add chicken breasts, cook for 2 minutes on each side and also transfer to a plate. Heat the pan once again over medium high heat, add stock, bacon, onions, salt and pepper, stir and bring to a simmer. Return chicken to pan as well, stir gently and simmer over medium heat for 20 minutes, turning meat halfway. Divide chicken on plates, drizzle the sauce over it and serve.

**Nutrition:** calories 223, fat 8, fiber 1, carbs 3, protein 26

# Chicken with Sausage and Mushrooms Mix

*Prep Time: 10 minutes | Cook Time: 1 hour | Servings: 6*

## Ingredients:

- 8 ounces mushrooms, chopped
- 1 pound Italian sausage, chopped
- 2 tablespoons avocado oil
- 6 cherry peppers, chopped
- 1 red bell pepper, chopped
- 1 red onion, sliced
- 2 tablespoons garlic, minced
- 2 cups cherry tomatoes, halved
- 4 chicken thighs
- Salt and black pepper to taste
- ½ cup chicken stock
- 1 tablespoon balsamic vinegar
- 2 teaspoons oregano, dried
- Some chopped parsley for serving

## Directions:

Heat a pan with half of the oil over medium heat, add sausages, stir, brown for a few minutes and transfer to a plate. Heat the pan again with remaining oil over medium heat, add chicken thighs, salt and pepper, cook for 3 minutes on each side and transfer to a plate. Heat the pan again over medium heat, add garlic, cherry peppers, mushrooms, onion and bell pepper, stir and cook for 4 minutes. Add stock, vinegar, salt, pepper, oregano, cherry tomatoes, chicken and sausage, stir and bake everything at 400 degrees F for 30 minutes. Sprinkle parsley, divide between plates and serve.

**Nutrition:** calories 340, fat 33, fiber 3, carbs 4, protein 20

# Chicken and Peppers Mix

*Prep Time: 10 minutes* | *Cook Time: 20 minutes* | *Servings: 4*

## Ingredients:

- 4 teaspoons pine nuts, toasted
- 1 pound chicken breasts, skinless, boneless
- 2 tablespoons white flour
- Cooking spray
- ¼ cup shallots, chopped
- ¼ cup roasted peppers, chopped
- 2 tablespoons capers, chopped
- 2 tablespoons black olives, pitted and sliced
- 1 cup orange juice
- 1 tablespoon lemon juice
- 1 cup chicken stock
- A pinch of salt and black pepper
- 2 tablespoons parsley, chopped

## Directions:

Pound chicken breasts into ½-inch thick pieces, add salt and pepper, dredge them in flour. Heat a pan over medium-high heat and grease with cooking spray. Add the chicken, cook for 2 minutes on each side and transfer to a plate. Heat up the same pan over medium heat, add the shallots and the rest of the ingredients except the parsley, stir and sauté for 5 minutes. Return the chicken to the pan, cook everything for 8 minutes more, divide between plates, sprinkle the parsley on top and serve.

**Nutrition:** calories 223, fat 10, fiber 5, carbs 15, protein 8

# Chicken and Pineapple Platter

*Prep Time: 10 minutes* | *Cook Time: 10 minutes* | *Servings: 4*

## Ingredients:

- 20 ounces canned pineapple slices
- A drizzle of olive oil
- 3 cups chicken thighs, boneless,
- skinless and cut into medium pieces
- 1 tablespoon smoked paprika

## Directions:

Heat a pan over medium high heat, add pineapple slices, cook them for a few minutes on each side, transfer to a cutting board, cool them down and cut into medium cubes. Heat another pan with a drizzle of oil over medium high heat, rub chicken pieces with paprika, add them to the pan, cook for 5 minutes on each side, arrange it on a platter, top with the pineapple and serve.

**Nutrition:** calories 120, fat 3, fiber 1, carbs 5, protein 2

# Orange Chicken Salad

*Prep Time: 10 minutes* | *Cook Time: 30 minutes* | *Servings: 4*

## Ingredients:

- 1 whole chicken, chopped
- 4 scallions, chopped
- 2 celery stalks, chopped
- 1 cup mandarin orange, chopped
- ¼ cup homemade mayo
- ½ cup yogurts
- 1 cup cashews, toasted and chopped
- A pinch of salt and black pepper

## Directions:

Put chicken pieces in a pot, add water to cover, add a pinch of salt, bring to a boil over medium heat, cook for 25 minutes, transfer to a cutting borad, cool down, discard bones, shred and transfer to a bowl. Add the rest of the ingredients, toss to coat well and keep in the fridge until you serve it.

**Nutrition:** calories 150, fat 3, fiber 3, carbs 7, protein 6

# Chicken with Chili Peppers

*Prep Time:* *10 minutes* | *Cook Time:* *1 hour and 10 minutes* | *Servings: 6*

## Ingredients:

- 1 cup white flour
- Salt and black pepper to taste
- 4 pounds chicken breast, skinless, boneless and cubed
- 4 ounces olive oil
- 4 ounces celery, chopped
- 1 tablespoon garlic, minced
- 8 ounces onion, chopped
- 5 ounces red bell pepper, chopped
- 7 ounces poblano pepper, chopped
- ¼ teaspoon cumin, ground
- 2 cups corn
- A pinch of cayenne pepper
- 1-quart chicken stock
- 1 teaspoon chili powder
- 16 ounces canned beans, drained
- ¼ cup cilantro, chopped

## Directions:

Dredge chicken pieces in flour. Heat a pan with the oil over medium high heat, add chicken, cook for 5 minutes on each side, transfer to a bowl and leave aside. Heat the pan again over medium high heat, add onion, celery, the chicken and the rest of the ingredients except the cilantro, stir and cook for 5 minutes more. Bring to a simmer, reduce heat to medium low, cover and cook for 1 hour. Add cilantro, stir, divide into bowls and serve.

**Nutrition:** calories 345, fat 12, fiber 3, carbs 9, protein 4

# Chicken, Apple and Cucumber Sandwich

*Prep Time:* *10 minutes* | *Cook Time:* *0 minutes* | *Servings: 6*

## Ingredients:

- ½ cup hot water
- 1 celery stalk, chopped
- ½ cup mayonnaise
- 1 red apple, cored and chopped
- ½ cup smoked chicken breast, skinless, boneless,
- cooked and shredded
- 1 teaspoon thyme, chopped
- 1 cucumber, sliced
- 12 whole grain bread slices, toasted
- Sunflower sprouts

## Directions:

In a bowl, mix chicken with celery and the other ingredients except the bread and the sprouts and stir well. Divide this into 6 bread slices, add sunflower sprouts on each, top with the other bread slices and serve.

**Nutrition:** calories 160, fat 7, fiber 2, carbs 10, protein 5

# Chicken with Honey and Peaches

*Prep Time:* *10 minutes* | *Cook Time:* *1 hour and 10 minutes* | *Servings: 4*

## Ingredients:

- 1 whole chicken, cut into medium pieces
- ¾ cup water
- 1/3 cup honey
- Salt and black pepper to taste
- ¼ cup olive oil
- 4 peaches, halved

## Directions:

Put the water in a saucepan, bring to a simmer over medium heat, add pepper and honey, whisk really well and leave aside. Rub chicken pieces with the oil, season with salt and pepper, place on preheated grill pan over medium high heat, brush with honey mixture, cook for 15 minutes, brush with the honey again, cook for 15 more minutes, flip once more, brush with the honey and cook for another 20 minutes. Divide chicken pieces on plates and keep warm. Brush peaches with remaining honey marinade, place them on your grill pan and cook for 4 minutes. Flip again and cook for 3 minutes more. Divide between plates next to chicken pieces and serve.

**Nutrition:** calories 500, fat 14, fiber 3, carbs 15, protein 10

# Lemon Chicken

*Prep Time:* 10 minutes | *Cook Time:* 45 minutes | *Servings:* 2

## Ingredients:

- 2 chicken breasts, skinless, boneless
- 2 garlic cloves, minced
- ½ teaspoon oregano, dried
- ¼ teaspoon thyme, dried
- Salt and black pepper to taste
- ¼ cup olive oil
- ¼ cup lemon juice

## Directions:

In a roasting pan, mix the chicken breasts with garlic and the other ingredients, toss and bake at 400 degrees F for 45 minutes. Divide everything between plates and serve right away.

**Nutrition:** calories 298, fat 14, fiber 1, carbs 4, protein 30

# Chicken and Black Beans Soup

*Prep Time:* 10 minutes | *Cook Time:* 1 hour and 10 minutes | *Servings:* 6

## Ingredients:

- 3 and ½ pounds small tomatoes, halved
- 2 tablespoons extra virgin olive oil + some more for frying
- 2 yellow onions, cut into wedges
- 1 chicken, cut into pieces
- 3 garlic cloves, chopped
- 3 red chili peppers, chopped
- 1 tablespoon coriander seeds, crushed
- 4 ounces canned black beans, drained
- 4 tablespoons chipotle paste
- Zest from 1 lime
- Juice from 1 lime
- Salt and black pepper to taste
- A handful coriander, chopped
- 2 avocados, pitted, peeled and chopped
- 3 ounces sour cream

## Directions:

Arrange tomatoes on a baking dish, add onions, chicken pieces, salt and pepper and 1 tablespoon oil, toss and bake at 350 degrees F fro 50 minutes. Transfer chicken to a bowl, cover with foil to keep warm and reserve cooking juices from the baking dish. Transfer baked onions and tomatoes to a blender and pulse well. Heat up a saucepan with the rest of the oil over medium high heat, add chilies, garlic and coriander, stir and cook for 3 minutes. Discard bones and skin from chicken pieces, shred meat, add to pan, also add lime zest, beans, chipotle paste, tomatoes mix and cooking juice, stir and cook for 5 minutes more. Ladle soup into bowls, add salt and pepper to taste, add some sour cream and lime juice on top, sprinkle coriander and avocado pieces and serve.

**Nutrition:** calories 253, fat 4, fiber 2, carbs 4, protein 4

# Creamy Chicken and Tomato Mix

*Prep Time:* 10 minutes | *Cook Time:* 20 minutes | *Servings:* 4

**Ingredients:**

- 5 chicken thighs
- 1 tablespoon olive oil
- 1 tablespoon thyme, chopped
- 2 garlic cloves, minced
- 1 teaspoon red pepper flakes, crushed
- ½ cup heavy cream
- ¾ cup chicken stock
- ½ cup sun dried tomatoes in olive oil, drained and chopped
- Salt and black pepper to taste
- ¼ cup parmesan cheese, grated
- Basil leaves, chopped for serving

**Directions:**

Heat a pan with the oil over medium high heat, add chicken, salt and pepper to taste, cook for 3 minutes on each side, transfer to a plate and leave aside for now. Return pan to heat, add thyme, garlic and pepper flakes, stir and cook for 1 minute. Add the rest of the ingredients except the basil, stir and bring to a simmer. Add chicken pieces, stir, place in the oven at 350 degrees F and bake for 15 minutes. Divide between plates and serve with basil sprinkled on top.

**Nutrition:** calories 212, fat 4, fiber 3, carbs 3, protein 3

# Chicken with Zucchini

*Prep Time:* 10 minutes | *Cook Time:* 30 minutes | *Servings:* 4

**Ingredients:**

- 14 ounces canned tomatoes, crushed
- 1 pound chicken breast, boneless and skinless
- 2 tablespoons olive oil
- Salt and black pepper to taste
- 2 red bell peppers, sliced
- 1 small yellow onion, sliced
- 2 garlic cloves, minced
- 2 zucchinis, chopped
- ½ teaspoon oregano, dried
- 1 cup chicken stock
- ¼ cup basil leaves, torn

**Directions:**

Heat a pan with the oil over medium high heat, add chicken breasts, salt and pepper, cook for 6 minutes on each side, transfer to a plate and leave aside for now. Return pan to heat, add peppers, zucchinis, garlic, oregano and onion, stir and cook for 10 minutes. Add tomatoes and stock, stir, bring to a boil, reduce heat and simmer for 10 minutes. Add chicken breasts, toss to coat, cook for 1 minute, transfer to plates, sprinkle basil and serve.

**Nutrition:** calories 253, fat 3, fiber 2, carbs 3, protein 3

# Creamy Chicken and Grapes

*Prep Time:* 10 minutes | *Cook Time:* 0 minutes | *Servings:* 6

**Ingredients:**

- 20 ounces chicken meat, already cooked and chopped
- ½ cup pecans, chopped
- 1 cup green grapes, seedless and cut in
- halves
- ½ cup celery, chopped
- ounces canned mandarin oranges, drained

*For the creamy cucumber salad dressing:*

- 1 cup Greek yogurt
- 1 cucumber, chopped
- 1 garlic clove, chopped
- Salt and white pepper to taste
- 1 teaspoon lemon juice

**Directions:**

In a bowl, mix cucumber with the chicken, salt, pepper to taste, lemon juice and the other ingredients, toss and keep in the fridge until you serve it.

**Nutrition:** calories 200, fat 3, fiber 1, carbs 2, protein 4, protein 8

# Chicken Salad with Ginger Marinade

*Prep Time: 30 minutes | Cook Time: 20 minutes | Servings: 4*

## Ingredients:

- 4 medium chicken breasts, boneless and skinless
- 2 eggplants, sliced
- Salt and black pepper to taste
- 1 tablespoon ginger, grated
- 1 tablespoon garlic,

*For the vinaigrette:*

- 1 teaspoon ginger, grated
- 2 teaspoons balsamic vinegar
- 2 teaspoons Dijon mustard

*For serving:*

- ½ lettuce head, leaves torn
- 1 pound cucumbers, sliced
- ¾ cup cilantro,

- minced
- 2 tablespoons balsamic vinegar
- 3 tablespoons olive oil
- 2 tablespoons red wine
- ¼ teaspoon chili paste

- 1 teaspoon brown sugar
- 3 tablespoons olive oil
- 1 tablespoon lime juice

- chopped
- ½ cup scallions, sliced
- 1 red chili pepper, chopped

## Directions:

In a bowl, mix 1 tablespoon grated ginger with 1 tablespoon minced garlic, 2 tablespoons balsamic vinegar, 3 tablespoons olive oil, 2 tablespoon red wine and ½ teaspoon chili paste, whisk, transfer half to another bowl and combine it with the eggplant slices. Place chicken breasts in another bowl, add the rest of the ginger marinade, toss and keep in the fridge for 30 minutes. Heat up a kitchen grill over medium high heat, add eggplant slices, cook for 3 minutes on each side and transfer them to a bowl. Arrange chicken breasts on grill, cook for 5 minutes, flip and cook for 2 more minutes, transfer them to a cutting board, leave aside for 4 minutes and then slice them. Arrange lettuce leaves on a platter, add chicken slices, grilled eggplant slices, cucumbers and scallions and some salt. In a bowl, mix 2 teaspoons balsamic vinegar with 1 teaspoon grated ginger, brown sugar, mustard, 3 tablespoons olive oil, salt to the taste and lime juice, stir, spread 1 tablespoon of this over the salad, add the chili and cilantro on top and serve.

**Nutrition:** calories 264, fat 14, fiber 6, carbs 8, protein 5

# Lemon Chicken and Eggplant Soup

*Prep Time: 10 minutes | Cook Time: 1 hour | Servings: 8*

## Ingredients:

- 2 cups eggplant, diced
- Salt and black pepper to taste
- ¼ cup olive oil + 1 tablespoon
- 1 cup yellow onion, chopped
- 2 tablespoons garlic, minced
- 1 red bell pepper, chopped
- 2 tablespoons hot paprika+ 2 teaspoons
- ¼ cup parsley,

- chopped
- 1 teaspoon turmeric
- 1 and ½ tablespoons oregano, chopped
- 4 cups chicken stock
- 1 pound chicken breast, skinless, boneless and cut into small pieces
- 1 cup half and half
- 1 and ½ tablespoons cornstarch
- 2 egg yolks
- ¼ cup lemon juice
- Lemon wedges for serving

## Directions:

In a bowl, mix eggplant pieces with ¼ cup oil, salt and pepper to taste, toss to coat, arrange on a baking sheet, bake at 400 degrees F for 20 minutes flipping halfway. Heat a saucepan with 1 tablespoon oil over medium heat, add garlic and onion, cover and cook for 10 minutes. Add bell pepper, paprika, ginger and turmeric, stir and cook uncovered for 3 minutes. Add the stock, chicken, eggplant pieces, oregano and parsley, stir, bring to a boil and simmer for 12 minutes. In a bowl, mix cornstarch with half and half and egg yolks - stir well. Add 1 cup soup, stir again and pour gradually into soup. Stir, add salt and pepper to taste and lemon juice. Ladle into soup bowls and serve with lemon wedges on the side.

**Nutrition:** calories 242, fat 3, fiber 2, carbs 5, protein 3

# Chicken and Buttery Lentil Soup

*Prep Time:* 10 minutes | *Cook Time:* 1 hour and 10 minutes | *Servings:* 8

## Ingredients:

- 4 tablespoons butter
- 2 celery stalks, chopped
- 2 carrots, chopped
- 1 yellow onion, chopped
- 2 tablespoons tomato paste
- 2 garlic cloves, chopped
- cups chicken stock
- 2 cups French lentils
- 1 pound chicken thighs, skinless and boneless
- Salt and black pepper to taste
- Grated parmesan for serving

## Directions:

Heat a Dutch oven with the butter over medium high heat, add onion, garlic, carrots, celery, salt and pepper, stir and cook for 10 minutes. Add tomato paste, stir and cook for 2 minutes. Add lentils, chicken stock and chicken thighs, stir, bring to a boil, cover oven, cook for 1 hour, transfer the meat to a plate and cool down. Transfer soup to a food processor, add more salt and pepper if needed and blend. Return soup to oven, shred chicken meat, add to oven., stir, divide into bowls, sprinkle the cheese on top and serve.

**Nutrition:** calories 231, fat 2, fiber 2, carbs 5, protein 3

# Chicken, Leeks and Rice Soup

*Prep Time:* 15 minutes | *Cook Time:* 1 hour and 20 minutes | *Servings:* 4

## Ingredients:

- 1 big chicken
- 3 tablespoons salt
- 4 cups water
- 1 leek, cut in quarters
- 2 bay leaves
- 1 carrot, cut into quarters
- 3 tablespoons olive
- oil
- 2/3 cup rice
- 2 cups yellow onion, chopped
- 2 eggs
- ½ cup lemon juice
- 1 teaspoon black pepper

## Directions:

Put chicken in a large saucepan, add water and 2 tablespoons salt, bring to a boil over medium high heat, reduce heat, add bay leaves, carrot and the leek and simmer for 1 hour. Heat a pan with the oil over medium high heat, add onion, stir and cook for 6 minutes, take off heat and leave aside for now. Transfer chicken to a cutting board and leave aside to cool down. Strain soup back into the saucepan. Add sautéed onion and rice, bring again to a boil over high heat, reduce temperature to low and simmer for 20 minutes. Discard chicken bones and skin, dice into big chunks and return to boiling soup. Meanwhile, in a bowl, mix lemon juice with eggs and black pepper and stir well. Add 2 cups boiling soup, whisk again well, pour into the pot, stir, divide into bowls and serve.

**Nutrition:** calories 242, fat 3, fiber 2, carbs 3, protein 3

# Chicken and Barley Soup

*Prep Time:* 10 minutes | *Cook Time:* 50 minutes | *Servings:* 6

## Ingredients:

- 4 chicken things, bone-in and skin on
- 1 tablespoon olive oil
- Salt and black pepper to taste
- 2 celery stalks, chopped
- 2 carrots, chopped
- 1 yellow onion, chopped
- cups chicken stock
- ½ cup parsley, chopped
- ½ cup barley
- 1 teaspoon lemon zest, grated

## Directions:

Heat up a large saucepan with the oil over medium high heat, add chicken, season with salt and pepper to taste, stir and cook for 8 minutes, take off heat and transfer to a plate. Return saucepan to medium heat, add onion, celery, carrots, salt and pepper, stir and cook for 5 minutes. Add stock, barley, return the chicken to pan, stir, bring to a boil and cook over medium heat for 40 minutes, In a small bowl, mix parsley with a pinch of salt, pepper and lemon zest and stir well. Take chicken out of the saucepan, discard bones and skin, shred, return to pan again, ladle into bowls, sprinkle the parsley mix on top and serve.

**Nutrition:** calories 213, fat 2, fiber 2, carbs 4, protein 5

# Herbed Chicken and Tomato Stew

*Prep Time:* 20 minutes | *Cook Time:* 40 minutes | *Servings:* 4

## Ingredients:

- 3 ½ pounds chicken, cut into 10 medium pieces
- 2 yellow onions, chopped
- 2 tablespoons olive oil
- 1 garlic clove, minced
- ¼ pint chicken stock, warm
- 1 tablespoon white flour
- 2 teaspoons mixed dried herbs (parsley and basil)
- 14 ounces canned tomatoes, chopped
- Salt and black pepper to taste

## Directions:

Heat a saucepan with the oil over medium high heat, add chicken meat, stir and brown it for 5 minutes, take off heat, transfer to a plate and set aside. Return saucepan to heat, add garlic and onion, stir and cook for 3 minutes. Add flour and the rest of the ingredients, also return the chicken, stir, reduce heat to medium and simmer the stew for 45 minutes. Transfer to plates and serve right away.

**Nutrition:** calories 200, fat 4, fiber 3, carbs 7, protein 12

# Chicken and Radishes

*Prep Time:* 10 minutes | *Cook Time:* 30 minutes | *Servings:* 4

## Ingredients:

- 4 chicken things, bone-in
- Salt and black pepper to taste
- 1 tablespoon olive oil
- 1 cup chicken stock
- 6 radishes, halved
- 1 teaspoon sugar
- 3 carrots, cut into thin sticks
- 2 tablespoon chives, chopped

## Directions:

Heat a Dutch oven with the oil over medium high heat, add chicken, salt and pepper to taste, stir and brown for 7 minutes on each side and discard excess grease. Add the rest of the ingredients except the chives, toss, reduce heat to medium, and simmer for 20 minutes. Take off heat, allow the chicken to cool down for 2-3 minutes, transfer to plates and serve with chopped chives sprinkled on top.

**Nutrition:** calories 237, fat 10, fiber 3, carbs 9, protein 29

# Chicken with Cheese and Cabbage Mix

*Prep Time: 10 minutes | Cook Time: 6 minutes | Servings: 4*

## Ingredients:

- 3 medium chicken breasts, skinless, boneless and cut into thin strips
- 4 ounces green cabbage, shredded
- 5 tablespoon extra virgin olive oil
- Salt and black pepper to taste
- 2 tablespoons sherry
- vinegar
- 1 tablespoon chives, chopped
- ¼ cup feta cheese, crumbled
- ¼ cup barbeque sauce
- 2 bacon slices, cooked and crumbled

## Directions:

In a bowl, mix the cabbage with 4 tablespoon oil with vinegar, salt and pepper to taste and stir well. Season chicken with salt and pepper, heat a pan with remaining oil over medium high heat, add chicken, cook for 6 minutes, take off heat, transfer to a bowl, add barbeque sauce and toss. Arrange between plates, add chicken strips, sprinkle cheese, chives and bacon and serve.

**Nutrition:** calories 200, fat 15, fiber 3, carbs 10, protein 33

# Parmesan Chicken and Zucchini Mix

*Prep Time: 10 minutes | Cook Time: 15 minutes | Servings: 4*

## Ingredients:

- 1 pound chicken breasts, cut into medium chunks
- 12 ounces zucchini, sliced
- 2 tablespoons olive oil
- 2 garlic cloves, minced
- 2 tablespoons parmesan, grated
- 1 tablespoon parsley, chopped
- Salt and black pepper to taste

## Directions:

In a bowl, mix chicken pieces with 1 tablespoon oil, some salt and pepper and toss to coat. Heat a pan over medium high heat, add chicken pieces, brown for 6 minutes on all sides, transfer to a plate and leave aside. Heat the pan with the remaining oil over medium heat, add zucchini slices, garlic, return the chicken, sprinkle the parmesan on top, stir and cook for 5 minutes. Divide between plates and serve with some parsley on top.

**Nutrition:** calories 212, fat 4, fiber 3, carbs 4, protein 7

# Chicken and Olives Soup

*Prep Time: 10 minutes | Cook Time: 40 minutes | Servings: 8*

## Ingredients:

- 1 tablespoon Greek seasoning
- A pinch of salt and black pepper
- 1 tablespoon capers
- 1 tablespoon olive oil
- 4 spring onions, chopped
- 1 garlic clove, minced
- 2 teaspoons basil, chopped
- 2 teaspoons oregano, chopped
- 1 cup brown rice
- 7 cups chicken stock
- ¼ cup kalamata olives, pitted and sliced
- ¼ cup sun-dried tomatoes, chopped
- 2 tablespoons lemon juice
- 2 teaspoons parsley, chopped
- 1 pound chicken breast boneless, skinless and cubed

## Directions:

Heat a saucepan with the oil over medium heat, add the chicken and brown for 2-3 minutes. Add capers, olives and the other ingredients except the parsley, stir, bring to a boil and simmer for 35 minutes. Add the parsley, stir, ladle the soup into bowls and serve.

**Nutrition:** calories 271, fat 5, fiber 1, carbs 13, protein 16

# Chicken and Creamy Mushroom Soup

*Prep Time:* 10 minutes | *Cook Time:* 30 minutes | *Servings:* 4

## Ingredients:

- 1 yellow onion, chopped
- 1 tablespoon butter
- 2 celery stalks, chopped
- 1 big garlic clove, minced
- 2 carrots chopped
- Salt and black pepper to taste
- 1 tablespoon thyme, chopped
- 1 pound red potatoes, cut into quarters
- 1 qtr. chicken stock
- 4 ounces Bella mushrooms, sliced
- 1 bay leaf
- 1 cup heavy cream
- 4 cups rotisserie chicken, shredded
- 2 tablespoons chives, chopped

## Directions:

Heat a Dutch oven with the butter over medium heat, add onions, celery, garlic, carrot and thyme, stir and cook for 5 minutes. Add the rest of the ingredients except the chicken, cream and chives, stir, bring to boil and simmer for 20 minutes. Add chicken, and cream, cook for 5 more minutes and discard bay leaf. Ladle into bowls serve with chives sprinkled on top.

**Nutrition:** calories 267, fat 6, fiber 4, carbs 7, protein 4

# Curry Chicken and Tomatoes Mix

*Prep Time:* 5 minutes | *Cook Time:* 6 hours and 10 minutes | *Servings:* 6

## Ingredients:

- 2 pounds chicken breasts, boneless and skinless
- 28 ounces canned tomatoes, chopped
- 28 ounces canned artichoke hearts, drained
- 1 ½ cups chicken stock
- 1 yellow onion, chopped
- ¼ cup white wine
- vinegar
- ½ cup kalamata olives, pitted and chopped
- 1 tablespoon curry powder
- 2 teaspoons thyme
- 2 teaspoons basil
- Salt and black pepper to taste
- ¼ cup parsley, chopped

## Directions:

Put chicken breasts in a slow cooker, add tomatoes and the rest of the ingredients, cover and cook on Low for 6 hours. Uncover, add more salt and pepper if needed, add parsley and stir gently.

**Nutrition:** calories 342, fat 3, fiber 3, carbs 5, protein 4

# Chicken with Tomato Rice Mix

*Prep Time:* 10 minutes | *Cook Time:* 6 hours | *Servings:* 4

## Ingredients:

- 3 already chicken breasts, already browned
- 56 ounces canned plum tomatoes and their juice
- 16 ounces canned chickpeas
- 2 garlic cloves, minced
- 1 yellow onion, chopped
- 1 cup Mediterranean olives, pitted
- 2 cups chicken stock
- 2 tablespoons capers
- 1 cup brown rice, cooked
- ¼ cup oregano, chopped
- Salt and black pepper to taste
- Feta cheese for serving

## Directions:

Put chicken breasts in a slow cooker, add the tomatoes, chickpeas and the other of the ingredients except the rice and cheese, cover and cook on Low for 6 hours. Transfer to plates and serve with brown rice on the side and crumbled feta cheese on top.

**Nutrition:** calories 300, fat 2, fiber 3, carbs 5, protein 4

# Chicken with Sun-dried Tomatoes and Mushrooms

*Prep Time: 10 minutes | Cook Time: 4 hours | Servings: 12*

## Ingredients:

- 1 tablespoon olive oil
- 12 chicken thighs
- Salt and black pepper to taste
- 1 yellow onion, chopped
- 1 ½ cups mushrooms, cut in quarters
- 2 zucchinis, chopped
- 15 ounces canned chickpeas
- 15 ounces canned tomatoes, chopped
- ½ cup sun dried tomatoes, chopped
- 1 cup kalamata olives, pitted
- 2 tablespoons lemon juice
- 3 garlic cloves, minced
- 2 tablespoons capers
- 1 teaspoon oregano, dried

## Directions:

Heat a pan with the olive oil over medium high heat, add chicken, season with salt and pepper, brown it on both sides, remove and leave aside for now. Put mushrooms, zucchini and onion in a slow cooker, add the meat and the rest of the ingredients, cover and cook on High for 4 hours. Divide between plates and serve right away!

**Nutrition:** calories 264, fat 4, fiber 3, carbs 4, protein 5

# Chicken with Olives and Dates

*Prep Time: 10 minutes | Cook Time: 1 hour and 50 minutes | Servings: 6*

## Ingredients:

- 12 chicken wings, halved
- 2 garlic cloves, minced
- Juice of 1 lemon
- Zest from 1 lemon
- 2 tablespoons olive oil
- 1 teaspoon cumin, ground
- Salt and pepper to taste
- A small bowl full of olives
- A small bowl full of dates
- A small bowl full of pickled chilies
- 

## Directions:

In a bowl, mix the chicken wings with lemon zest with lemon juice, garlic, olive oil, cumin, salt and pepper, toss and keep in the fridge for 1 hour. Put chicken wings on a baking tray, place in the oven and bake for 50 minutes at 350 degrees F. Take chicken wings out of oven, transfer to a platter and serve with small bowls full of olives, dates and pickled chilies on the side.

**Nutrition:** calories 321, fat 3, fiber 4, carbs 6, protein 8

# Chicken, Walnuts and Creamy Sauce

*Prep Time: 10 minutes | Cook Time: 40 minutes | Servings: 4*

## Ingredients:

- 4 chicken thighs
- 2 tablespoons olive oil
- ½ teaspoon sweet paprika
- 1 teaspoon cumin, ground
- 5 ounces hot chicken stock
- 6 ounces walnuts, chopped
- 1 yellow onion, chopped
- 2 garlic cloves, minced
- 1 ½ tablespoons heavy cream
- A handful coriander, chopped
- Juice of 1 lemon
- Salt and pepper to taste

## Directions:

Put chicken thighs in a baking dish, add paprika, cumin, salt, pepper and 1 tablespoon olive oil, toss and bake at 350 degrees F for 40 minutes. Heat a pan over medium high heat, add walnuts, cook for 3 minutes and leave aside. Heat up another pan with the remaining oil over medium high heat, add onion and garlic, stir and for 3-4 minutes. Transfer onion to a food processor, add walnuts and the stock and pulse well. Transfer paste to the pan, heat it up over medium heat, add cream, lemon juice, salt and pepper, whisk and pour into a bowl. Take chicken out of the oven, arrange on a platter and serve with the sauce drizzled all over.

**Nutrition:** calories 253, fat 4, fiber 5, carbs 7, protein 8

# Lime Chicken and Corn Salad

*Prep Time:* 10 minutes | *Cook Time:* 20 minutes | *Servings:* 2

### Ingredients:

- 2 tablespoons olive oil
- 2 ounces quinoa
- 2 ounces cherry tomatoes, cut in quarters
- 3 ounces sweet corn
- A handful coriander, chopped
- Lime juice from 1 lime
- Lime zest from 1 lime, grated
- Salt and black pepper to taste
- 2 spring onions, chopped
- 1 small red chili pepper, chopped
- 1 avocado, pitted, peeled and chopped
- 7 ounces chicken meat, roasted, skinless, boneless and chopped

### Directions:

Put some water in a pan, bring to a boil over medium high heat, add quinoa, stir and cook for 12 minutes. Meanwhile, put corn in a pan, heat over medium high heat, cook for 5 minutes and leave aside for now. Drain quinoa, transfer to a bowl, add add the meat and the rest of the ingredients, toss and serve.

**Nutrition:** calories 320, fat 4, fiber 4, carbs 5, protein 7

# Chicken Rolls

*Prep Time:* 10 minutes | *Cook Time:* 12 minutes | *Servings:* 4

### Ingredients:

- 4 chicken breast halves, skinless and boneless
- Salt and black pepper to taste
- 4 teaspoons olive oil
- 1 small cucumber, sliced
- 3 teaspoons cilantro, chopped
- 4 Greek whole wheat tortillas
- 4 tablespoons peanut sauce

### Directions:

Heat a grill pan over medium high heat, season chicken with salt and pepper, rub with the oil, add to the grill, cook for 6 minutes on each side, transfer to a cutting board, cool down and slice. In a bowl, mix cilantro with cucumber and stir. Spread 1 tablespoon peanut sauce on each tortilla, divide chicken and cucumber mix on each, fold, arrange on plates and serve.

**Nutrition:** calories 321, fat 3, fiber 4, carbs 7, protein 9

# Salsa Verde Chicken

*Prep Time:* 10 minutes | *Cook Time:* 43 minutes | *Servings:* 4

### Ingredients:

- 1 pound chicken breast, boneless and skinless
- 16 ounces Greek salsa verde
- Salt and black pepper to taste
- 1 tablespoon olive
- oil
- 1 ½ cups goat cheese, crumbled
- ¼ cup cilantro, chopped
- White rice for serving
- Juice from 1 lime

### Directions:

In a bowl, mix chicken with salt, pepper, and oil and toss to coat. Spread salsa in a baking dish, add chicken on top, place in the oven at 400 degrees F, cook for 40 minutes, add cheese and broil for 3 more minutes. Add lime juice, divide between plates, sprinkle cilantro and serve with white rice.

**Nutrition:** calories 300, fat 3, fiber 4, carbs 6, protein 7

# Thyme and Creamy Chicken

*Prep Time: 10 minutes | Cook Time: 50 minutes | Servings: 8*

## Ingredients:

- 3 tablespoons butter
- 8 chicken thighs, bone in, skin-on
- Salt and black pepper to taste
- 3 garlic cloves, minced
- 8 ounces mushrooms, halved
- ½ teaspoons thyme, dried
- 1 cup chicken stock
- ¼ cup heavy cream
- ½ teaspoon basil, dried
- ½ teaspoon oregano, dried
- 1 tablespoon mustard
- ¼ cup parmesan, grated

## Directions:

Heat a large saucepan with 2 tablespoons butter over medium high heat, add chicken thighs, salt and pepper to taste, cook for 3 minutes on each side, take off heat and transfer to a plate. Return saucepan to medium heat, add remaining butter, salt, pepper, mushroom and garlic, stir and cook for 6 minutes. Add chicken, stir and bake in the oven at 400 degrees F for 30 minutes. Take pan off heat, transfer chicken to plates and heat pan juices on the stove over medium heat. Add cream, mustard and parmesan, stir, bring to a boil, reduce heat to low and simmer for 10 minutes. Divide between plates and serve.

**Nutrition:** calories 290, fat 5, fiber 3, carbs 6, protein 7

# Vegetable Recipes

## Lemon Lentils

*Prep Time:* 10 minutes | *Cook Time:* 20 minutes | *Servings:* 6

### Ingredients:

- 1 cup brown lentils
- 1 cup carrots, chopped
- 1 cup red onions, chopped
- 2 tablespoons lemon juice
- ½ cup celery, cubed
- ¼ cup parsley, chopped
- 2 garlic cloves, minced
- A pinch of salt and black pepper
- ½ teaspoon thyme, dried
- ¼ cup olive oil

### Directions:

Place the lentils in a pot, add carrots, onions, celery, salt, pepper, thyme, cover with water, bring to a boil and simmer over medium heat for 20 minutes. Drain well, put the mix into a bowl, add garlic, parsley, salt, pepper and the oil, toss and serve.

**Nutrition:** calories 170, fat 7, fiber 3, carbs 12, protein 6

## Cabbage and Carrots Salad

*Prep Time:* 10 minutes | *Cook Time:* 0 minutes | *Servings:* 4

### Ingredients:

- 1 green cabbage head, shredded
- A pinch of salt and black pepper
- 3 carrots, shredded
- 1 yellow bell pepper, chopped
- 1 orange bell pepper, chopped
- 1 red bell pepper, chopped
- 8 kalamata olives, pitted and chopped
- 2 tablespoons white vinegar
- 2 tablespoons olive oil

### Directions:

In a bowl, mix the cabbage with salt, pepper and the other ingredients, toss and serve.

**Nutrition:** calories 150, fat 9, fiber 4, carbs 8, protein 8

## Pomegranate Salad

*Prep Time:* 10 minutes | *Cook Time:* 0 minutes | *Servings:* 3

### Ingredients:

- 3 big pears, cored and cut with a spiralizer
- ¾ cup pomegranate seeds
- 5 ounces arugula
- ¾ cup walnuts, chopped

*For the vinaigrette:*

- 1 tablespoon sesame oil
- 1 tablespoon olive oil
- 1 tablespoon maple syrup
- 1 teaspoon white sesame seeds
- 2 tablespoons apple cider vinegar
- 1 tablespoon soy sauce
- 1 garlic clove, minced
- A pinch of sea salt
- Black pepper to taste

### Directions:

In a bowl, mix the pears with the pomegranate seeds, arugula and all the other ingredients, toss to coat well and serve right away.

**Nutrition:** calories 200, fat 2, fiber 4, carbs 6, protein 9

# Bulgur Salad

*Prep Time:* 15 minutes | *Cook Time:* 0 minutes | *Servings:* 6

## Ingredients:

- 1 ½ cups hot water
- 1 cup bulgur
- Juice of 1 lime
- 4 tablespoons cilantro, chopped
- ½ cup cranberries, dried
- 1 lime, cut into wedges
- 1 and ½ teaspoons coriander, ground
- 1/3 cup almonds, sliced
- ¼ cup green onions, chopped
- ½ cup red bell peppers, chopped
- ½ cup carrots, grated
- 1 tablespoon olive oil
- A pinch of sea salt and black pepper

## Directions:

Place bulgur into a bowl, add boiling water to it, stir, cover and set aside for 15 minutes. Fluff bulgur with a fork and transfer to a salad bowl. Add the rest of the ingredients, stir and serve right away with lime wedges on the side.

**Nutrition:** calories 160, fat 3, fiber 3, carbs 7, protein 10

# Beans and Mixed Veggies Salad

*Prep Time:* 15 minutes | *Cook Time:* 0 minutes | *Servings:* 4

## Ingredients:

- 1 ½ cups cooked black beans
- ½ teaspoon garlic powder
- ½ teaspoon smoked paprika
- 2 teaspoons chili powder
- 1 teaspoon cumin
- 1 ½ cups chickpeas, cooked

*For the salad dressing:*

- 2 tablespoons lemon juice
- ¾ cup cashews, soaked for a couple of hours and drained
- ½ cup water
- 1 garlic clove, minced
- 1 tablespoon apple cider vinegar
- ½ teaspoon onion

- ¼ teaspoon cinnamon
- 1 lettuce head, chopped
- 1 red bell pepper, chopped
- 2 tomatoes, chopped
- 1 avocado, pitted, peeled and chopped
- 1 cup corn kernels, chopped

powder
- 1 teaspoon chives, chopped
- ½ teaspoon oregano, dried
- 1 teaspoon dill weed, dried
- 1 teaspoon cumin
- ½ teaspoon smoked paprika

## Directions:

In a blender, mix cashews with water, 2 tablespoons lemon juice, 1 tablespoon vinegar, 1 garlic clove, ½ teaspoon onion powder, dill, oregano, chives, 1 teaspoon cumin, a pinch of salt and ½ teaspoon paprika, blend well and leave aside for now. In a salad bowl, mix black beans with chili powder and the rest of the ingredients, and toss. Drizzle the dressing over salad, toss to coat and serve right away.

**Nutrition:** calories 300, fat 4, fiber 1, carbs 6, protein 13

## Lentil and Bread Salad

*Prep Time: 10 minutes | Cook Time: 0 minutes | Servings: 2*

**Ingredients:**

- 1 pita bread, cubed
- 1/3 cup canned and cooked green lentils, drained
- 2 teaspoons olive oil
- 1 carrot, grated
- 4 cups arugula
- 2 celery stalks,

- chopped
- 1 cucumber, sliced
- ¼ cup dates, pitted and chopped
- 1 radish, sliced
- 2 tablespoons sunflower seeds

*For the vinaigrette:*

- 1 tablespoon maple syrup
- 1 tablespoon Dijon mustard

- 2 tablespoons balsamic vinegar
- 2 tablespoons olive oil

**Directions:**

In a bowl, mix maple syrup with mustard, vinegar and olive oil and whisk well. In a salad bowl, mix green lentils with the pita cubes and the rest of the ingredients, add the vinaigrette as well, toss and serve.

**Nutrition:** calories 179, fat 4, fiber 3, carbs 6, protein 12

## Maple Chickpeas Mix

*Prep Time: 15 minutes | Cook Time: 0 minutes | Servings: 2*

**Ingredients:**

- 16 ounces canned chickpeas, drained
- 1 handful raisins
- 1 handful baby spinach leaves
- 1 tablespoon maple syrup
- ½ tablespoon lemon juice

- 4 tablespoons olive oil
- 1 teaspoon cumin, ground
- A pinch of sea salt
- Black pepper to taste
- ½ teaspoon chili flakes

**Directions:**

In a bowl, mix maple syrup with lemon juice, oil, cumin, a pinch of salt, black pepper and chili flakes and whisk well. In a salad bowl, mix chickpeas with spinach, the rest of the ingredients and the salad dressing, toss and serve.

**Nutrition:** calories 300, fat 3, fiber 6, carbs 12, protein 9

## Tomato and Olives Salad

*Prep Time: 10 minutes | Cook Time: 0 minutes | Servings: 4*

**Ingredients:**

- 1 handful kalamata olives, pitted and sliced
- 1 punnet cherry tomatoes, halved
- 4 tomatoes, chopped
- 1 and ½ cucumbers,

*For the salad dressing:*

- 1 teaspoon sugar
- 2 tablespoons balsamic vinegar
- ¼ cup olive oil
- 1 garlic clove, minced

- sliced
- 1 red onion, chopped
- 2 tablespoons oregano, chopped
- 1 tablespoon mint, chopped

- 2 teaspoons Italian herbs, dried
- 1 teaspoon soy sauce
- A pinch of sea salt
- Black pepper to the taste

**Directions:**

In a salad bowl, mix all tomatoes, olives, cucumbers, onion, mint and oregano and stir. In another bowl, mix sugar with vinegar and the rest of the ingredients, toss, add to salad and serve.

**Nutrition:** calories 140, fat 2, fiber 3, carbs 6, protein 12

## Bean Salad

*Prep Time: 10 minutes | Cook Time: 0 minutes | Servings: 4*

**Ingredients:**

- 15 ounces canned chickpeas, drained
- 15 ounces canned great northern beans, drained
- 2 tablespoons olive oil
- ½ cup spinach, chopped
- ½ cup cucumber,

- sliced
- 1 tablespoon basil, chopped
- 1 tablespoon parsley, chopped
- sun dried tomatoes, chopped
- A pinch of sea salt
- 2 tablespoon vinegar

**Directions:**

In a bowl, mix chickpeas with beans and the rest of the ingredients, toss and serve.

**Nutrition:** calories 140, fat 5, fiber 6, carbs 9, protein 15

# Lemon Avocado and Beans Mix

*Prep Time: 10 minutes | Cook Time: 0 minutes | Servings: 4*

**Ingredients:**

- 15 ounces canned white beans, drained
- 1 tomato, chopped
- 1 avocado, pitted, peeled and chopped
- ¼ sweet onion, chopped
- A pinch of sea salt
- Black pepper to taste
- ¼ cup lemon juice
- 1 and ½ tablespoons olive oil
- A handful basil, chopped
- 1 teaspoon garlic, minced
- 1 teaspoon mustard

**Directions:**

In a salad bowl, mix beans with tomato, avocado and the rest of the ingredients, toss to coat and serve.

**Nutrition:** calories 150, fat 3, fiber 2, carbs 6, protein 14

# Tomato and Avocado Salad

*Prep Time: 10 minutes | Cook Time: 0 minutes | Servings: 4*

**Ingredients:**

- 2 avocados, pitted, peeled and cubed
- 1 pint mixed cherry

*For the salad dressing:*

- 2 tablespoons olive oil
- 1 tablespoon lime juice
- ½ teaspoon lime
- tomatoes, halved
- 2 cups fresh corn
- 1 red onion, chopped

- zest, grated
- A pinch of salt
- Black pepper to taste
- ¼ cup cilantro, chopped

**Directions:**

In a bowl, mix oil with lime juice and zest, a pinch of salt and some black pepper and whisk well. In a salad bowl, mix the avocados with tomatoes and the rest of the ingredients, add the dressing, toss to coat and serve.

**Nutrition:** calories 120, fat 3, fiber 2, carbs 6, protein 9

# Black Beans Salad

*Prep Time: 10 minutes | Cook Time: 0 minutes | Servings: 4*

**Ingredients:**

- 1 cucumber, cut into chunks
- 15 ounces canned black beans, drained
- 1 cup corn
- 1 cup cherry tomatoes, halved
- 1 small red onion, chopped
- 3 tablespoons olive
- oil
- 4 ½ teaspoons orange marmalade
- 1 teaspoon agave nectar
- Salt and black pepper to taste
- ½ teaspoon cumin
- 1 tablespoon lemon juice

**Directions:**

In a bowl, mix beans with cucumber, corn, onion and tomatoes. In another bowl, mix the rest of the ingredients, whisk, pour over the salad, toss and serve.

**Nutrition:** calories 110, fat 0, fiber 3, carbs 6, protein 8

# Corn and Radish Salad

*Prep Time: 10 minutes | Cook Time: 0 minutes | Servings: 4*

**Ingredients:**

- 1 and ½ teaspoons agave nectar
- 2 tablespoons lime juice
- 1 jalapeno, chopped
- ¼ cup olive oil
- ¼ teaspoon cumin, ground
- A pinch of sea salt
- Black pepper to taste
- 4 cups fresh corn kernels
- ½ cup parsley, chopped
- 6 radishes, thinly sliced
- 1 red onion, chopped

**Directions:**

In a blender, mix agave nectar with lime juice, jalapeno, cumin, oil, salt and pepper and blend well. In a bowl mix the radishes with the rest of the ingredients, add the agave dressing as well, toss and serve.

**Nutrition:** calories 100, fat 0.4, fiber 0.8, carbs 1, protein 6

# Pepper and Arugula Salad

*Prep Time: 10 minutes | Cook Time: 0 minutes | Servings: 4*

### Ingredients:

- 1 red bell pepper, thinly sliced
- 2 cups corn
- Juice of 1 lemon
- Zest from 1 lemon,
- grated
- 8 cups arugula
- A pinch of sea salt
- Black pepper to taste

### Directions:

In a salad bowl, mix the arugula with the corn and the other ingredients, toss and serve.

**Nutrition:** calories 90, fat 0, fiber 1, carbs 1, protein 5

# Bulgur Salad

*Prep Time: 30 minutes | Cook Time: 0 minutes | Servings: 4*

### Ingredients:

- 1 cup bulgur
- 2 cups hot water
- A pinch of sea salt
- Black pepper to taste
- 2 cups corn
- 1 cucumber,
- chopped
- 2 tablespoons lemon juice
- 2 tablespoons balsamic vinegar
- ¼ cup olive oil

### Directions:

In a bowl, mix bulgur with water, cover, leave aside for 25 minutes, fluff with a fork and transfer to a salad bowl. Add corn and the rest of the ingredients, toss to coat well and serve.

**Nutrition:** calories 100, fat 0.5, fiber 2, carbs 2, protein 6

# Lettuce, Tomato and Pita Salad

*Prep Time: 10 minutes | Cook Time: 15 minutes | Servings: 6*

### Ingredients:

- 3 tablespoons olive oil
- 2 loaves pita bread
- 1 cucumber, chopped
- 1 heart lettuce, chopped
- 5 medium tomatoes,
- chopped
- ½ teaspoon sumac
- 5 green bell peppers, chopped
- 1 cup parsley, chopped
- 5 radishes, sliced

*For the dressing:*

- 1/3 cup olive oil
- Juice from 1 ½ limes
- Salt and black pepper to taste
- 1 teaspoon sumac
- ½ teaspoon cinnamon powder
- ¼ teaspoon allspice, ground

### Directions:

Heat a pan with 3 tablespoons olive oil over medium heat, break pita, place in pan, brown for 1-2 minutes, add salt, pepper and ½ teaspoon sumac, transfer to paper towels and leave aside. In a bowl, mix the lettuce with cucumber and the rest of the ingredients and toss. Toss and top with toasted pita. Serve right away.

**Nutrition:** calories 201, fat 3, fiber 2, carbs 5, protein 8

# Tomato and Cucumber Salad

*Prep Time: 30 minutes | Cook Time: 0 minutes | Servings: 6*

**Ingredients:**

- 1 pound tomatoes, chopped
- ¾ pound cucumbers, chopped
- 1 long green pepper, chopped
- 1 red onion, soaked in cold water and sliced
- 1 tablespoon dill weed, chopped
- ¼ cup parsley, chopped
- 2 tablespoons mint, chopped
- 1 teaspoon sumac
- Salt and black pepper to taste
- 3 tablespoons olive oil
- 3 tablespoons lemon juice
- 2 ounces feta cheese, crumbled
- 10 big black olives, pitted
- Pita bread for serving

**Directions:**

In a large salad bowl mix tomatoes with cucumber, green pepper and the rest of the ingredients except the pita and olives and toss well. Place in the fridge for 30 minutes and then serve with pita and black olives on top.

**Nutrition:** calories 241, fat 3, fiber 2, carbs 5, protein 6

# Rice Salad

*Prep Time: 10 minutes | Cook Time: 15 minutes | Servings: 4*

**Ingredients:**

- 1 cup green lentils
- ½ cup rice
- 4 tablespoons olive oil
- 1 yellow onion, sliced
- 1 carrot, grated
- 3 green onions, chopped
- 1 cup parsley, chopped
- ½ cup mint, chopped
- Juice of 1 lemon
- ½ cup corn
- Salt and black pepper to taste

**Directions:**

Boil rice and lentils in separate pots, drain water and cool them down. Heat a pan with the oil over medium high heat, add onions and carrots and cook for 15 minutes. Put lentils and rice in a bowl, add sautéed onions and carrots, add green onions as and the rest of the ingredients, toss and serve.

**Nutrition:** calories 200, fat 3, fiber 3, carbs 5, protein 7

# Peas, Corn and Couscous Salad

*Prep Time: 10 minutes | Cook Time: 20 minutes | Servings: 6*

**Ingredients:**

- 1 pound couscous
- 3 tablespoons olive oil
- 2 carrots, cubed
- ½ cup sweet peas
- ¼ cup parsley, chopped
- ½ cup sweet corn
- 1 tablespoon mint, chopped
- Salt to taste
- 1 red bell pepper, cut into strips

**Directions:**

Place couscous in a bowl, cover with water and leave aside for 10 minutes. Drain, add olive oil and stir well. Put some water and salt in a large saucepan, add carrots and sweet peas, bring to a boil over medium heat, boil for 4 minutes, drain water and put into the same bowl with the couscous. Add the rest of the ingredients, toss and serve.

**Nutrition:** calories 210, fat 2, fiber 2, carbs 4, protein 7

# Yogurt and Cucumber Salad

*Prep Time: 1 hour and 10 minutes | Cook Time: 0 minutes | Servings: 6*

**Ingredients:**

- 2 garlic cloves, minced
- Salt to taste
- 1 tablespoon wine vinegar
- 1 ½ cups Greek yogurt
- 1 tablespoon dill
- weed, chopped
- 3 medium cucumbers, sliced
- 1 tablespoon olive oil
- 1 tablespoon mint, chopped

**Directions:**

In a bowl, mix the cucumber with the garlic and the other ingredients, toss and keep in the fridge for 1 hour before serving.

**Nutrition:** calories 210, fat 1, fiber 2, carbs 5, protein 8

# Potato and Carrot Soup

*Prep Time: 10 minutes | Cook Time: 25 minutes | Servings: 2*

## Ingredients:

- 2 medium potatoes, peeled and cut into cubes
- 1 yellow onion, chopped
- 2 tablespoons butter
- 1 small carrot, cubed
- 1 ½ tablespoon flour
- 1 bay leaf
- 2 ½ cups chicken stock
- Salt and black pepper to taste

## Directions:

Heat a large saucepan with the butter over medium high heat, add onion and carrot, stir and cook for 3-4 minutes. Add potatoes and flour, whisk and cook for 5 more minutes. Add the rest of the ingredients, toss and cook for 15-20 minutes. Discard bay leaf, ladle into bowls and serve.

**Nutrition:** calories 198, fat 3, fiber 2, carbs 6, protein 8

# Tomato and Rice Soup

*Prep Time: 10 minutes | Cook Time: 20 minutes | Servings: 3*

## Ingredients:

- 4 medium tomatoes, grated
- 1 green bell pepper, chopped
- 1 garlic clove, minced
- 1 tablespoon olive oil
- ¼ cup white rice
- ½ teaspoon sweet paprika
- ½ tablespoon peppercorns
- Salt and black pepper to taste
- 3 cups hot water
- ½ bunch parsley, chopped

## Directions:

Heat a large saucepan with the olive oil over medium heat, add bell pepper and garlic, stir and cook for 5 minutes. Add paprika, tomatoes and the other ingredients, stir and cook over medium heat fro 15 minutes. Ladle into bowls and serve.

**Nutrition:** calories 200, fat 2, fiber 3, carbs 5, protein 7

# Creamy Eggplant and Tomato Soup

*Prep Time: 15 minutes | Cook Time: 1 hour and 30 minutes | Servings: 4*

## Ingredients:

- 1 big eggplant, sliced lengthwise
- 3 tomatoes, halved
- 1 yellow onion, halved
- 2 tablespoons olive oil
- 6 garlic cloves
- 4 cups chicken stock
- 1 tablespoon thyme, chopped
- 1 cup heavy cream
- Salt and black pepper to taste
- 3 and ½ ounces goat cheese, crumbled

## Directions:

Arrange tomatoes, eggplant, garlic and onion on a lined baking sheet, brush with oil and bake at 400 degrees F for 45 minutes. Scoop out pulp from veggies, transfer to a pan, heat over medium heat add thyme and stock and simmer for 45 minutes. Transfer soup to a blender, pulse well, return to saucepan, bring to a simmer, add salt and pepper and cream, stir, ladle into bowls and serve with goat cheese sprinkled on top.

**Nutrition:** calories 200, fat 3, fiber 3, carbs 5, protein 8

# Hot Tomato Soup

*Prep Time: 10 minutes | Cook Time: 35 minutes | Servings: 6*

## Ingredients:

- 6 big tomatoes, peeled and chopped
- 2 tablespoons olive oil
- 1 yellow onion, chopped
- 2 celery stalks, chopped
- 1 carrot, chopped
- 1 jalapeno, chopped
- 1 green bell pepper, chopped
- 2 garlic cloves, minced
- 3 fish fillets, cubed
- 4 cups chicken stock
- Salt and black pepper to taste
- A splash of balsamic vinegar
- A handful of basil leaves, chopped

## Directions:

Heat a large saucepan with the oil over medium high heat, add onion, celery, bell pepper, jalapeno, carrot and garlic, stir and cook for 10 minutes. Add the rest of the ingredients except the fish and basil, stir and simmer over medium heat for 15 minutes. Add fish cubes, stir and cook for 10 minutes more. Ladle into bowls, sprinkle basil on top and serve.

**Nutrition:** calories 198, fat 3, fiber 1, carbs 7, protein 10

# Broccoli Soup

*Prep Time: 30 minutes | Cook Time: 0 minutes | Servings: 2*

## Ingredients:

- 10 ounces mushrooms, chopped
- 1 broccoli head, florets separated and chopped
- 1 garlic clove, minced
- 1 tablespoon agave nectar
- 1 tablespoon balsamic vinegar
- 1 yellow onion, chopped
- 1 tablespoon olive oil
- A pinch of sea salt and black pepper
- 1 teaspoon basil, dried
- 1 avocado, peeled and pitted
- A pinch of red pepper flakes
- 1 and ½ cups water

## Directions:

In a blender, combine the mushrooms with broccoli, garlic and the other ingredients, pulse well, divide into bowls and keep in the fridge for 30 minutes before serving.

**Nutrition:** calories 182, fat 3, fiber 3, carbs 5, protein 8

# Salami and Mushroom Soup

*Prep Time: 10 minutes | Cook Time: 25 minutes | Servings: 4*

## Ingredients:

- 2 tablespoons butter, melted
- 2 tablespoons olive oil
- 1 yellow onion, chopped
- 3 ounces salami, chopped
- 1 pound brown mushrooms, sliced
- 3 tablespoons tomato paste
- ½ teaspoon garlic powder
- ½ tablespoon thyme, dried
- 1 teaspoon oregano, dried
- 1 teaspoon fennel seeds
- 6 cups chicken stock
- 3 tablespoons white flour
- 1 cup half and half
- 1 and ½ cups farro, cooked
- A pinch of salt and black pepper

## Directions:

Heat a pot with the oil and the butter over high heat, add the mushrooms, stir and sauté for 5 minutes. Add the salami and onions, stir, reduce heat to medium-low and cook for 5 minutes more. Add the rest of the ingredients except the half and half, stir and simmer for 15 more minutes. Add half and half, stir, ladle into bowls and serve.

**Nutrition:** calories 233, fat 13, fiber 6, carbs 9, protein 11

# Corn and Zucchini Soup

*Prep Time: 10 minutes | Cook Time: 0 minutes | Servings: 3*

## Ingredients:

- 1 small avocado, pitted and peeled
- 1 cup corn
- ½ zucchini, chopped
- 2 cups water
- A pinch of sea salt
- and black pepper
- 1 tablespoon white vinegar
- 1 tablespoon olive oil
- 1 teaspoon saffron

## Directions:

In a blender, mix avocado with corn and the other ingredients, pulse well, divide into bowls and serve.

**Nutrition:** calories 200, fat 2, fiber 3, carbs 5, protein 8

# Cucumber and Green Onions Soup

*Prep Time: 10 minutes | Cook Time: 0 minutes | Servings: 2*

## Ingredients:

- 2 cucumbers, peeled
- 2 green onions, chopped
- 1/3 cup dill weed, chopped
- 1 tablespoon lemon juice
- 1 teaspoon lemon juice
- A pinch of sea salt
- ½ cup water
- ½ cup hemp seeds
- A drizzle of olive oil

## Directions:

In a blender, mix cucumber with green onions, dill and the other ingredients, and pulse well. Divide into soup bowls and serve.

**Nutrition:** calories 187, fat 3, fiber 2, carbs 6, protein 4

# Milky Soup

*Prep Time: 10 minutes | Cook Time: 0 minutes | Servings: 3*

## Ingredients:

- 1 tablespoon olive oil
- 1 and ½ cups low fat milk
- 3 garlic cloves, grated
- A pinch of sea salt
- and white pepper
- ½ teaspoon apple cider vinegar
- A drizzle of olive oil for serving
- 1 tablespoon coriander, chopped

## Directions:

In a blender, mix olive oil with almond milk and the rest of the ingredients, pulse well, divide into bowls and serve.

**Nutrition:** calories 135, fat 3, fiber 5, carbs 2, protein 4

# Spinach Soup

*Prep Time: 10 minutes | Cook Time: 0 minutes | Servings: 2*

## Ingredients:

- 2 cups water
- ½ cups peanuts
- 1 cup spinach
- 1 cup broccoli florets
- A handful leek, chopped
- 1 teaspoon ginger, grated
- 1 garlic clove, minced
- A handful basil, chopped
- Juice of ½ lemon
- A pinch of sea salt and black pepper to taste

## Directions:

Put peanuts in a blender, pulse until you obtain a powder and then mix with the water. Add spinach and the other ingredients and pulse again. Divide into bowls and serve.

**Nutrition:** calories 112, fat 2, fiber 4, carbs 3, protein 3

# Stuffed Cabbage Wraps

*Prep Time: 10 minutes | Cook Time: 35 minutes | Servings: 6*

## Ingredients:

- 1 green cabbage, leaves separated
- 1 pound pork meat, ground
- A pinch of salt and black pepper
- Juice of 1 lemon
- 1 teaspoon cinnamon powder
- 2 tablespoons mint, dried and crushed
- 4 garlic cloves, minced

## Directions:

Fill a large pan with water, bring to a boil over medium-high heat, add the cabbage, cook for 3 minutes, drain and cool them down. In a bowl, mix the pork meat with salt, pepper and the rest of the ingredients and stir well. Arrange the cabbage leaves on a work surface, divide the pork mixture between the center of each, roll and seal edges. Arrange the cabbage rolls in a pot, cover them with water, bring to a boil over medium heat, cook for 30 minutes, divide between plates and serve.

**Nutrition:** calories 150, fat 2, fiber 3, carbs 5, protein 4

# Quinoa and Cherries Salad

*Prep Time:* 10 minutes | *Cook Time:* 12 minutes | *Servings:* 6

## Ingredients:

- 8 green tea bags
- 2 cups hot water
- 1 cup red quinoa
- ½ cup almonds, roasted and chopped
- ½ cup cherries, pitted
- ½ cup parsley, chopped
- A pinch of sea salt
- Black pepper to taste
- 2 tablespoons olive oil

## Directions:

Put tea bags in a bowl, add hot water, cover, leave aside for 10 minutes, discard the tea bags, transfer the tea to a pan and bring to a simmer over medium heat. Add quinoa, stir, cover, cook for 12 minutes, transfer to a bowl, fluff with a fork and then mix with cherries and the rest of the ingredients. Toss and serve.

**Nutrition:** calories 150, fat 2, fiber 3, carbs 5, protein 2

# Mango and Pasta Salad

*Prep Time:* 10 minutes | *Cook Time:* 6 minutes | *Servings:* 8

## Ingredients:

- 2 quarts water
- 12 ounces fusilli pasta
- A pinch of salt
- 1 avocado, pitted, peeled and chopped
- 1 cup red bell pepper, chopped
- 1 small cucumber, chopped
- 2 mangos, peeled
- and cubed
- Some black sesame seeds
- 1/3 cup olive oil
- 1 garlic clove, minced
- 2 tablespoons lime juice
- 1 teaspoon mustard
- Black pepper to taste

## Directions:

Put the water in a large saucepan, bring to a boil over medium high heat, add pasta, cook according to instructions and drain well. In a salad bowl, mix pasta with avocado and the rest of the ingredients, toss to coat and serve.

**Nutrition:** calories 243, fat 4, fiber 12, carbs 22, protein 6

# Fennel and Zucchini Soup

*Prep Time:* 2 hours and 10 minutes | *Cook Time:* 25 minutes | *Servings:* 6

## Ingredients:

- ½ cup fennel bulb, chopped
- ½ cup sweet onion, chopped
- 1 tablespoon olive oil
- 3 garlic cloves, minced
- 5 cups zucchini, chopped
- 1 cup water
- 2 cups veggie stock
- Salt to the taste
- 2 teaspoons white wine vinegar
- 1 teaspoon lemon juice
- 1 teaspoon lemon zest, grated

## Directions:

Heat a Dutch oven with the oil over medium heat, add onion, garlic and fennel, stir and cook for 5 minutes. Add zucchini, water and stock, stir, cook for 20 more minutes, transfer to a blender and pulse well. Add salt and the rest of the ingredients and pulse again. Leave the soup to cool down, cover and place in the fridge for 2 hours. Ladle into bowls and serve.

**Nutrition:** calories 200, fat 1, fiber 3, carbs 5, protein 8

# Stuffed Peppers

*Prep Time:* 10 minutes | *Cook Time:* 10 minutes | *Servings:* 6

## Ingredients:

- 2 big green bell peppers, cut into 6 wedges
- 2 tablespoons olive oil
- 1 garlic clove finely chopped
- 1 tablespoon lemon pepper
- ½ cup goats cheese

## Directions:

In a bowl, mix bell peppers with garlic, drizzle oil seal, toss to coat, leave aside for 10 minutes and grill over medium-high heat for 4 minutes. In a bowl, mix goats cheese with lemon pepper and whisk well. Stuff peppers with goats cheese, place on the preheated grill again, cook for 3 more minutes and serve.

**Nutrition:** calories 186, fat 4, fiber 2, carbs 7, protein 9

# Zucchini Pasta

*Prep Time: 10 minutes | Cook Time: 20 minutes | Servings: 4*

## Ingredients:

- 8 prosciutto slices, cut into thin strips
- Salt and black pepper to taste
- 5 tablespoons olive oil
- 2 zucchinis, quartered and chopped
- 1 yellow onion, chopped
- 1 cup corn kernels
- 1 pound penne
- 3 tablespoons mint, chopped
- ½ cup pecorino cheese, grated
- 2 teaspoons cider vinegar

## Directions:

Put water in a large saucepan, add salt, bring to a boil, add penne, cook according to instructions, drain, reserve ½ cup cooking liquid and leave pasta aside for now. Heat a pan with 2 tablespoons oil over medium heat, add prosciutto, stir, cook for 5 minutes, transfer to paper towels, drain fat and also leave aside for now. Heat the pan with 1 more tablespoon oil over medium heat, add onion, zucchini, corn, salt and pepper, stir and cook for 10 minutes. Add mint and half of the pecorino and stir well. Heat the pan with remaining oil over medium heat, add pasta, reserved cooking liquid, zucchini mix, vinegar, more salt and pepper, stir and cook for 1 minute. Divide between plates and serve with remaining cheese and prosciutto on top.

**Nutrition:** calories 168, fat 3, fiber 3, carbs 12, protein 4

# Beans and Corn Mix

*Prep Time: 1 hour and 10 minutes | Cook Time: 0 minutes | Servings: 8*

## Ingredients:

- 15 ounces canned cannellini beans, drained
- 15 ounces canned kidney beans, drained
- 15 ounces canned black beans, drained
- 1 green bell pepper, chopped
- 1 red bell pepper, chopped
- Salt and black pepper to taste
- 1 garlic clove, minced
- 10 ounces corn kernels
- ½ cup olive oil
- 1 red onion, chopped
- 2 tablespoons lime juice
- ½ cup red wine vinegar
- 1 tablespoon lemon juice
- 2 tablespoons sugar
- ½ tablespoon cumin, ground
- ¼ cup cilantro, chopped
- A dash of hot sauce
- ½ teaspoon chili powder

## Directions:

In a bowl, mix cannellini, kidney and black beans with all the other ingredients, toss to coat and keep in the fridge for 1 hour before serving.

**Nutrition:** calories 200, fat 4, fiber 2, carbs 6, protein 8

# Honey Lettuce and Corn Salad

*Prep Time: 10 minutes | Cook Time: 0 minutes | Servings: 8*

## Ingredients:

*For the salad dressing:*

- 2 tablespoons honey
- ¼ cup lime juice
- ½ teaspoon cumin
- 1 garlic clove, minced
- Salt and black pepper to taste
- 2 tablespoons canola oil
- 2 tablespoons olive oil

*For the salad:*

- 1 bell pepper, chopped
- 1 head lettuce, chopped
- 1 small red onion, chopped
- 1 zucchini, chopped
- 1 and ½ cups corn
- 4 tomatoes, chopped
- ½ cup cilantro, chopped
- 1 and ½ cups canned black beans, drained

## Directions:

In a bowl, mix cumin with honey, lime juice, garlic, salt and pepper, 2 tablespoons canola oil and 2 tablespoons olive oil and whisk. In a salad bowl, mix lettuce with bell pepper, red onion, the rest of the ingredients and the dressing, toss and serve.

**Nutrition:** calories 201, fat 4, fiber 3, carbs 7, protein 9

# Veggie and Fish Salad

*Prep Time: 10 minutes | Cook Time: 30 minutes | Servings: 2*

## Ingredients:

- 1 cup water
- ¾ cup quinoa, rinsed
- 1 red capsicum, chopped
- 3 yellow pan squash, chopped
- 1 baby eggplant, chopped
- 1 zucchini, chopped
- ½ sweet potato, chopped
- 1 tablespoon olive oil
- 1 red onion, cut into wedges
- 1 teaspoon hot paprika
- 2 teaspoons cumin, ground
- Salt and black pepper to taste
- 2 medium snapper fillets, boneless and skinless
- 4 cups baby spinach

*For the salad dressing:*

- 2 tablespoons coriander, chopped
- ¼ cup lime juice
- ¼ cup olive oil

## Directions:

Put quinoa in a small saucepan, add the water, leave aside for 15 minutes, bring to a boil over medium heat, cook for 15 minutes, take off heat, leave aside for another 10 minutes and fluff with a fork. Place capsicum, squash, eggplant, zucchini, spinach, sweet potato and red onion on a baking tray, mix with 1 tablespoon oil, toss and bake at 400 degrees F for 15 minutes. Place fish in another baking tray, season with salt, pepper, hot paprika and cumin, place in the oven at 400 degrees F, bake for 10 minutes, take out of the oven and flake it. Meanwhile, in a small bowl, mix coriander with salt, pepper, ¼ cup oil and lime juice and whisk very well. In a salad bowl, mix quinoa with roasted veggies, fish, salt, pepper and the salad dressing, toss and serve.

**Nutrition:** calories 185, fat 4, fiber 2, carbs 6, protein 8

## Saffron Bean Soup

*Prep Time: 10 minutes | Cook Time: 1 hour | Servings: 4*

### Ingredients:

- 1 tomato, chopped
- 1 garlic clove, minced
- 2 cups fava beans, dried
- 4 cups water
- 1 small yellow onion, chopped
- 1 tablespoon olive oil
- Salt and black pepper to taste
- ¼ teaspoon cumin, ground
- ¼ teaspoon saffron threads, crushed

### Directions:

Put beans in a large saucepan, add the water, bring to a boil over high heat, reduce temperature to medium low, cover and cook for 40 minutes. In a food processor, mix garlic with salt, pepper, tomato and onion and pulse well. Heat another saucepan with the oil over medium high heat, add tomato mix, stir and cook for 5 minutes. Add beans, their liquid and the rest of the ingredients, stir, cook for 10 minutes more, ladle into bowls and serve.

**Nutrition:** calories 213, fat 3, fiber 2, carbs 3, protein 8

## Parmesan Mushroom Quinoa

*Prep Time: 10 minutes | Cook Time: 25 minutes | Servings: 4*

### Ingredients:

- 2 tablespoons olive oil
- Salt and black pepper to the taste
- 16 ounces mushrooms
- 1 cup quinoa
- 2 cups water
- ½ cup parmesan, grated
- ¼ cup parsley, chopped
- ¼ cup green onions, chopped
- 1 garlic clove, minced
- 3 teaspoons lemon juice
- 2 tablespoons pepitas, toasted

### Directions:

Arrange mushrooms on a lined baking sheet, add 1 tablespoon oil, salt and pepper, toss, and bake at 425 degrees F for 18 minutes. Put water and quinoa in a pan, bring to a boil over medium high heat, reduce temperature, cook for 20 minutes, take off heat, cover, leave aside for 5 minutes and fluff with a fork. Add parmesan, parsley, salt, pepper, green onions, lemon juice and remaining oil and toss to coat. Divide quinoa on plates, add mushrooms on top, sprinkle pepitas all over and serve.

**Nutrition:** calories 132, fat 6, fiber 3, carbs 10, protein 7

## Feta Stuffed Peppers

*Prep Time: 10 minutes | Cook Time: 20 minutes | Servings: 4*

### Ingredients:

- 1 zucchini, chopped
- 4 red peppers, cut in halves
- 2 tablespoons olive oil
- 17 ounces already cooked quinoa
- 3 ounces feta cheese, crumbled
- Salt and black pepper to taste
- A handful parsley, finely chopped

### Directions:

Place peppers on a lined baking sheet, drizzle 1 tablespoon oil, season with salt and pepper, place in the oven at 350 degrees F and cook for 15 minutes. Heat a pan with remaining oil over medium heat, add zucchini and the rest of the ingredients and stir. Take peppers out of oven, divide quinoa mix between them, place in the oven again and cook for 5 minutes more. Serve hot.

**Nutrition:** calories 245, fat 8, fiber 11, carbs 33, protein 11

## Cheese and Bean Toast

*Prep Time: 15 minutes | Cook Time: 5 minutes | Servings: 2*

### Ingredients:

- 12 ounces broad bean
- 3.5 ounces feta cheese, crumbled
- 1 tablespoon olive oil
- 2 tablespoons mint leaves, chopped
- Salt and black
- pepper to taste
- 2 ounces mixed salad leaves
- 10 cherry tomatoes, cut in halves
- 1 teaspoon lemon juice
- 4 baguette slices

### Directions:

Put some water in a saucepan, bring to a boil over medium high heat, add beans, cook for 4 minutes, drain, put into a bowl, add half of the oil, salt, pepper, mint and cheese and toss. In another bowl, mix tomatoes with the rest of the ingredients except the bread slices Divide this on serving plates, add toasted bread slices and top them with beans mix. Serve right away.

**Nutrition:** calories 354, fat 12, fiber 11, carbs 23, protein 20

# Butter and Breadcrumbs Spinach

*Prep Time:* 10 minutes | *Cook Time:* 5 minutes | *Servings:* 4

## Ingredients:

- 1 tablespoon butter
- Zest from 1 lemon
- 3 tablespoons bread crumbs
- 2 garlic cloves,
- minced
- 17 ounces spinach
- 1 red chili, chopped
- Salt and black pepper to taste

## Directions:

Heat a pan with the butter over medium high heat, add breadcrumbs, garlic and the other ingredients except the spinach, stir, cook for 3 minutes and transfer to a bowl. Heat the pan again over medium heat, add spinach, stir and cook for 2 minutes. Divide spinach on plates, top with bread crumbs mix and serve.

**Nutrition:** calories 160, fat 7, fiber 3, carbs 20, protein 7

# Roasted Peppers Mix

*Prep Time:* 10 minutes | *Cook Time:* 1 hour and 10 minutes | *Servings:* 4

## Ingredients:

- 2 ounces canned anchovy, sliced
- 4 red bell peppers, deseeded and cut in halves
- 8 cherry tomatoes cut in halves
- 2 rosemary sprigs
- 2 garlic cloves, minced
- Salt and black pepper to taste
- 2 tablespoon olive oil

## Directions:

Place peppers in a baking dish, add the oil, salt and pepper, toss to coat, place in the oven at 300 degrees F and cook for 40 minutes. Take peppers out of the oven, divide the rest of the ingredients in each, place in the oven again and cook for 30 minutes more and serve them warm.

**Nutrition:** calories 156, fat 11, fiber 3, carbs 13, protein 4

# Hot Asparagus and Cheese Mix

*Prep Time:* 10 minutes | *Cook Time:* 15 minutes | *Servings:* 4

## Ingredients:

- 2 pounds fresh asparagus, trimmed
- ¼ cup olive oil
- Salt and black pepper to taste
- 1 teaspoon lemon zest
- 4 garlic cloves, minced
- ½ teaspoon oregano,
- dried
- ¼ teaspoon red pepper flakes
- 4 ounces feta cheese, crumbled
- 2 tablespoons parsley, finely chopped
- Juice of 1 lemon

## Directions:

Heat a pan with the oil over medium high heat, add lemon zest, garlic, pepper flakes and oregano, stir and cook for 2 minutes. Place asparagus on a lined baking sheet, add oil mix, cheese, salt, pepper, lemon juice and parsley, place in the oven at 400 degrees F and roast for 13 minutes. Divide between plates and serve hot.

**Nutrition:** calories 300, fat 23, fiber 5, carbs 12, protein 12

# Oregano Stuffed Eggplant and Cheese

*Prep Time:* 10 minutes | *Cook Time:* 1 hour | *Servings:* 4

## Ingredients:

- 4 small eggplants cut into halves lengthwise
- Salt and black pepper to taste
- 10 tablespoons olive oil
- 2 ½ pounds tomatoes, cut in halves and grated
- 1 green bell pepper, chopped
- 1 yellow onion, chopped
- 1 tablespoon garlic, minced
- ½ cup cauliflower, chopped
- 1 teaspoon oregano, chopped
- ½ cup parsley, chopped
- 3 ounces feta cheese, crumbled

## Directions:

Place eggplant halves on a lined baking sheet, add salt, pepper and 4 tablespoons oil, place them in the oven at 375 degrees F and roast for 35 minutes. Heat a pan with 3 tablespoons oil over medium high heat, add onion, stir and cook for 5 minutes. Add bell pepper, garlic, parsley, tomato, salt, pepper, oregano, cheese and cauliflower, stir, cook for 5 minutes and take off the heat. Take eggplant halves out of the oven, divide tomato mix in each half, drizzle remaining oil over them, place in the oven again and roast for 10 minutes more before serving.

**Nutrition:** calories 240, fat 4, fiber, 2, carbs 19, protein 2

# Veggie Spaghetti

*Prep Time:* 10 minutes | *Cook Time:* 15 minutes | *Servings:* 4

## Ingredients:

- 2 zucchinis cut in rounds
- 1 pound plum tomatoes cut in halves
- Salt and black pepper to taste
- 2 small eggplants cut into rounds
- 1 red onion, sliced
- 1 red bell pepper, roughly chopped
- 1 garlic head
- ¼ cup olive oil
- 1 teaspoon herbs de Provence
- ¾ cup kalamata olives, pitted and chopped
- 2 tablespoons basil, chopped
- 12 ounces spaghetti
- 2 teaspoons marjoram, chopped
- ½ cup feta cheese, crumbled

## Directions:

In a bowl, mix tomatoes with eggplant, red pepper, zucchini, garlic and onion with herbs, salt, pepper and 3 tablespoons oil, toss, place them on preheated grill, cook for 8 minutes, chop them except the garlic, transfer to a bowl, add half of the olives and toss. Put garlic in a food processor, add the rest of the olives and the oil and blend well. Put water in a saucepan, bring to a boil over medium high heat, add salt, add spaghetti, cook according to instructions, drain and reserve ½ cup of cooking water. In a bowl, mix veggies with half of the garlic sauce, basil, marjoram and pasta, stir and transfer everything to a pan. Heat over medium heat, add reserved cooking liquid and the rest of the garlic sauce, stir, divide between plates, sprinkle the cheese on top and serve.

**Nutrition:** calories 340, fat 23, fiber 11, carbs 32, protein 13

# Balsamic Eggplant

*Prep Time:* 10 minutes | *Cook Time:* 10 minutes | *Servings:* 4

## Ingredients:

- ½ tablespoon balsamic vinegar
- ½ tablespoon red wine vinegar
- 1 tablespoon currants, dried
- 1 garlic clove
- Salt and black pepper to taste
- 2 tablespoons pine nuts, toasted and chopped
- 1 red bell pepper
- 1 and ½ tablespoons
- olive oil
- 1 tablespoon marjoram, chopped
- 3 tablespoons parsley, chopped
- A pinch of cayenne pepper
- For the eggplants:
- 1 eggplant, cut into rounds
- 3 tablespoons olive oil
- Salt and black pepper to taste

## Directions:

In a bowl, mix wine vinegar with balsamic and currants then stir. In a mortar and pestle mix garlic with salt and pepper and pound until you obtain a paste. Grill bell pepper on a grill pan, transfer to a bowl, cover, leave aside for a few minutes, peel, chop it and add to the currants. Also add garlic paste, 1 ½ tablespoons oil, cayenne pepper, marjoram, nuts and parsley, stir and leave aside. Heat your grill pan over medium high heat, brush eggplant pieces with 3 tablespoons oil, season with salt and pepper, place them on the grill, cook for 4 minutes on each side and serve with the relish spread all over.

**Nutrition:** calories 140, fat 12, fiber 4, carbs 7, protein 2

# Eggplant Bowls

*Prep Time:* 10 minutes | *Cook Time:* 35 minutes | *Servings:* 12

## Ingredients:

- 2 big eggplants cut in halves
- 30 garlic cloves
- 2 tablespoons lemon juice
- 1 teaspoon lemon zest, grated
- 4 tablespoons olive oil
- 1 tablespoon parsley, chopped
- Salt and black pepper to taste

## Directions:

Put eggplant halves on a lined baking sheet, arrange garlic cloves, drizzle 2 tablespoons oil over them, season with salt and pepper, place in the oven at 350 degrees F and roast for 35 minutes. Take eggplants and garlic out of the oven, leave aside to cool down, peel, chop flesh of both eggplants and garlic and transfer to a bowl. Add the rest of the ingredients, toss, divide into smaller bowls and keep in the fridge until serving.

**Nutrition:** calories 20, fat 3, fiber 1, carbs 3, protein 0

# Stuffed Avocado

*Prep Time: 10 minutes* | *Cook Time: 7 minutes* | *Servings: 4*

## Ingredients:

- 1 and ½ teaspoons paprika
- 1 teaspoon cayenne pepper
- Salt and black pepper to taste
- ½ teaspoon garlic powder
- ½ teaspoon onion powder
- ½ teaspoon thyme
- ½ teaspoon basil
- 1 tablespoon hot sauce
- Juice from 2 limes
- 2 tablespoons olive oil
- 3 tablespoons cilantro, chopped
- 2 avocados, cut in halves and pitted
- 20 shrimp, peeled and deveined
- ¼ cup red onion, chopped
- 1 tomato, chopped
- 1 red chili pepper, chopped

## Directions:

Drizzle juice from 1 lime over avocado halves, brush them with 1 tablespoon oil, leave aside for 10 minutes, place them on preheated grill, cook over medium-high heat for 1-2 minutes and transfer to a platter. In a bowl, mix remaining lime juice with 1 tablespoon oil, hot sauce, cilantro, salt, pepper and tomato and stir. In another bowl, mix paprika with salt, pepper, onion and garlic powder, cayenne, basil and thyme and stir. Arrange shrimp on skewers, place them on preheated grill pan over medium high heat, add seasoning mix, cook for 3 minutes on each side, transfer to a cutting board, discard skewers, chop shrimp and add to the bowl with the veggies. Stuff the avocado halves with the shrimp mix and serve.

**Nutrition:** calories 234, fat 12, fiber 4, carbs 12, protein 22

# Garlic Roasted Beets

*Prep Time: 10 minutes* | *Cook Time: 1 hour* | *Servings: 4*

## Ingredients:

- 2 garlic cloves, minced
- 2 pounds beets
- Salt and black pepper to taste
- 2 tablespoons extra virgin olive oil
- A handful cilantro, chopped

## Directions:

Put beets on a lined baking sheet, place in the oven at 400 degrees F and bake for 1 hour. Cool them down, peeled, cut into cubes, transfer to a bowl, add the rest of the ingredients, toss and serve.

**Nutrition:** calories 150, fat 4, fiber 7, carbs 22, protein 4

# Beet Cakes

*Prep Time: 10 minutes* | *Cook Time: 35 minutes* | *Servings: 6*

## Ingredients:

- 3 beets
- 4 tablespoons olive oil
- Salt and black pepper to taste
- 1 yellow onion, chopped
- 2 teaspoons cumin, ground
- ¼ teaspoon allspice, ground
- 1 cup milk
- 1 cup chickpea flour
- 3 tablespoons already cooked chickpeas
- Vegetable oil for frying
- 2 tablespoons lemon juice

## Directions:

Heat a pan with 1 tablespoon olive oil over medium high heat, add onion, allspice and cumin, stir, cook for 4 minutes, take off heat and transfer to a bowl. Put beets in a saucepan, add water to cover, bring to a boil over medium heat, cook for 20 minutes, drain, cool down, peel and grate. Put milk in a saucepan, bring to a boil over medium heat, add chickpea flour, salt, pepper and the rest of the oil, whisk well until you obtain a paste, cook over low heat for 8 minutes, take off the heat and cool down. Mix and mix with grated beets, sautéed onions, lemon juice and chickpeas, stir, shape medium cakes out of this mix, arrange them on a baking sheet, flatten then and cool them down in the fridge. Heat a pan with the vegetable oil over medium high heat, add beets balls, cook for 4 minutes, transfer to paper towels, drain grease and arrange on a platter. Serve with Greek yogurt on the side.

**Nutrition:** calories 140, fat 4, fiber 6, carbs 20, protein 4

# Beet Spread

*Prep Time: 30 minutes | Cook Time: 1 hour | Servings: 6*

## Ingredients:

- 3 beets
- 3 tablespoons tahini
- 3 tablespoons olive oil
- 1 teaspoon cumin, ground
- 1 tablespoon apple
- cider vinegar
- 3 garlic cloves, roasted
- Salt and black pepper to taste
- Sesame seeds, toasted for serving

## Directions:

Arrange beet on a baking dish, add 1 tablespoon oil, rub them, cover with foil, place in the oven at 425 degrees F and bake for 1 hour. Take beets out of the oven, leave them to cool down, peel, chop them, transfer to a blender, add the rest of the ingredients except the sesame seeds and pulse well. Transfer to a bowl, keep in the fridge for 30 minutes, sprinkle sesame seeds on top and serve.

**Nutrition:** calories 50, fat 3, fiber 1, carbs 4, protein 2

# Roasted Broccoli

*Prep Time: 10 minutes | Cook Time: 10 minutes | Servings: 4*

## Ingredients:

- 12 ounces broccoli, cut into small florets
- 1 tablespoon olive oil
- Salt and black pepper to taste
- 1 cup cherry tomatoes cut in halves
- 2 garlic cloves, minced
- ½ teaspoon lemon zest, grated
- 10 black olives, pitted and chopped
- 1 tablespoon lemon juice
- 1 teaspoon oregano, dried
- 2 teaspoons capers, drained

## Directions:

In a bowl, mix broccoli with salt, pepper, tomatoes, garlic and oil, toss, arrange on a lined baking sheet and bake at 450 degrees F for 10 minutes. In a bowl, mix capers with lemon zest, lemon juice, oregano and olives and stir gently. Divide roasted broccoli mix on plates, add capers and olives mix on top and serve.

**Nutrition:** calories 90, fat 7, fiber 3, carbs 6, protein 4

# Broccoli and Walnuts Macaroni

*Prep Time: 10 minutes | Cook Time: 12 minutes | Servings: 4*

## Ingredients:

- 1 and ½ pounds broccoli, stalks and florets chopped
- ¼ cup olive oil
- Salt and black pepper to taste
- ¾ pound macaroni
- 3 garlic cloves,
- minced
- ½ cup walnuts, chopped
- 4 anchovy fillets, drained
- ¼ cup parmesan, grated

## Directions:

Put water and some salt in a saucepan, bring to a boil over medium high heat, add broccoli stalks, stir, cook for 3 minutes, add macaroni and cook for 5 more minutes. Add broccoli florets, stir, cook for 3 minutes more and drain everything. Heat a pan with the oil over medium high heat, add, garlic, anchovies and walnuts, stir and cook for 4 minutes. Add pasta, broccoli florets and stalks, salt, pepper and parmesan, stir well for 1 minute, take off heat and divide between plates.

**Nutrition:** calories 256, fat 7, fiber 5, carbs 42, protein 14

# Broccoli and Tomato Mix

*Prep Time: 10 minutes | Cook Time: 10 minutes | Servings: 4*

## Ingredients:

- 1 broccoli head, florets separated and roughly chopped
- 1 tablespoon extra-virgin olive oil
- 1 yellow onion, chopped
- 1 garlic clove, minced
- ½ pound tomatoes,
- chopped
- ¼ pint chicken stock
- 8 stuffed olives
- 1 tablespoon oregano, chopped
- 1 tablespoon parsley, chopped
- Salt and black pepper to taste

## Directions:

Heat a pan with the oil over medium high heat, add garlic and onion, stir and cook for 3 minutes. Add broccoli, tomatoes and the other ingredients, stir, cover and cook for 7 minutes more. Divide between plates and serve hot.

**Nutrition:** calories 100, fat 1, fiber 3, carbs 3, protein 5

# Lemon Brussels Sprouts

*Prep Time: 10 minutes* | *Cook Time: 10 minutes* | *Servings: 4*

## Ingredients:

- 1 pound Brussels sprouts
- 2 teaspoons lemon juice
- 3 tablespoons olive oil
- Salt and black pepper to taste
- 1 tablespoon
- mustard
- 2 garlic cloves, minced
- 1 tablespoon lemon zest
- 1 tablespoon parsley, chopped
- 2 tablespoons parmesan, grated

## Directions:

Put Brussels sprouts in a steamer basket and place over saucepan with water, and bring to a boil over medium high heat, cover, steam for 10 minutes and transfer sprouts to a bowl. In a separate bowl, mix oil with, salt, pepper and the other ingredients except the parmesan and whisk. Add over Brussels sprouts, toss to coat, divide among plates and serve with the parmesan sprinkled on top.

**Nutrition:** calories 145, fat 11, fiber 3.3, carbs 9, protein 5

# Balsamic Brussels Sprouts

*Prep Time: 10 minutes* | *Cook Time: 20 minutes* | *Servings: 4*

## Ingredients:

- 2 tablespoons balsamic vinegar
- 1 and ½ pounds Brussels sprouts
- Salt and black
- pepper to taste
- 3 tablespoons olive oil
- 2 teaspoons honey

## Directions:

In a bowl, mix Brussels sprouts with 2 tablespoons oil, salt and pepper, toss to coat, arrange on a lined baking sheet and bake at 425 degrees F for 20 minutes. Transfer to a bowl, add the rest of the ingredients, toss and serve.

**Nutrition:** calories 200, fat 8, fiber 3, carbs 7, protein 5

# Cheesy Squash

*Prep Time: 10 minutes* | *Cook Time: 10 minutes* | *Servings: 4*

## Ingredients:

- 1 tablespoon extra-virgin olive oil
- ¼ cup yellow onion, chopped
- 1 summer squash, sliced
- 1 garlic clove, minced
- 1 zucchini, thinly
- sliced
- ½ teaspoon oregano, dried
- Salt and black pepper to taste
- 1 plum tomato, chopped
- ¼ cup feta cheese, crumbled

## Directions:

Heat a pan with the oil over medium high heat, add onion, stir and cook for 2 minutes. Add squash, garlic and zucchini, stir and cook for 8 minutes. Add the rest of the ingredients, toss, cook for 1 more minute, take off heat and divide between plates.

**Nutrition:** calories 70, fat 5, fiber 2, carbs 4, protein 4

# Salad Recipes

## Chickpea Salad

*Prep Time:* 10 minutes | *Cook Time:* 30 minutes | *Servings:* 4

### Ingredients:

- 15 ounces canned chickpeas, drained
- Salt and black pepper to taste
- 1 tablespoon extra-virgin olive oil
- 1 avocado, pitted, peeled and chopped
- ½ teaspoon lime juice
- 2 ounces feta cheese, crumbled
- 2 scallions, chopped

### Directions:

Place chickpeas on a lined baking sheet, add salt, pepper and oil, toss to coat, place in the oven at 400 degrees F and bake for 30 minutes. In a bowl mix avocado with lime juice, mash, divide between plates, add roasted chickpeas and the other ingredients on top and serve.

**Nutrition:** calories 230, fat 12, fiber 12, carbs 34, protein 13

## Orange and Lettuce Salad

*Prep Time:* 10 minutes | *Cook Time:* 0 minutes | *Servings:* 4

### Ingredients:

- 1 and ½ teaspoons orange zest, grated
- ¼ cup orange juice
- 2 oranges, peeled and sliced
- 3 tablespoons white wine vinegar
- ¾ teaspoon thyme, chopped
- 2 teaspoons rosemary, chopped
- ¼ cup olive oil
- Salt and black
- pepper to taste
- 10 ounces baby romaine lettuce, chopped
- 1 pear, cored and cut into medium wedges
- 4 ounces mozzarella, cut into medium pieces
- 1/3 cup red onion, chopped
- 4 dates, pitted and chopped

### Directions:

In a bowl, mix orange juice with zest, vinegar, thyme, rosemary, oil, salt and pepper and whisk well. In another bowl, combine the rest of the ingredients with the vinaigrette, toss and serve.

**Nutrition:** calories 230, fat 12, fiber 7, carbs 32, protein 8

## Halloumi Salad

*Prep Time:* 15 minutes | *Cook Time:* 4 minutes | *Servings:* 4

### Ingredients:

- 8 ounces halloumi cheese, cubed
- 1 tablespoon capers, drained and chopped
- 1 and ½ tablespoons red wine vinegar
- 1 teaspoon honey
- 1 teaspoon lemon zest, grated
- 1 teaspoon parsley, chopped
- ½ teaspoon garlic, minced
- Salt and black pepper to taste
- 5 ounces arugula
- 5 tablespoons olive oil
- ¼ cup pistachios, chopped

### Directions:

Put halloumi in a bowl, add hot water to cover, leave aside for 15 minutes, drain and pat dry well. Heat a pan with 2 tablespoons oil over medium high heat, add halloumi, stir, cook for 4 minutes, transfer to paper towels, drain excess grease and put in a salad bowl. Add all the other ingredients, toss to coat and serve.

**Nutrition:** calories 230, fat 23, fiber 3, carbs 8, protein 16

# Herbed Radish and Pistachio Salad

*Prep Time: 30 minutes* | *Cook Time: 0 minutes* | *Servings: 4*

## Ingredients:

- 5 tablespoons olive oil
- 1/3 cup tahini
- ½ cup raisins
- 4 tablespoons lemon juice
- 1 tablespoon water
- ¼ cup chives, chopped
- ¾ cup parsley, chopped
- ¼ cup cilantro, chopped
- Salt and black pepper to taste
- ¼ cup fennel, chopped
- ¼ cup dill, chopped
- ¼ cup mint leaves, torn
- 3 radishes, cut into matchsticks
- ¼ cup pistachios, toasted
- ¼ cup tarragon, chopped
- 1 tablespoon sesame seeds, toasted

## Directions:

Put raisins in a bowl, add warm water to cover, leave aside for 30 minutes, drain and put in a bowl. In a small bowl, mix tahini with 3 tablespoons lemon juice, 3 tablespoons oil, salt, pepper and 1 tablespoon water and whisk well. Arrange this on serving plates and leave them aside for now. In a salad bowl, mix parsley with cilantro, and the other ingredients except the pistachios and radishes and toss. Divide this on tahini mix, top with raisins, pistachios and radishes and serve.

**Nutrition:** calories 240, fat 22, fiber 2, carbs 18, protein 4

# Chicken Salad

*Prep Time: 10 minutes* | *Cook Time: 5 minutes* | *Servings: 4*

## Ingredients:

*For the chicken:*
- 1 tablespoon oregano, chopped
- 2 garlic cloves, minced
- 5 chicken breast halves, skinless and boneless
- 1 tablespoons lemon

*For the salad:*
- 2 pints cherry tomatoes cut in halves
- 1 small red onion, thinly sliced
- 1 cucumber, sliced
- 1 ½ tablespoons olive oil
- 1/3 cup black olives,

  zest
- ¼ teaspoon water
- Salt and black pepper to taste
- 2 tablespoons parsley, chopped
- A drizzle of olive oil
- 6 lemon wedges

  pitted and cut in halves
- 1 cup tzatziki sauce
- Salt and black pepper to taste
- 1 teaspoon oregano, chopped
- 4 pitas, toasted

## Directions:

In a mortar, mix garlic with water, salt, pepper 1 teaspoon lemon zest and 1 tablespoon oregano and stir well. Rub chicken pieces with this mix, drizzle them with some oil, put them on preheated grill pan over medium high heat, cook for 4 minutes, flip, cook for 1 minutes more, transfer to a plate, squeeze 2 lemon wedges over them, sprinkle parsley on top and cool down. In a salad bowl, mix tomatoes with olives, onion and cucumber. Add the rest of the ingredients except the pitas, tzatziki and remaining lemon wedges and toss. Drizzle tzatziki all over and serve with pitas and the remaining lemon wedges.

**Nutrition:** calories 400, fat 22, fiber 4, carbs 34, protein 34

# Steak Salad

*Prep Time: 5 hours* | *Cook Time: 10 minutes* | *Servings: 4*

## Ingredients:

- 3 garlic cloves, minced
- 5 ½ tablespoons olive oil
- 2 teaspoons red wine vinegar
- 1 tablespoons oregano, chopped
- Salt and black pepper to taste
- 2 tablespoons parsley, chopped
- 1 pound beef meat, sliced
- 1 tablespoon lemon juice
- 1 tablespoon capers, chopped
- 1 teaspoon thyme, chopped
- 7 ounces feta cheese, cubed
- ¼ teaspoon red chili flakes
- 5 ounces baby spinach
- 2 cucumbers, thinly sliced
- 1 ½ cups cherry tomatoes cut in halves
- ½ cup kalamata olives, pitted and cut in halves

## Directions:

In a bowl, mix the beef with 3 tablespoons oil with vinegar, oregano, garlic, salt and pepper, toss and keep in the fridge for 4 hours. In another bowl, mix remaining oil with the cheese, thyme, parsley, capers, lemon juice and chili flakes, toss and leave aside for 1 hour. Heat your kitchen grill pan over medium high heat, add beef pieces, grill for 8 minutes, turning every 2 minutes, transfer them to a cutting board, leave aside for cool down, thinly slice and season with salt and pepper to taste. In a salad bowl, mix spinach with tomatoes, cucumber and olives, add the feta and its marinade, salt and pepper, toss, divide between plates, top with the steak and serve.

**Nutrition:** calories 340, fat 32, fiber 4, carbs 11, protein 34

# Potato and Orange Salad

**Cook Time:** 50 minutes | **Servings:** 6

## Ingredients:

- 4 sweet potatoes
- 3 tablespoons olive oil
- ¼ cup olive oil
- 1/3 cup orange juice
- 1 tablespoon orange juice
- 2 tablespoons pomegranate molasses
- ½ teaspoon sumac, ground
- 1 tablespoon red wine vinegar
- ½ teaspoon sugar
- Salt and black pepper to taste
- 1 tablespoon orange zest, grated
- 3 tablespoons honey
- 2 tablespoons mint, chopped
- 1/3 cup pistachios, chopped
- 1 cup Greek yogurt
- 1/3 cup pomegranate seeds

## Directions:

Put potatoes on a lined baking sheet, place in the oven at 350 degrees F, bake for 40 minutes, leave them aside for 1 hour to cool down, peel them, cut into wedges and put on a cutting board. In a bowl, mix ¼ cup oil with 1 tablespoon orange juice, sugar, vinegar, pomegranate molasses, sumac, salt and pepper and whisk. In another bowl, mix the rest of the orange juice with orange zest, honey, salt, pepper and the remaining oil and whisk well again. In a third bowl mix yogurt with some salt and pepper and with the mint and whisk. Brush potato wedges with the honey mix, add some salt, place on your kitchen grill pan heated over medium high heat, cook for 3 minutes and transfer to serving plates. Add the rest of the ingredients, drizzle the vinaigrette and yogurt sauce all over and serve.

**Nutrition:** calories 240, fat 14, fiber 3, carbs 32, protein 5

# Cucumber and Feta Salad

*Prep Time:* 5 minutes | *Cook Time:* 0 minutes | *Servings:* 4

## Ingredients:

- 2 tablespoons olive oil
- 3 tablespoons red wine vinegar
- 1 teaspoon oregano, dried
- 3 cucumbers, peeled and thinly sliced
- Salt and black pepper to taste
- 1 small red onion, chopped
- ¼ cup feta cheese, crumbled
- 1 tablespoon dill, chopped

## Directions:

In a bowl, mix the cucumbers with the onion and the other ingredients, toss and serve.

**Nutrition:** calories 53, fat 0.3, fiber 0.5, carbs 11, protein 1

# Greek Cabbage and Mint Salad

*Prep Time:* 10 minutes | *Cook Time:* 2 minutes | *Servings:* 4

## Ingredients:

- 1 teaspoon cumin, ground
- 1 small red onion, chopped
- 1 tablespoon olive oil
- 1 teaspoon coriander, ground
- 2 tablespoons lemon juice
- 2 teaspoons honey
- 1 tablespoon lemon
- zest, grated
- Salt and black pepper to taste
- 1 cup Greek yogurt
- 1 cabbage head, cut into halves and thinly sliced
- ½ cup mint, chopped
- 2 carrots, cut into thin strips
- ¼ cup pistachios, chopped

## Directions:

Put the onion in a bowl, add water to cover, leave aside for 20 minutes, drain and put in a bowl. Heat a pan over medium high heat, add oil cumin and coriander, stir, cook for 2 minutes, take off heat and leave aside to cool down. Add salt, pepper, lemon juice, lemon zest, honey and yogurt and stir well. In a salad bowl, mix cabbage with onion, mint, carrots, pistachios, salt, pepper and the salad dressing, toss and leave aside for 10 minutes before serving.

**Nutrition:** calories 139, fat 5, fiber 5, carbs 13, protein 5

# Carrot Salad

*Prep Time:* 10 minutes | *Cook Time:* 0 minutes | *Servings:* 6

## Ingredients:

- Juice of 1 lemon
- 5 tablespoons olive oil
- 1 teaspoon ginger, grated
- 1 tablespoon apple cider vinegar
- 8 carrots, peeled and grated
- Salt and black pepper to taste
- ½ cup almonds,
- toasted and sliced
- ¼ cup black raisins
- 1/3 cup pistachios, toasted
- 1 red chili pepper, chopped
- ½ cup mint, chopped
- 1 tablespoon sumac, ground
- ½ cup parsley, chopped

## Directions:

In a salad bowl, mix carrots with almonds, raisins and the rest of the ingredients, toss well and serve.

**Nutrition:** calories 100, fat 4, fiber 4, carbs 1, protein 4

# Chickpeas and Bread Salad

*Prep Time:* 10 minutes | *Cook Time:* 7 minutes | *Servings:* 4

## Ingredients:

- 1 shallot, chopped
- ¼ cup lemon juice
- 5 ounces bread, cubed
- ½ teaspoon sugar
- 7 tablespoons olive oil
- Salt and black pepper to the taste
- 15 ounces canned chickpeas, drained
- 1/3 cup mint, chopped
- 8 ounces cherry tomatoes cut in halves
- 6 ounces feta cheese, crumbled
- 6 ounces snap peas, cut in quarters
- 3 ounces baby arugula

## Directions:

Arrange the bread cubes in the oven at 350 degrees F, bake for 7 minutes and set aside to cool down. In a bowl, mix the oil, with mint, sugar with shallot, lemon juice, salt and pepper, whisk well and set aside for 10 minutes. In a salad bowl, mix tomatoes with snap peas, chickpeas, cheese, arugula, bread and the vinaigrette, toss to coat and serve.

**Nutrition:** calories 340, fat 23, fiber 12, carbs 23, protein 25

# Minty Fennel and Almond Salad

*Prep Time: 10 minutes | Cook Time: 0 minutes | Servings: 4*

## Ingredients:

- ½ cup almonds, toasted and sliced
- 3 tablespoons lemon juice
- 2 fennel bulbs, trimmed, cut in
- halves, cored and shaved crosswise
- Salt and black pepper to taste
- ¼ cup mint, torn
- ¼ cup olive oil

## Directions:

In a bowl, mix the fennel with the almonds and the other ingredients, toss and serve.

**Nutrition:** calories 200, fat 12, fiber 9, carbs 19, protein 4

# Greens and Olives Salad

*Prep Time: 10 minutes | Cook Time: 8 minutes | Servings: 4*

## Ingredients:

- ½ loaf sourdough bread, cubed
- ¼ teaspoon paprika
- 2 tablespoons Manchego, grated
- 9 tablespoons olive oil
- 1 and ½ tablespoons sherry vinegar
- Salt and black pepper to taste
- 1 teaspoon mustard
- 5 cups baby greens
- ¾ cup green olives, pitted and chopped
- 12 thin slices ham, torn

## Directions:

In a bowl, mix 6 tablespoons oil with Manchego, paprika and bread cubes, toss to coat, arrange on a lined baking sheet, place in the oven at 400 degrees F and bake for 8 minutes. In a bowl, mix mustard with salt, pepper, remaining oil and the vinegar and whisk well. In a salad bowl, mix the greens with the bread and all the other ingredients, add the vinaigrette, toss and serve.

**Nutrition:** calories 250, fat 14, fiber 2, carbs 15, protein 9

# Tomato Salad

*Prep Time: 10 minutes | Cook Time: 0 minutes | Servings: 4*

## Ingredients:

- 2 cups cherry tomatoes cut in halves
- 1 and ½ cups watermelon, chopped
- 2 cups baby arugula
- 3 small cucumbers, chopped
- ¼ cup basil, torn
- ¾ cup feta cheese, cubed
- 1 tablespoon lemon juice
- Salt and black pepper to taste
- 1 tablespoon olive oil

## Directions:

In a salad bowl, mix the tomatoes with the watermelon and the other ingredients, toss to coat and serve.

**Nutrition:** calories 140, fat 4, fiber 2, carbs 10, protein 5

# Farro, Beans and Radicchio Salad

*Prep Time: 10 minutes | Cook Time: 35 minutes | Servings: 8*

## Ingredients:

- 7 cups water
- 3 cups pearled farro
- Salt and black pepper to taste
- ½ cup black olives, pitted and chopped
- 1/3 cup red wine vinegar
- ½ cup olive oil
- 1 tablespoons olive oil
- 1 teaspoon lemon zest, grated
- 1 cup fennel, chopped
- 1 cup jarred artichoke hearts, drained
- 1 cup cooked cannellini beans
- 1 cup radicchio, shredded
- ¼ cup basil leaves, chopped
- ¾ cup pine nuts, toasted

## Directions:

Put the water in a large saucepan, bring to a boil over high heat, add salt and farro, stir, reduce heat to medium-low, cook for 35 minutes, drain, spread on a lined baking sheet, combine with 1 tablespoon oil, salt and pepper, toss and leave aside for now. In a bowl, mix remaining oil with the vinegar, lemon zest, olives, salt and pepper and whisk well. Transfer farro to a salad bowl, add fennel, artichokes, cannellini beans, radicchio, basil, nuts, salt and pepper and the vinaigrette, toss and keep in the fridge until you serve.

**Nutrition:** calories 340, fat 21, fiber 9, carbs 45, protein 11

# Orange Asparagus and Pistachios Salad

*Prep Time: 10 minutes | Cook Time: 0 minutes | Servings: 4*

## Ingredients:

- 8 slices of prosciutto, chopped
- 2 oranges, peeled, cut into segments
- 1 tablespoon orange juice
- 1 pound asparagus, trimmed
- ½ cup water
- 5 tablespoons olive oil
- ½ cup pistachios, roasted and chopped
- Salt and black pepper to taste
- 1-ounce parmesan cheese, grated

## Directions:

Put asparagus in a heatproof dish, add the water, salt, pepper and 1 tablespoon olive oil, toss to coat, place in your microwave and cook on High for 5 minutes. Divide asparagus on serving plates; add all the other ingredients, toss and serve.

**Nutrition:** calories 230, fat 12, fiber 4, carbs 12, protein 14

# Arugula Salad

*Prep Time: 10 minutes | Cook Time: 0 minutes | Servings: 4*

## Ingredients:

- 1 teaspoon lemon zest, grated
- 4 cups baby arugula
- 2 tablespoons olive oil
- Salt and black pepper to taste
- 4 ounces prosciutto,
- cut into strips
- 2 ounces mozzarella, shredded
- 4 teaspoons balsamic vinegar
- ½ cup almonds, toasted and chopped

## Directions:

In a bowl, mix the arugula with mozzarella and the rest of the ingredients, toss and serve.

**Nutrition:** calories 140, fat 6, fiber 3, carbs 8, protein 3

# Potato and Artichoke Salad

*Prep Time: 10 minutes | Cook Time: 20 minutes | Servings: 8*

## Ingredients:

- ¼ cup lemon juice
- Salt and black pepper to the taste
- 2 teaspoons Dijon mustard
- ¼ cup olive oil
- 2 garlic cloves, minced and mashed
- ½ teaspoon red pepper flakes
- 2 teaspoons marjoram, chopped
- For the salad:
- ¼ cup rice vinegar
- 1 tablespoon olive oil
- 3 and ¼ pounds baby red potatoes
- 2 cup frozen artichoke hearts
- Salt and black pepper to taste
- ¾ cup mint, chopped
- 1 cup black olives, pitted and chopped

## Directions:

In a bowl, mix lemon juice with salt, pepper, mustard, ¼ cup oil, 2 garlic cloves, marjoram and pepper flakes and whisk well. In a bowl, mix vinegar with salt and whisk. Put potatoes in a large saucepan, add salt and water to cover, bring to a boil over high heat, reduce temperature, cook for 10 minutes, take off heat, drain, cool them down, peel and cut them into chunks. Put potatoes in a salad bowl, add rice vinegar mixed with salt and toss to coat. Heat a pan with 1 tablespoon oil over medium high heat, add artichoke hearts, cook for 1-2 minutes, add over the potatoes, also add olives, mint and the vinaigrette, toss and serve.

**Nutrition:** calories 145, fat 4, fiber 3, carbs 11, protein 4

# Bulgur Salad

*Prep Time:* 10 minutes | *Cook Time:* 1 hour | *Servings:* 6

## Ingredients:

- 1 cup red grapes, cut in quarters
- 1 cup bulgur
- 1 cup celery, chopped
- 3 tablespoons dried currants
- ¼ cup parsley, chopped
- 1/3 cup walnuts, toasted and chopped
- 3 tablespoons walnut oil
- 3 tablespoons balsamic vinegar
- Salt and black pepper to taste
- 2 tablespoons shallot, minced
- 1 cup water

## Directions:

Put the water in a large saucepan, bring to a boil over medium high heat, add bulgur, take off heat and leave aside for 1 hour. Fluff bulgur and transfer to a bowl. Add the rest of the ingredients, toss and serve.

**Nutrition:** calories 220, fat 11, fiber 6, carbs 24, protein 5

# Hot Chickpea and Mint Salad

*Prep Time:* 10 minutes | *Cook Time:* 1 hour and 30 minutes | *Servings:* 4

## Ingredients:

- 3 cups canned chickpeas, drained
- 2 bay leaves
- ¼ teaspoon turmeric
- Salt and black pepper to taste
- 1 yellow onion, cut in half
- 3 potatoes
- 1 cup yogurt
- ¼ cup sour cream
- 1 tablespoon ginger, grated
- 1 teaspoon fennel seeds, toasted and ground
- 1 ½ teaspoons cumin, toasted and ground
- 1 cucumber, chopped
- 1 hot green chili pepper, chopped
- 1 red onion, chopped
- ¼ cup mint, chopped
- ¼ cup cilantro, chopped
- 8 cups water

## Directions:

Put beans in a saucepan, add the water over them, bring to a boil over medium high heat, add bay leaves, yellow onion, salt, pepper and turmeric, stir, reduce to medium and cook for 1 hour and 30 minutes, take off heat and leave aside to cool down. Meanwhile, put potatoes in another saucepan, add salt, bring to a boil over high heat, cook for 20 minutes, drain, leave aside to cool down, peel and cut them into small cubes. In a bowl, mix beans with potatoes and all the remaining ingredients, toss, leave aside for 15 minutes and serve.

**Nutrition:** calories 210, fat 4, fiber 8, carbs 32, protein 8

# Dessert Recipes

## Banana Shake

*Prep Time:* 5 minutes | *Cook Time:* 0 minutes | *Servings:* 2

### Ingredients:

- 2 medium bananas, peeled
- 2 teaspoons cocoa powder
- ½ big avocado, mashed
- ¾ cup low fat milk
- A pinch of salt

### Directions:

Put bananas in a blender and pulse a few times. Add the rest of the ingredients, pulse again, divide into 2 glass and serve right away.

**Nutrition:** calories 185, fat 3, fiber 4, carbs 6, protein 7

## Lemon Bars

*Prep Time:* 30 minutes | *Cook Time:* 0 minutes | *Servings:* 4

### Ingredients:

- 1 cup olive oil
- 1 and ½ bananas, peeled and chopped
- A pinch of salt
- 1/3 cup agave syrup
- ¼ cup lemon juice
- A pinch of lemon zest, grated
- 3 kiwis, peeled and chopped
- Raw hemp seeds for the crust

### Directions:

In a food processor, mix bananas with kiwis, almost all oil, a pinch of salt, agave syrup, lemon juice and a pinch of lemon zest, pulse and spread into a pan after you've greased with the rest of the oil and sprinkled with hemp seeds all over. Keep in the fridge for 30 minutes, slice and serve bars.

**Nutrition:** calories 187, fat 3, fiber 3, carbs 4, protein 4

## Lemon Berry Cobbler

*Prep Time:* 10 minutes | *Cook Time:* 30 minutes | *Servings:* 6

### Ingredients:

- ¾ cup sugar
- 6 cups strawberries, halved
- 1/8 teaspoon baking powder
- 1 tablespoon lemon juice
- ½ cup spelled flour
- 1/8 teaspoon baking soda
- A pinch of salt
- ½ cup water
- 3 and ½ tablespoon olive oil
- Cooking spray

### Directions:

Grease a baking dish with some cooking spray and leave aside. In a bowl, mix strawberries with half of palm sugar, sprinkle some flour and add lemon juice, whisk and pour into the baking dish. In another bowl, mix flour with remaining sugar, a pinch of salt, baking powder, soda, ½ cup water and the oil and stir well with your hands. Spread over strawberries, bake at 375 degrees F for 30 minutes, cool down and serve.

**Nutrition:** calories 221, fat 3, fiber 3, carbs 6, protein 9

# Buttery Black Tea Cake

*Prep Time: 10 minutes | Cook Time: 35 minutes | Servings: 12*

## Ingredients:

- 6 tablespoons black tea powder
- 2 cups low fat milk
- ½ cup butter
- 2 cups sugar
- 4 eggs
- 2 teaspoons vanilla

*For the cream:*

- 6 tablespoons honey
- 4 cups sugar

- extract
- ½ cup olive oil
- 3 and ½ cups flour
- 1 teaspoon baking soda
- 3 teaspoons baking powder

- 1 cup butter, soft

## Directions:

Put the milk in a saucepan, heat up up over medium heat, add the tea, stir, take off the heat and cool down In a bowl, mix ½ cup butter with 2 cups sugar, eggs, vegetable oil, vanilla extract, 3 and ½ cups flour, baking powder and baking soda and stir. Pour this into 2 greased round pans, place in the oven at 350 degrees F and bake for 30 minutes. Leave cakes to cool down. In a bowl, mix 1 cup butter with honey and 4 cups sugar and stir well. Arrange one cake on a platter, spread the cream all over, top with the other cake and keep in the fridge until you serve it.

**Nutrition:** calories 200, fat 4, fiber 4, carbs 6, protein 2

# Creamy Pudding

*Prep Time: 2 hours and 10 minutes | Cook Time: 5 minutes | Servings: 6*

## Ingredients:

- 14 ounces milk
- 2 tablespoons green tea powder
- 14 ounces heavy

- cream
- 3 tablespoons sugar
- 1 teaspoon gelatin powder

## Directions:

Put the milk in a pan, add sugar and the rest of the ingredients except the cream, bring to a simmer and cook for 2 minutes. Cool the mix down, add heavy cream, stir, divide into cups and keep in the fridge for 2 hours before serving.

**Nutrition:** calories 120, fat 3, fiber 3, carbs 7, protein 4

# Apple and Vanilla Pie

*Prep Time: 10 minutes | Cook Time: 1 hour and 5 minutes | Servings: 8*

## Ingredients:

- ½ cup sugar
- 4 apples, peeled, cored and cut into chunks

- 1 cup flour
- 3 eggs
- 1 teaspoon vanilla extract

## Directions:

Arrange apple pieces on the bottom of a lined spring form pan, add eggs mixed with vanilla, sugar and flour and stir well again. Pour over apples, place in the oven at 375 digress F and bake for 1 hour. Flip pie upside down when it's done, slice and serve.

**Nutrition:** calories 200, fat 4, fiber 3, carbs 6, protein 8

# Lemony Apricot Cream Bowls

*Prep Time: 2 hours and 10 minutes | Cook Time: 0 minutes | Servings: 4*

## Ingredients:

- ¾ cup apricot pulp
- 1 cup low fat milk
- ½ cup whipping cream
- 3 eggs, whites and yolks separated
- 1/3 cup sugar

- 1 teaspoon lemon juice
- ½ teaspoon vanilla
- 1 package gelatin
- 1 tablespoon warm water

## Directions:

In a bowl, mix warm water with gelatin and whisk well In another bowl, mix sugar with egg yolks and milk whisk well, put under the preheated broiler, cook until it thickens, add the gelatin, stir and leave this aside to cool down. In a food processor, mix the apricot pulp with lemon juice and vanilla and pulse well. Add this to gelatin mix and stir well. In a bowl, beat egg white using your mixer. Add this to gelatin mix and stir everything. Divide into molds and serve after you've kept in the fridge for 2 hours.

**Nutrition:** calories 129, fat 4, fiber 6, carbs 8, protein 9

## Cherry and Yogurt Mix

*Prep Time: 4 hours and 10 minutes | Cook Time: 2 minutes | Servings: 4*

### Ingredients:

- 1 tablespoon gelatin
- ¼ cup water
- 2 cups sour cherry puree
- 1/3 cup sugar
- 1 cup Greek yogurt
- ½ teaspoon vanilla extract
- 1 cup cold heavy cream

### Directions:

In a small pot, combine the gelatin with the water, set aside for 1 minute and then slowly heat up over medium-low heat for 2 minutes. In a blender, mix the sour cherry puree with the cream, gelatin, sugar, vanilla and the yogurt, pulse well, divide into bowls and keep in the fridge for 4 hours before serving.

**Nutrition:** calories 190, fat 13, fiber 5, carbs 8, protein 8

## Lemon Plum and Butter Cake

*Prep Time: 1 hour and 20 minutes | Cook Time: 40 minutes | Servings: 8*

### Ingredients:

- 7 ounces flour
- 1 package dried yeast
- 1 ounce butter, soft
- A pinch of salt
- 1 egg, whisked
- 5 tablespoons sugar
- 3 ounces warm milk
- 1 and ¾ pounds plums, pitted and cut in quarters
- Zest from 1 lemon, grated
- 1 ounce almond flakes

### Directions:

In a bowl, mix yeast with butter, flour, a pinch of salt, 3 tablespoons sugar, milk and egg and stir until you obtain a dough. Arrange the dough in a spring form pan which you've greased with some of the butter, cover and leave aside for 1 hour. Arrange plums on top of the butter, sprinkle the rest of the sugar, place in the oven at 350 degrees F, bake for 40 minutes, cool down, sprinkle almond flakes and lemon zest on top, slice and serve.

**Nutrition:** calories 192, fat 4, fiber 2, carbs 6, protein 7

## Lentil and Raisins Cookies

*Prep Time: 10 minutes | Cook Time: 25 minutes | Servings: 36*

### Ingredients:

- 1 cup water
- 1 cup lentils, cooked, drained and rinsed
- 1 cup white flour
- 1 teaspoon cinnamon
- 1 cup whole wheat flour
- 1 teaspoon baking powder
- ½ teaspoon nutmeg, ground
- A pinch of salt
- 1 cup butter, soft
- ½ cup brown sugar
- ½ cup white sugar
- 1 egg
- 2 teaspoons almond extract
- 1 cup raisins
- 1 cup rolled oats
- 1 cup coconut, unsweetened and shredded

### Directions:

Put lentils in a saucepan, add the water, bring to a boil over medium heat, cook for 15 minutes, take off heat, leave aside to cool down and mash them to create a paste. In a bowl, mix white and whole wheat flour with salt, cinnamon, baking powder and nutmeg and stir. In a bowl, mix butter with white and brown sugar, egg, almond extract, lentils mix and flour and stir until you obtain a dough. Add oats, raisins and coconut and stir gently. Scoop tablespoons of dough on 2 lined baking sheets, place them in the oven at 350 degrees F, bake for 18 minutes, cool them down and serve.

**Nutrition:** calories 154, fat 2, fiber 2, carbs 4, protein 7

# Banana and Lentils Brownies

*Prep Time: 10 minutes | Cook Time: 15 minutes | Servings: 8*

## Ingredients:

- 28 ounces canned lentils, rinsed and drained
- 12 dates
- 1 tablespoon honey
- 1 banana, peeled and chopped
- ½ teaspoon baking soda
- 4 tablespoons almond butter
- 2 tablespoons cocoa powder

## Directions:

Put lentils in a food processor, blend, add dates, butter, banana, cocoa, baking soda and honey and blend again. Pour this into a greased pan, spread evenly, place in the oven at 375 degrees F and bake for 15 minutes. Take brownies out of the oven, cut, arrange on a platter and serve them cold.

**Nutrition:** calories 162, fat 4, fiber 2, carbs 3, protein 4

# Lemony Ice Cream

*Prep Time: 3 hours and 10 minutes | Cook Time: 1 hour and 20 minutes | Servings: 4*

## Ingredients:

- ½ cup red lentils, rinsed
- Juice of ½ lemon
- ½ cup sugar
- 1 and ½ cups water
- A pinch of salt
- 3 cups almond milk
- ½ cup honey
- Juice from 2 limes
- 2 teaspoons cardamom, ground
- 1 teaspoon rose water
- 3 drops vanilla extract

## Directions:

Heat a pan over medium high heat with the water, sugar, some salt and lemon juice, stir well, bring to a boil and mix with the lentils. Reduce heat to low and simmer for 1 hour and 20 minutes. Drain lentils, put them into to a blender, add the almond milk, honey, lime juice, cardamom, rosewater and vanilla extract and pulse well. Transfer the mix to a container and keep in the freezer for 3 hours before serving.

**Nutrition:** calories 144, fat 4, fiber 3, carbs 5, protein 4

# Apple Cupcakes

*Prep Time: 10 minutes | Cook Time: 20 minutes | Servings: 4*

## Ingredients:

- 4 tablespoons butter
- 4 eggs
- ½ cup pure applesauce
- 2 teaspoons cinnamon powder
- 1 teaspoon vanilla extract
- ½ apple, cored and sliced
- 4 teaspoons maple syrup
- ¾ cup almond flour
- ½ teaspoon baking powder
- Cinnamon powder for serving
- A pinch of salt

## Directions:

Heat a pan with butter over medium heat, add applesauce, vanilla, eggs and maple syrup, stir, take off heat and leave aside to cool down. Add the rest of the ingredients except the apples and cinnamon, whisk, pour in a cupcake pan, place in the oven at 350 degrees F and bake for 20 minutes. Cool them down, transfer to a platter, top with apple slices and cinnamon and serve!

**Nutrition:** calories 150, fat 3, fiber 1, carbs 5, protein 4

# Nutmeg and Butter Rhubarb Pie

*Prep Time: 30 minutes | Cook Time: 1 hour | Servings: 6*

**Ingredients:**

- 1 and ¼ cups almond flour
- 8 tablespoons butter
- A pinch of salt

*For the filling:*

- 3 cups rhubarb, chopped
- 3 tablespoons almond flour
- 1 and ½ cups sugar
- 2 eggs

- 5 tablespoons cold water
- 1 teaspoon sugar

- A pinch of salt
- ½ teaspoon nutmeg, ground
- 1 tablespoon butter
- 2 tablespoons low fat milk

**Directions:**

In a bowl, mix 1 ¼ cups flour with salt, 1 teaspoon sugar, cold water and 8 tablespoons butter. and knead until you obtain a dough. Transfer dough to a floured working surface, shape a disk, flatten, wrap in plastic, keep in the fridge for about 30 minutes and then roll into a pie plate. In a bowl, mix rhubarb with a pinch of salt, 1 ½ cups sugar, nutmeg, 3 tablespoons flour and whisk. In a second bowl, whisk eggs with milk. Add this to rhubarb mix, stir well, pour into pie crust and bake in the oven for 50 minutes at 400 degrees F. Cut and serve it cold.

**Nutrition:** calories 200, fat 2, fiber 1, carbs 6, protein 3

# Couscous Pudding

*Prep Time: 15 minutes | Cook Time: 2 minutes | Servings: 4*

**Ingredients:**

- 1 cup couscous
- 2 tablespoons rose water
- 2 cups fruit juice
- 3 tablespoons butter
- ¼ cup pistachio, grated

- ¼ cup almonds, blanched
- ½ cup sugar
- 1 tablespoon cinnamon powder
- ½ cup pomegranate seeds

**Directions:**

In a large saucepan, mix fruit juice with rose water and couscous, bring to a boil over medium heat, cover, take off heat, leave aside for 15 minutes and fluff with a fork. Add melted butter, almonds and pistachios, stir, divide into bowls, sprinkle the remaining ingredients on top and serve.

**Nutrition:** calories 200, fat 2, fiber 2, carbs 4, protein 7

# Apricot Ice Cream

*Prep Time: 2 hours and 10 minutes | Cook Time: 10 minutes | Servings: 4*

**Ingredients:**

- 2 cups sparkling wine
- 1 cup palm sugar
- 2 strips lemon peel

- A pinch of salt
- 1 ½ pounds apricots pitted and cut in halves

**Directions:**

Heat a saucepan over medium heat, add sugar, wine, apricots, lemon peel and a pinch of salt, stir bring to a simmer, cook for 10 minutes, take off heat and discard lemon peel. Transfer this cold to a blender, pulse, transfer to a casserole, freeze for 2 hours and serve

**Nutrition:** calories 172, fat 4, fiber 3, carbs 6, protein 6

# Apple and Cranberry Sweet Mix

*Prep Time: 10 minutes | Cook Time: 40 minutes | Servings: 4*

**Ingredients:**

- 2 cup cranberries
- 3 cups apple, cubed
- A drizzle of olive oil
- ½ cup sugar
- 1/3 cup almond
- flour
- 1 cup oats
- ¼ canola oil
- ½ cup palm sugar

**Directions:**

In a bowl, mix apples with cranberries and ½ cup sugar and stir well. In another bowl, mix flour with oats, canola oil and ½ cup sugar, stir and pour into a baking dish greased with a drizzle of olive oil. Sprinkle flour mix on top, place in the oven at 350 degrees F, bake for 40 minutes, cool down and serve.

**Nutrition:** calories 202, fat 2, fiber 3, carbs 4, protein 2

# Lemon Pie

*Prep Time: 1 hour | Cook Time: 45 minutes | Servings: 6*

**Ingredients:**

*For the crust:*

- 2 tablespoons sugar
- 2 cups white flour
- A pinch of salt
- 3 tablespoons ice
- water
- 12 tablespoons cold butter

*For the filling:*

- 2 eggs, whisked
- 1 and ¼ cup sugar
- 10 tablespoons melted and chilled
- butter
- Juice from 2 lemons
- Zest of 2 lemons, grated

**Directions:**

In a bowl, mix 2 cups flour with a pinch of salt, 2 tablespoons sugar, 12 tablespoons butter and the water knead until you obtain a firm dough, shape a ball, wrap in plastic and keep in the fridge for 1 hour. Transfer dough to a floured working surface, flatten it, arrange on the bottom of a tart pan, prick with a fork, cover with foil and keep in the fridge for 20 minutes. Fill this with pie weights, place in the oven at 375 degrees F and bake shell for 15 minutes. Get rid of the pie weights, bake 5 more minutes and leave aside for now. In a bowl, mix 1 and ¼ cup sugar with eggs, 10 tablespoons butter, lemon juice and lemon zest and whisk well. Pour this into pie crust, spread evenly, place in the oven, bake for 25 minutes, cool down and serve it.

**Nutrition:** calories 182, fat 4, fiber 1, carbs 2, protein 3

# Berry and Yogurt Bowls

*Prep Time: 10 minutes | Cook Time: 5 minutes | Servings: 8*

**Ingredients:**

- 1 and ½ cups blueberries
- 1 and ½ cups strawberries, cut in quarters
- 2 tablespoons
- cornstarch
- 3 tablespoons sugar
- 1 and ½ cups pure apple juice
- Vanilla Greek yogurt for serving

**Directions:**

In a heat proof dish, mix blueberries with strawberries and 2 tablespoons sugar. Heat apple juice in a saucepan over medium high heat, add cornstarch, stir, boil for 2 minutes, cool down for 10 minutes, pour over the fruits, add the rest of the sugar as well, cover and keep in the fridge for 10 minutes. Spoon fruit mix in small bowl, top with Greek yogurt and serve!

**Nutrition:** calories 174, fat 3, fiber 3, carbs 3, protein 5

# Mandarin Pudding

*Prep Time: 20 minutes | Cook Time: 2 hours and 35 minutes | Servings: 8*

**Ingredients:**

- 1 mandarin, peeled and sliced
- Juice from 2 mandarins
- 2 tablespoons brown sugar
- 4 ounces butter, soft
- 2 eggs, whisked
- ¾ cup sugar
- ¾ cup white flour
- ¾ cup almonds, ground
- Honey for serving

**Directions:**

Grease a loaf pan with some butter, sprinkle the brown sugar on the bottom, and arrange slices from mandarin on top In a bowl, mix butter with sugar, eggs, almonds, flour and mandarin juice and whisk using your mixer. Spoon mix over mandarin slices, place pan in a slow cooker, cover and cook on High for 2 hours and 30 minutes. Uncover, leave aside for a few minutes transfer to a plate and serve with honey on top.

**Nutrition:** calories 162, fat 3, fiber 2, carbs 3, protein 6

# Berry Jars

*Prep Time: 20 minutes | Cook Time: 1 hour and 30 minutes | Servings: 6*

### Ingredients:

- Olive oil cooking spray
- ¼ cup sugar + 4 tablespoons
- 1 ½ cup almond flour
- 1 teaspoon baking powder
- A pinch of salt
- ¼ teaspoon baking soda
- 1/3 cup butter
- 1 cup low fat buttermilk
- 1 egg, whisked
- 2 cups strawberries, sliced
- 1 tablespoon rum
- 1 tablespoon mint, chopped
- 1 teaspoon lime zest, grated
- ½ cup whipping cream

### Directions:

Grease 6 small jars with olive oil cooking spray and leave them aside for now. In a bowl, mix flour with ¼ cup sugar, baking powder, salt, baking soda, buttermilk and eggs and mix. Spoon this dough into jars, cover with foil, arrange them in a slow cooker, add some water to the bottom, cover and cook on High for 1 hour and 30 minutes. In a bowl mix strawberries with 3 tablespoons sugar, rum, mint and lime zest, stir and leave aside in a cold place. In another bowl, mix whipping cream with 1 tablespoon sugar and stir. Uncover slow cooker, take jars out, divide strawberry mix and whipped cream on top and serve.

**Nutrition:** calories 164, fat 2, fiber 3, carbs 5, protein 2

# Olive Oil Cake

*Prep Time: 10 minutes | Cook Time: 20 minutes | Servings: 12*

### Ingredients:

- 3 cups almond flour
- 3 teaspoons baking powder
- ½ cup cornstarch
- 1 teaspoon baking soda
- 1 cup olive oil
- 1 and ½ cup low fat milk
- 1 and 2/3 cup sugar
- 2 cups water
- ¼ cup lemon juice
- 2 teaspoons vanilla extract

### Directions:

In a bowl, mix flour with the oil and the other ingredients and whisk well. Pour into a greased baking dish, place in the oven at 357 degrees F and bake for 20 minutes. Leave cake to cool down, cut and serve!

**Nutrition:** calories 246, fat 3, fiber 1, carbs 6, protein 2

# Pumpkin Bowls

*Prep Time: 3 minutes | Cook Time: 4 minutes | Servings: 1*

### Ingredients:

- 1 apple, peeled, cored and chopped
- ¼ cup canned pumpkin flesh
- 2 tablespoons water
- A pinch of pumpkin spice

### Directions:

In a bowl, mix some apple slices with some of the pumpkin flesh. Sprinkle pumpkin spice, layer the rest of the apples and pumpkin flesh, top with pumpkin spice again, add water, microwave for 4 minutes and serve.

**Nutrition:** calories 99, fat 0.4, fiber 3, carbs 5, protein 1

# Berry Smoothie

*Prep Time: 5 minutes | Cook Time: 0 minutes | Servings: 2*

### Ingredients:

- 1 and ½ cup low fat milk
- 1 cup blueberries
- 4 big strawberries, chopped
- ½ banana, peeled
- 2 tablespoons hemp seeds
- 1 and ½ tablespoons chia seeds
- A handful spinach
- 1 teaspoon cinnamon

### Directions:

Put blueberries in a blender and mix well. Add the rest of the ingredients, pulse again, pour into a glass and serve.

**Nutrition:** calories 121, fat 2, fiber 3, carbs 6, protein 5

# Minty Strawberry Smoothie

*Prep Time: 6 minutes | Cook Time: 0 minutes | Servings: 2*

**Ingredients:**

- ½ banana, peeled
- 2 cups strawberries, halved
- 3 tablespoons spearmint
- 1 ½ cups coconut
- water
- ½ avocado, pitted and peeled
- 1 date, chopped
- Ice cubes for serving

**Directions:**

Put banana in a blender and pulse a few times. Add the rest of the ingredients and blend some more. Pour into a glass and enjoy!

**Nutrition:** calories 100, fat 0, fiber 1, carbs 2, protein 3

# Cold Melon Bowls

*Prep Time: 15 minutes | Cook Time: 0 minutes | Servings: 2*

**Ingredients:**

- 2 ripe melons, peeled and cubed
- Equal parts lime
- juice and pure maple syrup
- Ice for serving

**Directions:**

Place melon cubes in a bowl add lime, add the rest of the ingredients, and toss. Cover and keep in the fridge until you serve. Divide into bowl and serve with ice.

**Nutrition:** calories 78, fat 0, fiber 0, carbs 0, protein 2

# Vanilla Fruit Cake

*Prep Time: 10 minutes | Cook Time: 40 minutes | Servings: 8*

**Ingredients:**

- 1 cup whole wheat flour
- 1 and ½ teaspoon baking powder
- ½ cup cornmeal
- A pinch of salt
- 2 eggs
- 2/3 cup sugar
- ½ cup extra virgin
- olive oil
- 1/3 cup low fat milk
- 1 teaspoon vanilla extract
- 1 teaspoon lemon zest, grated
- 1 ¾ cup red grapes, halved

**Directions:**

In a bowl, mix flour with cornmeal, a pinch of salt and baking powder, stir and leave aside. In another bowl, mix eggs with sugar and blend using a kitchen mixer for 5 minutes. Add oil, milk, vanilla and lemon zest and stir again. Add flour to this mix and half of the grapes and stir. Grease a baking pan, pour the batter in it, place in the oven at 350 degrees F for 10 minutes, arrange the remaining grapes on top, bake for 30 minutes more, cool down, slice and serve.

**Nutrition:** calories 120, fat 2, fiber 2, carbs 4, protein 4

# Cherry Sorbet and Compote

*Prep Time: 2 hours and 20 minutes | Cook Time: 0 minutes | Servings: 7*

**Ingredients:**

- ½ cup cocoa powder
- ¾ cup red cherry jam
- ¼ cup sugar
- 2 cups water
- A pinch of salt

*For the compote:*

- ¼ cup sugar
- 1 pound cherries,
- pitted and halved

**Directions:**

In a pan, mix cherry jam with cocoa, sugar and a pinch of salt, stir, bring to a boil over medium heat, add the water, stir again, remove from heat and leave aside to cool down. Whisk sorbet again, pour in a casserole dish and keep in the freezer for 1 hour. In a bowl, mix ¼ cup sugar with cherries, toss to coat, leave aside for 1 hour and serve with the sorbet.

**Nutrition:** calories 197, fat 1, fiber 3, carbs 5, protein 1

# Cinnamon Rice Pudding

*Prep Time:* 15 minutes | *Cook Time:* 45 minutes | *Servings:* 6

## Ingredients:

- ½ cup basmati rice
- 4 cups milk
- ¼ cup raisins
- 3 tablespoons sugar
- ½ teaspoon cardamom
- ¼ teaspoon

- cinnamon powder
- ½ teaspoon rose water
- ¼ cup almonds, chopped
- 1 tablespoon orange zest, grated

## Directions:

Soak rice in some water for 10 minutes, drain and leave aside. In a pan, mix sugar with milk, stir, bring to a boil at a medium high temperature, add rice and the other ingredients except the orange zest and almonds, stir and cook over medium heat for 45 minutes. In a bowl, mix orange zest with almonds. Pour rice pudding into bowls, sprinkle almond mix on top and serve cold.

**Nutrition:** calories 120, fat 1, fiber 2, carbs 2, protein 3

# Orange Cake

*Prep Time:* 10 minutes | *Cook Time:* 1 hour and 10 minutes | *Servings:* 4

## Ingredients:

- 8 eggs, whisked
- 3 pounds ricotta cheese
- ½ pound sugar
- Zest from 1 lemon,

- grated
- Zest from 1 orange, grated
- Butter for the pan

## Directions:

In a bowl, mix eggs with sugar, cheese, lemon and orange zest and stir very well. Grease a baking pan with some butter, pour the eggs mixture, place in the oven at 425 degrees F, bake for 30 minutes, reduce heat to 380 degrees F, cool for another 40 minutes, cool down, slice and serve.

**Nutrition:** calories 110, fat 3, fiber 2, carbs 3, protein 4

# Mixed Fruit Bowls

*Prep Time:* 10 minutes | *Cook Time:* 0 minutes | *Servings:* 4

## Ingredients:

- 1 cup apples, chopped
- 1 cup pineapple, chopped
- 1 cup banana, peeled and chopped
- 1 cup melon, peeled and chopped
- 1 cup papaya, peeled

- and chopped
- ½ teaspoon vanilla powder
- ¾ cup cashews, soaked for 6 hours and drained
- Stevia to taste
- Some cold water

## Directions:

Put cashews in a food processor, add stevia and vanilla, blend, transfer to a bowl and keep in the fridge for now. In a bowl, arrange a layer of fruits and then add a layer of cashew paste. Repeat with the remaining layers of fruits and paste and serve right away!

**Nutrition:** calories 140, fat 1, fiber 1, carbs 3, protein 2

# Lemon Pancakes

*Prep Time:* 10 minutes | *Cook Time:* 5 minutes | *Servings:* 4

## Ingredients:

- 1 tablespoon lemon juice
- Zest of 2 lemons, grated
- 2 cups milk
- 1 teaspoon almond extract
- 1 teaspoon vanilla extract
- 1 cup whole wheat flour

- 1/3 cup oat bran
- 2/3 cups all-purpose flour
- 1 and ½ teaspoon baking powder
- 2 tablespoons sugar
- A pinch of salt
- ¼ cup olive oil
- ½ cup silver almonds, chopped

## Directions:

In a bowl, mix almond milk with lemon zest, lemon juice and the other ingredients except some of the oil and whisk. Heat a pan over medium high heat, grease with some olive oil, drop 1/3 cup pancakes batter, spread evenly, cook for 2 minutes, flip and cook another 2 minutes, transfer to a plate and leave aside. Repeat this with the rest of the batter and serve pancakes right away.

**Nutrition:** calories 80, fat 1, fiber 2, carbs 5, protein 3

# Chocolate Cups

*Prep Time: 2 hours and 10 minutes | Cook Time: 0 minutes | Servings: 6*

## Ingredients:

- 5 tablespoons almond flour
- ½ cup soft butter
- 1 cup, chocolate, chopped
- 1 teaspoon matcha powder + some
- more for the topping
- 3 tablespoons sugar
- 1 teaspoon coconut oil
- A pinch of salt
- Cocoa nibs

## Directions:

In a bowl, mix butter with almond flour, sugar and matcha powder, stir, cover and keep in the fridge for 10 minutes. Put chocolate in a bowl, place it over another bowl filled with boiling water, stir until it melts, mix with the oil and spoon 2 teaspoons of this in a muffin tray. Take 1 tablespoon matcha mix, shape a ball, place in a muffin liner, press to flatten it, repeat this with the rest of the mix, and top each with 1 tablespoon melted chocolate. In a small bowl, mix a pinch of sea salt with a pinch of matcha powder, stir and sprinkle all over muffins. Add cocoa nibs on top, place them in the freezer and keep there until they are firm.

**Nutrition:** calories 230, fat 2, fiber 1, carbs 4, protein 3

# Orange Bowl

*Prep Time: 30 minutes | Cook Time: 0 minutes | Servings: 4*

## Ingredients:

- 3 cups oranges, peeled and cut into segments
- ½ cup low fat milk
- ¼ cup sugar

## Directions:

Put the oranges in a blender, add the rest of the ingredients, pulse well, transfer to bowls and keep in the freezer for 20 minutes before serving.

**Nutrition:** calories 160, fat 2, fiber 2, carbs 3, protein 1

# Cocoa Ice Cream

*Prep Time: 10 minutes | Cook Time: 5 minutes | Servings: 4*

## Ingredients:

- 2 cups water
- 1/3 cup brown sugar
- 2/3 cup white sugar
- A pinch of salt
- ¾ cup cocoa powder
- 6 ounces dark chocolate, chopped
- Zest and juice from 1 lemon

## Directions:

Put 1 ½ cups water in a saucepan, heat up over medium heat, add brown and white sugar, a pinch of salt and cocoa powder, stir, bring to a boil, simmer for 1 minute, take off the heat and combine with the rest of the ingredients. Leave aside to cool down, transfer to your ice cream maker process. Serve when it's done.

**Nutrition:** calories 160, fat 3, fiber 3, carbs 7, protein 10

# Pecan and Pineapple Cake

*Prep Time: 10 minutes | Cook Time: 40 minutes | Servings: 8*

## Ingredients:

- 3 cups white flour
- ¼ cup olive oil
- 1 ½ cup butter
- 1 teaspoon vanilla extract
- 2 ¼ cups sugar
- 1 ¼ cup natural apple sauce
- 2 teaspoons baking powder
- 1 ¼ cups low fat milk
- A pinch of salt
- 2 tablespoons white vinegar
- 1 ½ cups brown sugar
- 16 pecans
- 16 pineapple slices

## Directions:

Grease 2 cake pans with olive oil, sprinkle some flour and brown sugar and coat well. Pour ½ cup melted butter and spread evenly. Put 1 pineapple slice in the middle of each pan, divide rest of the slices in a circle around the edges of cake pans and divide the pecans in the middle of each pineapple slice. In a bowl, mix milk with white vinegar, whisk and leave aside as well. Put remaining butter in a bowl, add white sugar, apple sauce and vanilla and whisk using your hand mixer. In a bowl, mix flour with a pinch of salt and baking powder, stir and add to milk mix.. Pour over pineapples, arrange, place pans in the oven at 350 degrees F and bake for 40 minutes. Take cakes out of the oven, leave them aside for 10 minutes, invert them on platters, cut and serve.

**Nutrition:** calories 200, fat 1, fiber 2, carbs 6, protein 4

# Maple Fudge

*Prep Time:* 3 hours and 10 minutes | *Cook Time:* 0 minutes | *Servings:* 6

## Ingredients:

- 1/3 cup natural cashew butter
- 1 and ½ tablespoons olive oil
- 2 tablespoons butter
- 5 tablespoons lemon
- juice
- ½ teaspoon lemon zest, grated
- A pinch of salt
- 1 tablespoons maple syrup

## Directions:

In a bowl, mix cashew butter with butter, oil, and the rest of te ingredients and whisk well. Line a muffin tray with parchment paper, scoop 1 tablespoon of lemon fudge mix in each of the muffin tins and keep in the freezer for 3 hours before serving.

**Nutrition:** calories 72, fat 4, fiber 1, carbs 3, protein 1

# Maple Tart

*Prep Time:* 2 hours and 10 minutes | *Cook Time:* 15 minutes | *Servings:* 6

## Ingredients:

*For the crust:*

- 2 cups graham cracker crumbs
- 7 tablespoons olive oil

*For the filling:*

- ¼ cup maple syrup
- 14 ounces low fat milk
- Zest from 1 lemon
- Juice of 1 lemon

*For the topping:*

- ½ pint blueberries
- ½ pint cherries
- 1 pint strawberries, halved

## Directions:

Put crackers in a blender and pulse a few times. Heat a pan with the oil over medium high heat, add crumbled graham crackers and stir well. Press well on the bottom of a tart pan, place in the oven at 350 degrees F, bake for 10 minutes and completely cool it down. Put the milk in a bowl, add maple syrup, lemon zest and lemon juice and stir well. Pour coconut milk mixture into tart crust, spread evenly and place in the freezer for 2 hours. Spread blueberries, cherries and strawberries on top and keep in the fridge until you serve it.

**Nutrition:** calories 130, fat 4, fiber 1, carbs 6, protein 9

# Almond Tangerine Cake

*Prep Time:* 10 minutes | *Cook Time:* 20 minutes | *Servings:* 8

## Ingredients:

- ¾ cup sugar
- 2 cups almond flour
- ¼ cup olive oil
- ½ cup low fat milk
- 1 teaspoon cider vinegar
- ½ teaspoon vanilla
- extract
- Juice and zest of 2 lemons
- Juice and zest from 1 tangerine
- Tangerine segments, for serving

## Directions:

Put flour in a bowl, mix with salt and sugar and stir. Add the rest of the ingredients except the tangerine segments and whisk. Pour into a greased cake pan, place in the oven at 375 degrees F and bake for 20 minutes. Transfer cake to a platter, cut and put the tangerine segments on top.

**Nutrition:** calories 190, fat 1, fiber 1, carbs 4, protein 4

# Blueberry and Oats Mix

*Prep Time:* 10 minutes | *Cook Time:* 30 minutes | *Servings:* 6

## Ingredients:

- 2 cups garbanzo bean flour
- 2 cups rolled oats
- 8 cups blueberries
- 1 stick butter
- 1 cup walnuts,
- chopped
- 3 tablespoons maple syrup
- A pinch of salt
- 2 tablespoons rosemary, chopped

## Directions:

Arrange blueberries in a greased baking pan and leave aside. Meanwhile, in a food processor, mix rolled oats the other ingredients and pulse well. Layer this mix over blueberries, place everything in the oven at 350 degrees F and bake for 30 minutes. Take dessert out of the oven, leave aside to cool down, cut and serve.

**Nutrition:** calories 150, fat 3, fiber 2, carbs 7, protein 4

# Yogurt Mousse

*Prep Time: 8 hours* | *Cook Time: 3 minutes* | *Servings: 4*

## Ingredients:

- 2 cups yogurt
- ¼ cup honey
- A pinch of salt
- ½ vanilla bean
- ¾ cup heavy cream
- 2 tablespoons water
- For the berries:
- 1 tablespoon honey
- ¼ cup balsamic
- vinegar
- A pinch of black pepper
- 2 cups mixed blueberries and raspberries
- 4 amaretto cookies, crushed

## Directions:

Strain yogurt, spoon into a cheesecloth, press, cover and keep in the fridge for 4 hours. Heat a pan with the water and a pinch of salt over medium high heat, add ¼ cup honey, vanilla seeds and the bean, stir, bring to a boil, cook for 2 minutes, take off heat, leave aside to cool down for 10 minutes and discard vanilla bean. Mix cream with a mixer, add yogurt and whisk for 3 minutes. Divide into dessert glasses, cover and keep in the fridge for 4 hours. Heat up a pan over medium heat, add vinegar and the rest of the ingredients except the cookies, stir, bring to a boil and simmer for 2 minutes. Pour over yogurt mousse. Garnish each glass with crumbled amaretto cookies and serve.

**Nutrition:** calories 340, fat 21, fiber 3, carbs 43, protein 6

# Minty Peaches

*Prep Time: 10 minutes* | *Cook Time: 5 minutes* | *Servings: 4*

## Ingredients:

- 1/3 cup almonds, toasted
- 1/3 cup pistachios, toasted
- 1 tablespoon cumin seeds
- 1 tablespoon caraway seeds
- 1 tablespoon cumin seeds
- 1 teaspoon crushed pepper
- 2 teaspoons salt
- 3 tablespoons
- sesame seeds, toasted
- 1 teaspoon mint
- 1 teaspoon nigella seeds
- ½ teaspoon marjoram, dried
- 1 teaspoon lemon zest, grated
- 4 peaches, halved
- A drizzle of olive oil
- Whipped cream
- Blueberries

## Directions:

In a food processor, mix pistachios with almonds and the rest of the ingredients except the cream, berries, oil and the peaches and ground everything well. Heat a grill pan over medium high heat, add peach halves, brush them with some oil, grill for 4 minutes and divide between plates. Add some of the nut mix and serve with blueberries and whipped cream.

**Nutrition:** calories 70, fat 1, fiber 4, carbs 17, protein 1

# Orange and Almond Cake

*Prep Time:* 10 minutes | *Cook Time:* 40 minutes | *Servings:* 10

## Ingredients:

- ½ pound almonds, blanched and ground
- Zest from 1 lemon, grated
- Zest from 1 orange, grated
- 1 ¼ cups sugar
- 6 eggs, whites and yolks separated
- 4 drops almond extract
- Confectioner's sugar

## Directions:

Beat egg yolks with a mixer well and combine with the rest of the ingredients except the confectioner's sugar. Stir well, pour this into a greased baking dish, place in the oven at 350 degrees F and bake for 40 minutes. Take cake out of oven, leave it to cool down, slice, dust confectioners' sugar on top and serve.

**Nutrition:** calories 200, fat 0, fiber 0, carbs 23, protein 6

# Hazelnut Cake

*Prep Time:* 10 minutes | *Cook Time:* 40 minutes | *Servings:* 10

## Ingredients:

*For the syrup:*
- 1 ¼ cups sugar
- 2/3 cup water
- 2 ½ tablespoons orange water

*For the cake:*
- 2 ¼ cups hazelnut flour
- 5 eggs, whites and yolks separated
- 1 cup sugar
- 2 tablespoons
- 2 ½ tablespoons orange juice
- Zest from 1 orange, grated

- confectioners' sugar for serving
- 1 1/3 cups Greek yogurt for serving
- Pulp from 4 passion fruits

## Directions:

Put the water in a large saucepan, bring to a boil over medium high heat, add 1 and ¼ cups sugar, orange juice, zest and the water, stir, boil for 10 minutes and take off the heat. In a bowl, beat egg yolks with 1 cup sugar and hazelnut flour using your mixer. In another bowl, beat egg whites using your mixer as well. Combine the 2 mixtures, stir, pour into a lined baking pan and bake at 350 degrees F for 30 minutes. Take cake out of the oven, leave it to cool down a bit, slice and serve with the orange sauce, with yogurt, confectioners' sugar dusted on top and passion fruit pulp on the side.

**Nutrition:** calories 234, fat 1, fiber 2, carbs 4, protein 7

## Raisins and Semolina Bowls

*Prep Time: 10 minutes | Cook Time: 7 minutes | Servings: 18*

**Ingredients:**

- 2 cups semolina, ground
- 1 cup olive oil
- 4 cups hot water
- 2 ½ cups water
- 1 cup raisins
- 1 teaspoon cinnamon powder

**Directions:**

Heat a pan with the oil over medium high heat, add semolina and brown it for 3 minutes stirring often. Add sugar and hot water, stir and cook until it thickens. Divide into bowls, sprinkle raisins and cinnamon and serve.

**Nutrition:** calories 240, fat 12, fiber 1, carbs 32, protein 3

## Lemon Ice Cream

*Prep Time: 2 hours | Cook Time: 0 | Servings: 8*

**Ingredients:**

- 2/3 cup heavy cream
- 4 and ¼ cups Greek yogurt
- 2/3 cup sugar
- 6 tablespoons lemon juice

**Directions:**

In an ice cream maker, mix yogurt with cream and the other ingredients, whisk well, place in your freezer for 2 hours and then serve.

**Nutrition:** calories 134, fat 7, fiber 0, carbs 16, protein 1

## Vanilla Nectarines

*Prep Time: 10 minutes | Cook Time: 30 minutes | Servings: 3*

**Ingredients:**

- 3 teaspoons brown sugar
- 3 nectarines, cut into halves and stones removed
- 1 teaspoon vanilla extract
- 6 tablespoons yogurt
- 3 tablespoons honey

**Directions:**

Place nectarines on a lined baking sheet, add brown sugar and the other ingredients except the yogurt, place in the oven at 350 degrees F and bake for 30 minutes tossing them halfway. Serve them with Greek yogurt on top.

**Nutrition:** calories 221, fat 7, fiber 3, carbs 55, protein 2

## Cocoa Berry Pudding

*Prep Time: 10 minutes | Cook Time: 0 minutes | Servings: 1*

**Ingredients:**

- 1 tablespoon cocoa powder
- ¾ cup Greek yogurt
- 5 drops vanilla
- stevia
- 4 tablespoons strawberry jam

**Directions:**

In a bowl, mix yogurt with cocoa powder and the other ingredients except the jam and whisk well. Top with strawberry jam and keep in the fridge until you serve.

**Nutrition:** calories 113, fat 4, fiber 2, carbs 14, protein 12

# Lemon Bread Pudding

*Prep Time:* 10 minutes | *Cook Time:* 40 minutes | *Servings:* 6

## Ingredients:

- 12 ounces bread, sliced
- 1.5-ounce sultanas
- 2 tablespoons lemon marmalade
- 4 eggs
- 1.5 ounces sugar
- 1 pint milk
- 3 tablespoons brandy
- 4 allspice berries, crushed
- ¼ teaspoon nutmeg, grated

## Directions:

Place half bread slices in a baking dish, spread marmalade over them, sprinkle the sultanas and arrange the rest of the bread slices. In a bowl, mix eggs with milk, nutmeg, allspice, sugar and brandy, whisk well, pour over the pudding and bake at 350 degrees F for 40 minutes. Take bread pudding out of the oven, leave it aside to cool down, slice, arrange on plates and serve.

**Nutrition:** calories 300, fat 12, fiber 1, carbs 32, protein 24

# Corn Pudding

*Prep Time:* 10 minutes | *Cook Time:* 5 minutes | *Servings:* 4

## Ingredients:

- ¾ cup sugar
- 2 and ½ cups milk
- ¼ cup cornstarch
- 3 egg yolks, whisked
- Juice from 2 lemons
- A pinch of salt
- Zest of 2 lemons, grated
- 2 tablespoons butter
- Whipped cream

## Directions:

In a bowl, mix cornstarch with sugar, milk and the rest of the ingredients except the butter, whipped cream and lemon juice, whisk and cook over medium heat for 5 minutes. Take off heat, add butter and lemon juice, stir, divide into 4 ramekins and serve cold with the cream on top.

**Nutrition:** calories 200, fat 2, fiber 1, carbs 4, protein 1

# Conclusion

Your journey to better living doesn't end here; in fact, it's just beginning! Choosing the Mediterranean diet is a monumental step towards enhanced health and wellbeing. Remember, with this diet, you're not cutting out delectable meals; instead, you're redefining them with nourishing ingredients that provide as much taste as they do health benefits.

Isn't it fascinating? The Mediterranean diet isn't just a food regimen - it's a vibrant invitation to a healthier, fulfilling, and potentially longer life. It's a life choice that espouses the virtues of wholesomeness, nutrition, and notably, culinary delight.

Having made this decisive choice, all you need now is this extraordinary cookbook to kickstart your journey. Immerse yourself in our trove of dreamy recipes, each a beautiful testament to the essence of Mediterranean cuisine!

So, grab your copy, roll up your sleeves, and ignite the stoves. A world of tantalizing Mediterranean flavors awaits you. It's time to cook, eat, and share the best meals of your life. Here's to joyful cooking, mouthwatering meals, and a healthier, happier you! Cheers to living the Mediterranean way!

Made in the USA
Las Vegas, NV
22 September 2024

95648504R00098